Texas Eats 240

Take A Tasty Tour Of Texas, With 240 Best Texas Recipes!

(Texas Eats - Volume 1)

Lucas Neill

Copyright: Published in the United States by Lucas Neill / © LUCAS NEILL

Published on November 20, 2018

All rights reserved. No part of this publication may be reproduced, stored in retrieval system, copied in any form or by any means, electronic, mechanical, photocopying, recording or otherwise transmitted without written permission from the publisher. Please do not participate in or encourage piracy of this material in any way. You must not circulate this book in any format. LUCAS NEILL does not control or direct users' actions and is not responsible for the information or content shared, harm and/or actions of the book readers.

In accordance with the U.S. Copyright Act of 1976, the scanning, uploading and electronic sharing of any part of this book without the permission of the publisher constitute unlawful piracy and theft of the author's intellectual property. If you would like to use material from the book (other than just simply for reviewing the book), prior permission must be obtained by contacting the author at *cheflucasneill@gmail.com*

Thank you for your support of the author's rights.

Contents

- CONTENTS 3
- INTRODUCTION 7
- **CHAPTER 1: HOUSTON RECIPES** 8
  1. Aunt Doras Colombian Chicken with Potatoes 8
  2. Banh Bao 9
  3. Crispy Baked Basa 9
  4. Frozen Strawberry Smoothie Bars 10
  5. Fusion Chili 10
  6. Grilled Stuffed Red Snapper 11
  7. Johns Chili 12
  8. Ninfas Green Tomato Salsa 12
  9. Pancetta Wrapped Shrimp with Chipotle Vinaigrette and Cilantro Oil 13
  10. Queso Catfish 13
  11. Sausage Jalapeno Poppers 14
  12. Shrimp Kisses 15
  13. Soul Smothered Chicken 15
  14. Spicy Soup 16
  15. Tex Mex Shark and Shrimp 16
  16. Texas Smoked Flounder 17
  17. TexMex Corn Chowder 17
  18. Ultimate Gulf Coast Gumbo 18
- **CHAPTER 2: DALLAS RECIPES** 19
  19. Baby Does Cheese Soup with Beer 19
  20. Baked Chicken Reuben 20
  21. Best Ever Cowboy Caviar 20
  22. Bethanys Frito Pie 21
  23. Brazilian Grilled Pineapple 21
  24. Cowboy Bread 21
  25. Cowboy Caviar 22
  26. Cowboy Cookie Mix in a Jar 22
  27. Cowboy Cookies Dunkin Platters 23
  28. Cowboy Cookies II 23
  29. Cowboy Cookies III 24
  30. Cowboy Dip 24
  31. Cowboy Kale 25
  32. Cowboy Margaritas 25
  33. Cowboy Mashed Potatoes 25
  34. Cowboy Mexican Dip 26
  35. Cowboy Oatmeal Cookies 26
  36. Cowboy Skillet New Potato Medley Italian Sausage Eggs 27
  37. Cowboy Stew I 27
  38. DallasStyle Sloppy Joes 28
  39. Easy Cowboy Beans Frijoles Charros ... 28
  40. Grandmas Cowboy Cookies 29
  41. Greek Cowboy Hash and Eggs 29
  42. Harriet and Marlos Cowboy Stew 30
  43. Holy Hot Mango Daiquiri Batman 31
  44. Rich Mexican Corn 31
  45. Tangy Cowboy Caviar 32
  46. Texas Cowboy Stew 32
  47. Uptown Cowboy Caviar 33
  48. Vincents Famous Garlic Coleslaw 33
  49. Winter Blossoms Often Requested Ham Salad 34
- **CHAPTER 3: AMAZING TEXAS RECIPES** 35
  50. Addictive Texas Trash 35
  51. Aunt Blanches Blueberry Muffins 36
  52. Baked Beans Texas Ranger 36
  53. Beaumont Ranch Potato Salad 37
  54. Beer Can Chicken Texas Style 37
  55. BestEver Texas Caviar 38
  56. Big Kevs Texas Style Long Island Iced Tea 39
  57. Boudreauxs Zydeco Stomp Gumbo 39
  58. Brisket with BBQ Sauce 40
  59. Capidotada Mexican Bread Pudding ... 40
  60. Cattlemans Beans 41
  61. Cheapskate Stew 42
  62. Cheesy Chicken Toast Sandwich 42
  63. Chilled Vegetable Salad 43
  64. ChoriQueso 43
  65. Cinnamon Brown Sugar Butter 44
  66. Classic Texas Caviar 44
  67. Cowboy Jacks Beer Bread 44

68. Crispy French Toast 45
69. Critter Fritter Casserole 45
70. Daddys If Theyda had This at the Alamo we wouldha WON Texas Chili 46
71. Dakotas Texas Style Chili 47
72. Davids Mesquite Smoked Texas Brisket 47
73. Dinner Rolls Made With Healthy Coconut Oil 48
74. Ds Famous Salsa 49
75. Easy Armadillo Eggs 49
76. Easy Texas Caviar 49
77. Easy Texas Chili 50
78. Embarrassingly Easy Barbecue Chicken 50
79. Fiesta Grilled Chicken 51
80. Fort Worth Fish Tacos 51
81. Fried Cabbage Texas Style 52
82. German Texas Chili 53
83. Grampa Daves Texas Chainsaw BarBQue Sauce 54
84. Grand Margarita 54
85. Healthy Turkey Tex Mex Chili 54
86. Hearty Meat Sauce 55
87. Hill Country Turkey Chili with Beans .. 56
88. Hollys Texas Brisket 56
89. Honey Smoked Turkey 57
90. Jalapeno Ranch Salad Dressing 57
91. Jamoncillo de Leche Mexican Fudge 58
92. Jesses Hot Sauce 58
93. KCs Smoked Brisket 59
94. Kens Texas Chili 59
95. King Beef Oven Brisket 60
96. King Ranch Chicken Casserole 60
97. Kristins Turkey Butternut Squash Casserole 61
98. Lemon Butter Chicken 62
99. Mamas TexasStyle Peach Cobbler 62
100. Margarita Balls II 63
101. Marks Surprise Meatloaf 63
102. Mexican Corn 64
103. Mexican Rice 64
104. Mock Chicken Patties 65
105. Moms Chili 65
106. Moms Favorite Baked Mac and Cheese 65
107. Moms Texas Hash 66
108. Mr Goodbar Frosting 67
109. Ninas Texas Chili 67
110. OnePot Texas Borracho Beans 68
111. Peanut Butter Sheet Cake 68
112. Pecan Pie I 69
113. Pineapple and Basil Sorbet 69
114. Port Wine Jelly 70
115. Potato and Bean Enchiladas 70
116. Queso Cheese Dip 71
117. Quick Texas Stew 72
118. Randys Texas Tea 72
119. Razors Carne Guizida 73
120. Real Deal TexMex Queso 73
121. Red Cabbage Slow Slaw 74
122. San Antonio Salad 74
123. Sangria White 75
124. Sauteed Patty Pan Squash 75
125. Seven Layer Tex Mex Dip 76
126. Simple Texas Salsa 76
127. Slow Cooker Carolina BBQ 77
128. Slow Cooker Texas Pulled Pork 77
129. SlowCooked TexasStyle Beef Brisket ... 78
130. South Texas Borracho Beans 78
131. South Texas Carne Guisada 79
132. South Texas Tartar Sauce 79
133. Southern TexasStyle Beef Barbacoa 80
134. Speedy French Onion Soup 80
135. Spicy BBQ Chicken 81
136. Spicy Cranberry Pecan Cornbread Stuffing 81
137. Spicy Fish Soup 82
138. Spinach Noodle Casserole 82
139. Super TexMex Chicken Chop Salad 83
140. Tejano Style Shrimp Cocktail 84
141. Terrys Texas Pinto Beans 84
142. Tex Mex Black Bean Dip 84
143. Tex Mex Dip 85
144. Tex Mex Meatloaf 85
145. Tex Mex Potato Soup 86
146. Tex Mex Stir Fry 86
147. Texan Chicken and Rice Casserole 87
148. Texas BBQ Chicken 88
149. Texas BBQ Rub 88
150. Texas Beef Soup 89
151. Texas Boiled Beer Shrimp 89
152. Texas Brazil Nut Fruitcake 89
153. Texas Brisket 90

154. Texas Brownies I 90
155. Texas Brownies II 91
156. Texas Caviar 92
157. Texas Caviar I 92
158. Texas Caviar II 93
159. Texas Caviar with Avocado 93
160. Texas Chicken Quesadillas 93
161. Texas Chicken Vegetable Soup 94
162. Texas Chili Beef Slices 94
163. Texas Chili Dog 95
164. Texas Chocolate Frosting 96
165. Texas Chocolate Mini Cake Bites 96
166. Texas Chocolate Sheet Cake 97
167. Texas Christmas Pickles 97
168. Texas Coleslaw 98
169. Texas Corn Chowder with Venison 98
170. Texas Cowboy Chili Beans 99
171. Texas Crabgrass 99
172. Texas Curried Chicken 100
173. Texas Egg Rolls 100
174. Texas Eggs 101
175. Texas Enchilada Sauce 101
176. Texas Firehouse Dip 102
177. Texas Ground Turkey Burrito 102
178. Texas Hash 102
179. Texas Hash in the Microwave 103
180. Texas Hickory BBQ Chicken 103
181. Texas Hot Sauce 104
182. Texas Hot Wiener Sauce Ulster County New York Style 105
183. Texas Hotdog Sauce 105
184. Texas Hurricane 106
185. Texas Jambalaya 106
186. Texas Lime in the Coconut Muffins ... 107
187. Texas Lizzies 107
188. Texas Mess 108
189. Texas New Mexico Chili 108
190. Texas Pecan Candy Cake 109
191. Texas Pie 109
192. Texas Pork Ribs 110
193. Texas Praline Cake 111
194. Texas Praline Coffee Cake 111
195. Texas Pralines 112
196. Texas Ranch Chicken 112
197. Texas Ranch Potato Salad 113
198. Texas Rice 113
199. Texas Sheet Cake I 114
200. Texas Sheet Cake V 114
201. Texas Sheet Cake VI 115
202. Texas Slaw 116
203. Texas Smoked Barbecue Meatloaf 116
204. Texas Stuffed Grilled Burgers 117
205. Texas Stuffed Mushrooms 118
206. Texas Style Chicken Tequila 118
207. Texas Taco Soup 119
208. Texas Tea III 120
209. Texas Tomatillo Avocado Sauce 120
210. Texas Tornado Cake 120
211. Texas Wild Pork Roast for Two 121
212. Texas Yum Yum 121
213. TexasStyle Baked Beans 122
214. TexasStyle Chili Rice 122
215. Texatini 123
216. TexiFied Black Beans and Brown Rice 123
217. TexMex Beef and Cheese Enchiladas 124
218. TexMex Beef Bowl with Avocado Cilantro Dressing 124
219. TexMex Burger with Cajun Mayo 125
220. TexMex Chicken Tamale Pie 126
221. TexMex Eggs Benedict with Grilled Potato Slabs and AvocadoLime Hollandaise ... 126
222. TexMex Enchiladas 128
223. TexMex Macaroni and Cheese 128
224. TexMex Migas 129
225. TexMex Pasta Salad 129
226. TexMex Patty Melts 130
227. TexMex Pork 130
228. TexMex Sheet Cake 131
229. TexMex Squash Bake 132
230. TexMex Tuna Salad 132
231. TexMex Turkey Chili with Black Beans Corn and Butternut Squash 133
232. TexMex Turkey Soup 133
233. The Best Natural Peach Jam or Filling 134
234. Trays Spicy Texas Chili 135
235. Vietnamese Beef and Red Cabbage Bowl 136
236. West TexasStyle Buffalo Chili 136
237. White Texas Sheet Cake 137
238. Yeah ILivedinTexas Smoked Brisket . 137
239. Yum Yum Cake II 138
240. Zekes Tortilla Soup 139

INDEX 140	
CONCLUSION 148	
LUCAS NEILL 148	

Introduction

***

The culinary scene in the United States has never been passive. In my 25 years of experience in cooking and writing, it's always been dynamic and active. Nowadays, the American food culture has become more interesting and livelier. We enthusiastically read food magazines, cookbooks, and cooking columns. We buy the fresher, tasty, and more varied food items in supermarkets. We buy local produce from farmers' markets is an exciting change that has become widespread now. Lastly, we always go for the best ingredients available, such as free-range chickens, stone-ground flours and meals, fragrant fresh herbs, and extra virgin olive oils.

For this American cookbook series, I explored the food cultures in Asia, the Caribbean, Europe, Latin America, and North Africa. I had much interest in the so-called exotic cuisines that were quickly becoming popular. Americans were searching outside the country for inspiration and sustenance, and this curiosity was really something worth supporting. It was an awesome experience traveling the world, sampling new dishes and picking up ideas, and then trying out all I had gathered back home right in my own kitchen. Soon after I was done writing the American cookbook series, I looked inward with a newfound passion for local American foods. I felt a spark burning while I was starting my book tour in the Pacific Northwest. Maybe the colorful Pacific oysters in the Pike Place Market in Seattle had to do with it. Or perhaps, it was the season's first Copper River salmon, grilled to perfection and paired with an Oregon Pinot Noir that's flowery and fruity. Or it could be my first time to sample caramelized Kasu cod at Seattle's Dahlia Lounge. I can't tell for sure. All I knew was that I had to begin writing the U.S Cookbook. You are handling the book "Texas Eats 240 Volume 1"

Excited as I was to go back home, my desire for traveling to find more ideas grew stronger. I wished to have more trips so that I could taste the food offerings in every place's fine-dining restaurants, diners, inns, and luncheonettes. I wished to see for myself the harvest of grains, fish, veggies, and fruits, as well as to join the celebration of these harvests at county fairs and local festivals. In the process, I wished to find remarkable home-cooked food and meet some talented yet unknown home cooks. Throughout the next three years, my research adventures took me from Maine to the Florida Panhandle, from Chesapeake Bay crab cakes to crab Louis on San Francisco's Fisherman's Wharf where I had a buffalo dish in South Dakota, and wild boar in Texas hill country. I fished the icy Gulf of Alaska and visited the pineapple groves in Hawaii, looking for the oldest and newest, most authentic, boldest, and of course, the best American dishes.

You also see more different types of American recipes such as:

- ✓ *Cajun Cookbook*
- ✓ *Hawaii Cookbook*
- ✓ *The Southern Cookbook*
- ✓ *Tex-Mex Cookbook*
- ✓ *Tasting the United States*
- ✓ ...

Thank you for choosing "Texas Eats 240 Volume 1". I really hope that each book in the series will be always your best friend in your little kitchen.

Let's live happily and have a tasty tour to Texas!

Enjoy each page of the book,

Chapter 1: Houston Recipes

***

1. Aunt Doras Colombian Chicken with Potatoes

"I learned this recipe when visiting my Colombian family members in Houston, Texas. The sauce that the chicken cooks in is chock full of flavor. Cumin, curry, black pepper, turmeric, pimenton (paprika), and seasoning salt make the chicken's sauce tasty enough to lick your plate! Serve with rice."

Serving: 6 | Prep: 20 m | Cook: 2 h | Ready in: 2 h 20 m

Ingredients

- 1 1/2 teaspoons olive oil
- 1 large onion, sliced
- 6 cloves garlic, chopped
- 1 red bell pepper, sliced
- 1 green bell pepper, sliced
- 11 fluid ounces beef broth
- 1 1/2 tablespoons ground cumin
- 1 tablespoon curry powder
- 1 tablespoon seasoning salt
- 1 1/2 teaspoons garlic powder
- 1 1/2 teaspoons ground turmeric
- 1 1/2 teaspoons pimenton (paprika)
- 1 1/2 teaspoons dried oregano
- 1 1/2 teaspoons ground black pepper
- 6 chicken thighs
- 4 potatoes, peeled and quartered

Direction

- Heat olive oil in a deep skillet over high heat. Add onions and garlic; cook and stir until onions are softened, about 5 minutes. Stir in red and green bell peppers; cook and stir until peppers are firm but tender, 5 to 7 minutes. Mix in beef broth, cumin, curry powder, seasoning salt, garlic powder, turmeric, pimenton, oregano, and pepper.
- Submerge chicken thighs, skin side down, half way into broth mixture; stir to coat chicken. Bring to a boil; cover and reduce heat to low. Simmer until chicken is no longer pink, about 40 minutes.
- Stir potatoes into the chicken mixture until mostly submerged; check that chicken thighs

are still skin side down. Bring to a boil; cover. Reduce heat; simmer until potatoes are soft and chicken is cooked through, about 1 hour.

Nutrition Information

- Calories: 357 calories
- Total Fat: 14.1 g
- Cholesterol: 71 mg
- Sodium: 716 mg
- Total Carbohydrate: 33.8 g
- Protein: 24.2 g

2. Banh Bao

"I'm a Vietnamese living in Indiana who had to find a recipe for one of my favorite Vietnamese snacks, banh bao. They are a variation on the Chinese cha siu bao (Chinese pork buns). I would like to thank Houston Wok for providing Ms. SkimmyJeans' moist filling recipe and Miss Adventure[at]home for a tasty bun recipe. Combined, this is my ultimate banh bao recipe."

Serving: 18 | Prep: 25 m | Cook: 30 m | Ready in: 1 h 30 m

Ingredients

- Filling:
- 1 pound ground pork
- 2 shallots, minced
- 2 tablespoons fish sauce
- 1 1/2 tablespoons oyster sauce
- 1 tablespoon soy sauce
- Dough:
- 4 1/2 cups self-rising flour
- 1 1/2 cups milk
- 3/4 cup white sugar
- 3 links Chinese sausages, sliced on the diagonal
- 4 hard-boiled eggs, peeled and quartered
- waxed paper

Direction

- Mix pork, shallots, fish sauce, oyster sauce, and soy sauce together in a large bowl. Let mixture marinate in the refrigerator, about 30 minutes.
- Combine self-rising flour, milk, and sugar in another large bowl; knead until dough is smooth and no longer sticky. Cover dough with cheesecloth; let rest, about 5 minutes.
- Divide dough into 18 balls. Roll out each ball into a circle with a rolling pin on a floured work surface. Place a spoonful of the pork mixture in the center; top with 2 sausage slices and an egg quarter. Gather the edges of each circle together like a coin purse; twist and pinch to seal the bun.
- Cut waxed paper into eighteen 2-inch squares. Place each bun on a waxed paper square. Arrange 1 inch apart in a steamer; cover with lid.
- Steam buns until puffed up, about 30 minutes.

Nutrition Information

- Calories: 277 calories
- Total Fat: 9.6 g
- Cholesterol: 65 mg
- Sodium: 736 mg
- Total Carbohydrate: 34.6 g
- Protein: 12.9 g

3. Crispy Baked Basa

"Basa is a new fish that is common in many markets here in Houston. It is a mild, tasty fish."

Serving: 4 | Prep: 15 m | Cook: 15 m | Ready in: 30 m

Ingredients

- 1/4 cup mayonnaise
- 1 tablespoon stone ground mustard
- 1 teaspoon capers
- 1 teaspoon ketchup
- 1/4 teaspoon paprika
- 1/4 teaspoon hot pepper sauce
- 1 pound swai fish
- 1 1/2 tablespoons olive oil
- 1 cup finely crushed plain Melba toast rounds

- salt and pepper to taste
- 1 clove garlic, minced
- 1 lemon, sliced

Direction

- Preheat oven to 375 degrees F (190 degrees C).
- In a bowl, thoroughly blend the mayonnaise, mustard, capers, ketchup, paprika, and hot pepper sauce.
- Brush the basa fillets with about 1 tablespoon olive oil, and roll in the crushed Melba toast to coat. Season with salt and pepper. Use a kitchen sprayer to lightly spray the coated fish with remaining olive oil. Arrange the fish in a baking dish and top with garlic and lemon slices.
- Bake 15 minutes in the preheated oven, or until fish is easily flaked with a fork and coating is lightly browned. Serve with the mayonnaise sauce mixture.

Nutrition Information

- Calories: 338 calories
- Total Fat: 24.9 g
- Cholesterol: 59 mg
- Sodium: 380 mg
- Total Carbohydrate: 10.5 g
- Protein: 19.1 g

4. Frozen Strawberry Smoothie Bars

"With the hot Houston summer in full force, I wanted a cool treat that I'd feel good about giving my kids a couple times a day. I came up with this yummy alternative to ice pops and ice cream bars. The number of servings may vary depending on the size of your popsicle molds."

Serving: 6 | Prep: 10 m | Ready in: 12 h 10 m

Ingredients

- 8 fresh strawberries, hulled and quartered
- 1/4 cup plain yogurt
- 1/4 cup apple juice
- 2 tablespoons honey

Direction

- Blend strawberries, yogurt, apple juice, and honey in a blender until smooth.
- Pour blended mixture into ice pop molds; freeze until solid, about 12 hours.

Nutrition Information

- Calories: 38 calories
- Total Fat: 0.2 g
- Cholesterol: < 1 mg
- Sodium: 8 mg
- Total Carbohydrate: 8.9 g
- Protein: 0.7 g

5. Fusion Chili

"A true fusion of 'Tex' and 'Mex' style chili. I've made this recipe dozens of times, and it is great. Each bite slowly delivers a sweet flavor followed by dry heat afterwards. It takes a while to prepare, but well worth it. You can use any type of beans you like, and try different dried chile varieties."

Serving: 12 | Prep: 1 h | Cook: 3 h 30 m | Ready in: 4 h 30 m

Ingredients

- 10 dried ancho chiles - chopped, stemmed and seeded
- 1/2 cup water
- 1/4 cup white wine vinegar
- 3 pounds hot Italian sausage, casings removed
- 3 pounds ground beef
- 1 white onion, diced
- 1 red onion, diced
- 1 sweet onion, diced
- 1 cup diced celery
- 1 cup diced carrots
- 10 cloves garlic, sliced
- 1 teaspoon salt
- 1 teaspoon black pepper
- 1 (6 ounce) can tomato paste

- 1 cup dry red wine
- 4 (14.5 ounce) cans diced tomatoes
- 1/4 cup Worcestershire sauce
- 1/4 cup hot pepper sauce
- 1 tablespoon chili powder
- 2 teaspoons ground cumin
- 1 tablespoon chopped fresh parsley
- 1/2 cup honey
- 1 (16 ounce) can kidney beans, drained
- 1 (16 ounce) can pinto beans, drained

Direction

- In a small bowl, soak chiles in water and vinegar for 30 minutes. After soaking, puree in a blender or food processor until very smooth, about 5 minutes; set aside.
- Place sausage and ground beef in a large, deep skillet. Cook over medium high heat until evenly brown. Remove meat from pan, and set aside. In a large pot, Heat 3 to 4 tablespoons of the meat drippings over medium heat. Sauté white onion, red onion, sweet onion, celery, carrots and garlic until onions are soft and translucent. Season with salt and black pepper. Stir in tomato paste, and allow to caramelize. Pour in wine to deglaze the pot, scraping up any bits stuck to the bottom.
- Stir in cooked meat, tomatoes, Worcestershire sauce and hot pepper sauce. Season with chili powder, cumin and parsley. Bring to a boil, then stir in blended chile mixture and honey. Carefully mix in kidney beans pinto beans without breaking them. Cover, and simmer for 3 hours. Stir and scrape the bottom every hour or so.

Nutrition Information

- Calories: 977 calories
- Total Fat: 67.7 g
- Cholesterol: 183 mg
- Sodium: 1735 mg
- Total Carbohydrate: 45.4 g
- Protein: 43.2 g

6. Grilled Stuffed Red Snapper

"You can either stuff the fish with the seafood filling or simplify this recipe for yourself by spooning the stuffing on top of each fish fillet."

Serving: 6 | Prep: 20 m | Cook: 30 m | Ready in: 50 m

Ingredients

- 3 tablespoons butter
- 3/4 cup fresh bread crumbs
- 1/4 cup chopped green onions
- 1/4 cup celery, diced
- 1 clove garlic, minced
- 4 ounces cooked shrimp
- 4 ounces cooked crabmeat
- 1 tablespoon chopped fresh parsley
- 1/8 teaspoon salt
- 1/8 teaspoon ground black pepper
- 6 (4 ounce) fillets red snapper

Direction

- Preheat coals in a covered grill to high heat.
- To Make Stuffing: Melt 2 tablespoons butter or margarine in a skillet. Add the bread crumbs. Sauté and stir the mixture over medium-high heat till the bread crumbs are browned. Remove the bread crumbs to a mixing bowl.
- Melt 1 tablespoon butter or margarine in the skillet and sauté the onions, celery and garlic until tender; add to bread crumbs in mixing bowl, then stir in shrimp, crab, parsley, salt and pepper and toss gently.
- Cut foil to form a double-thickness 18x12-inch rectangle. Lay the fish fillets on the double thickness of foil. Mound the stuffing on top of the fillets.
- Curl up the edges of the foil to form a tray. In a covered grill, arrange the preheated coals at either side of the grill. Test for medium heat above the center of the grill. Place the fish in foil in the center of the grill rack. Cover and grill for 20 to 25 minutes or just until the fish flakes easily.

Nutrition Information

- Calories: 258 calories
- Total Fat: 8.4 g
- Cholesterol: 107 mg
- Sodium: 356 mg
- Total Carbohydrate: 10.6 g
- Protein: 33.1 g

7. Johns Chili

"Good chili from the great ol' state of TEXAS. Hope you enjoy this favorite of our family."

Serving: 12 | Prep: 25 m | Cook: 5 h 20 m | Ready in: 5 h 45 m

Ingredients

- 1 tablespoon olive oil
- 1 red bell pepper, finely chopped
- 1 yellow bell pepper, finely chopped
- 1 green bell pepper, finely chopped
- 1 orange bell pepper, finely chopped
- 1 large red onion, finely chopped
- 1 stalk celery, chopped
- 2 pounds ground pork
- 2 pounds ground beef
- 8 serrano chile peppers, diced
- 3 (14.5 ounce) cans diced tomatoes
- 1 (4.5 ounce) can diced green chile peppers
- 3 (6 ounce) cans tomato paste
- 2 (15 ounce) cans kidney beans
- 6 tablespoons minced garlic
- 1 fluid ounce key lime juice
- 4 fluid ounces tequila
- 16 fluid ounces beer
- 2 1/2 tablespoons chili powder
- salt and pepper to taste

Direction

- Heat the olive oil in a large pot over medium heat. Stir in the red bell pepper, yellow bell pepper, green bell pepper, orange bell pepper, onion, and celery. Cook until tender. Place pork and beef in the pot, and cook until evenly brown. Drain grease.
- Mix serrano chile peppers, diced tomatoes, green chile peppers, tomato paste, kidney beans, garlic, lime juice, tequila, and beer into the pot. Season with chili powder, salt, and pepper. Bring to a boil. Reduce heat to medium-low, and simmer 5 hours.

Nutrition Information

- Calories: 485 calories
- Total Fat: 21.7 g
- Cholesterol: 95 mg
- Sodium: 877 mg
- Total Carbohydrate: 30.5 g
- Protein: 33.9 g

8. Ninfas Green Tomato Salsa

"A famous green salsa recipe in Houston. Guaranteed to be loved by all."

Serving: 40 | Prep: 15 m | Cook: 10 m | Ready in: 25 m

Ingredients

- 3 green tomatoes, chopped
- 4 fresh tomatillos - husked, rinsed, and chopped
- 1 jalapeno pepper, chopped
- 3 small garlic cloves
- 3 avocados - peeled, pitted, and sliced
- 4 sprigs cilantro
- 1 teaspoon salt
- 1 1/2 cups sour cream

Direction

- Stir tomatoes, tomatillos, jalapeno pepper, and garlic together in a saucepan; bring to a boil, reduce heat to low, and cook at a simmer until the tomatoes and tomatillos soften, 10 to 15 minutes. Remove saucepan from heat and let tomato mixture cool slightly.
- Pour cooled tomato mixture into a blender pitcher; add avocado slices, cilantro, and salt.

- Blend the mixture until smooth; transfer to a bowl.
- Stir sour cream into the blended mixture until smooth.

Nutrition Information

- Calories: 46 calories
- Total Fat: 4.1 g
- Cholesterol: 4 mg
- Sodium: 65 mg
- Total Carbohydrate: 2.4 g
- Protein: 0.7 g

9. Pancetta Wrapped Shrimp with Chipotle Vinaigrette and Cilantro Oil

"This dish makes a hearty and filling main dish and is also great to serve as an appetizer or hors d'oeuvre."

Serving: 8 | Prep: 30 m | Cook: 10 m | Ready in: 40 m

Ingredients

- 1 bunch cilantro, rinsed
- 1 cup canola oil
- 1 teaspoon honey
- 4 teaspoons fresh lime juice
- Salt to taste
- 1 canned chipotle pepper
- 1 tablespoon adobo sauce from canned chipotle peppers
- 1/4 cup fresh lemon juice
- 1/2 cup rice vinegar
- 1 clove garlic
- 1 cup canola oil
- Salt to taste
- 3 pounds extra-large shrimp (16-20), peeled and deveined, tail left on
- 2 pounds thinly sliced pancetta

Direction

- Prepare cilantro oil by pureeing cilantro, canola oil, honey, lime juice, and salt to taste until smooth; pour into a bowl or bottle, and set aside.
- Prepare the chipotle vinaigrette by pureeing the chipotle pepper, adobo sauce, lemon juice, rice vinegar, and garlic in a blender until smooth. With the blender running, slowly pour in the canola oil, and puree until creamy. Season to taste with salt, and set aside.
- Preheat a grill for medium heat.
- Cut the pancetta slices in half. Wrap a half slice of pancetta around each shrimp to cover. Grill until the pancetta has crisped, and the shrimp has turned opaque, 2 to 3 minutes per side. Drain on paper towels.
- To serve, arrange cooked shrimp on a warmed serving platter or individual plates, and drizzle with chipotle vinaigrette and cilantro oil.

Nutrition Information

- Calories: 839 calories
- Total Fat: 73.2 g
- Cholesterol: 300 mg
- Sodium: 1183 mg
- Total Carbohydrate: 2.8 g
- Protein: 41.9 g

10. Queso Catfish

"A deliciously crunchy and spicy way to serve catfish inspired by a similar dish I had in Beaumont, TX."

Serving: 4 | Prep: 40 m | Cook: 10 m | Ready in: 50 m

Ingredients

- 4 (6 ounce) fillets catfish
- 1/4 cup lime juice
- 1/2 cup cheap beer
- 1/4 cup yellow cornmeal
- 1 cup finely crushed tortilla chips
- 1/2 teaspoon salt
- 1/4 teaspoon cayenne pepper
- 2 tablespoons lime juice
- 2 tablespoons canola oil

- 4 ounces processed cheese, cubed
- 1 teaspoon chili powder
- 1 teaspoon ground cumin
- 1/2 chipotle pepper, minced
- 2 tablespoons chopped fresh cilantro (optional)

Direction

- In a shallow dish, stir together 1/4 cup of lime juice and beer. Place fish in the dish, and turn to coat. Marinate for 30 minutes.
- Preheat the oven to 400 degrees F (200 degrees C). Coat a roasting rack with cooking spray, and place over a baking sheet.
- Rinse fish with cold water, and pat dry. Discard the marinade. In one dish, stir together the cornmeal, tortilla chip crumbs, salt and pepper. In another dish, stir together 2 tablespoons of lime juice and canola oil. Dip fillets into the lime and oil, then into the cornmeal mixture to coat. Place the fish onto the roasting rack.
- Bake fish for 8 to 10 minutes, or until it flakes easily with a fork. While the fish is baking, combine the processed cheese, chili powder, cumin, and chipotle pepper in a small saucepan over medium-low heat. Cook and stir until melted and smooth.
- Place fish onto serving plates, and spoon the cheese sauce over them. Top with a sprinkling of cilantro leaves, if desired.

Nutrition Information

- Calories: 442 calories
- Total Fat: 26.5 g
- Cholesterol: 106 mg
- Sodium: 796 mg
- Total Carbohydrate: 17.2 g
- Protein: 31.3 g

11. Sausage Jalapeno Poppers

"This is a recipe for stuffed jalapenos I had at a baby shower in Texas. I loved them and have made them for every party since. They are always anxiously requested, a HIT AT EVERY PARTY!!!! Use toothpicks to secure the bacon around the stuffed jalapenos. Be sure to use a pan that won't let the bacon drip all over the oven while cooking!"

Serving: 20 | Prep: 1 h | Cook: 20 m | Ready in: 1 h 20 m

Ingredients

- 2 (12 ounce) packages ground sausage
- 2 (8 ounce) packages cream cheese, softened
- 30 jalapeno chile peppers
- 1 pound sliced bacon, cut in half

Direction

- Preheat oven to 375 degrees F (190 degrees C).
- Place ground sausage in a large, deep skillet. Cook over medium high heat until evenly brown.
- Drain sausage and place in a medium bowl. Mix with the cream cheese.
- Cut jalapenos in half lengthwise. Remove the seeds. Stuff each jalapeno half with equal portions of the sausage and cream cheese mixture. Wrap with half slices of bacon. Secure bacon with toothpicks.
- Arrange wrapped jalapenos in a large, shallow baking dish. Bake in the preheated oven 20 minutes, or until the bacon is evenly brown.

Nutrition Information

- Calories: 189 calories
- Total Fat: 18.2 g
- Cholesterol: 40 mg
- Sodium: 256 mg
- Total Carbohydrate: 2 g
- Protein: 4.6 g

12. Shrimp Kisses

"A perfect blend of shrimp, bacon, and cheese baked in the oven. What could be better?"

Serving: 8 | Prep: 20 m | Cook: 10 m | Ready in: 30 m

Ingredients

- 1 (8 ounce) package Monterey Jack cheese, cut into strips
- 40 large shrimp - peeled, deveined and butterflied
- 20 slices bacon, cut in half

Direction

- Preheat the oven to 450 degrees F (220 degrees C).
- Place a small piece of cheese into the butterflied opening of each shrimp. Wrap half of a slice of bacon around each one to conceal the cheese, securing with toothpicks. Place on a cookie sheet.
- Bake for 10 to 15 minutes in the preheated oven, until bacon is browned.

Nutrition Information

- Calories: 284 calories
- Total Fat: 16.9 g
- Cholesterol: 205 mg
- Sodium: 753 mg
- Total Carbohydrate: 0.4 g
- Protein: 30.7 g

13. Soul Smothered Chicken

"You can't just go to any restaurant and get smothered chicken like you would if you went down to the urban neighborhoods in Houston. This meal of browned chicken in a savory chicken gravy sauce is best when served over a bed of white rice."

Serving: 8 | Prep: 15 m | Cook: 1 h | Ready in: 1 h 15 m

Ingredients

- 1/2 cup butter
- 1 whole chicken, cut into pieces
- 1 teaspoon salt
- 1/2 teaspoon ground black pepper
- 3/4 cup all-purpose flour
- 3 cups chopped yellow onions
- 1 cup chopped celery
- 3 cloves garlic, chopped
- 2 cups chopped carrots
- 3 cups chicken broth
- 3 tablespoons all-purpose flour
- 1/4 teaspoon cayenne pepper
- 2 teaspoons salt
- 1/4 teaspoon ground black pepper

Direction

- Melt the butter in a large skillet over medium-high heat. Season chicken pieces with 1 teaspoon salt and 1/2 teaspoon pepper. Dredge in 3/4 cup flour, place in the skillet, and brown on all sides. Set chicken aside, and drain skillet, reserving about 1 tablespoon butter.
- Reduce skillet heat to medium-low, and stir in onions, celery, garlic, and carrots. Cook 5 minutes, until tender. Stir in the flour, and cook 5 minutes more. Pour in the chicken broth, season with cayenne pepper, and remaining salt and pepper. Bring to a boil, and reduce heat to low.
- Return chicken to the skillet, cover, and continue cooking 30 minutes, until chicken juices run clear and gravy has thickened.

Nutrition Information

- Calories: 365 calories
- Total Fat: 22.9 g
- Cholesterol: 77 mg
- Sodium: 1035 mg
- Total Carbohydrate: 21.2 g
- Protein: 18.5 g

14. Spicy Soup

"This is a great soup that I got while visiting Houston. It has quickly become a family favorite!"

Serving: 4 | Prep: 15 m | Cook: 25 m | Ready in: 40 m

Ingredients

- 1 teaspoon unsalted butter
- 1/4 cup chopped celery
- 2 cloves garlic, chopped
- 1 tablespoon all-purpose flour
- 3 1/2 cups chicken broth
- 1 1/2 cups chopped broccoli
- 1 1/2 cups cauliflower, chopped
- 2 tablespoons peanut butter
- 1/4 teaspoon salt
- 1/4 teaspoon crushed red pepper flakes
- 2 green onions, chopped
- 1/4 cup heavy cream

Direction

- Melt butter in a saucepan over medium heat; cook and stir celery and garlic until garlic is fragrant, about 5 minutes.
- Stir in flour to make a roux; cook for 1 minute.
- Stir in chicken broth, broccoli, cauliflower, peanut butter, salt, and red pepper flakes. Simmer for 15-20 minutes.
- Mix in green onions and heavy cream just before serving.

Nutrition Information

- Calories: 142 calories
- Total Fat: 10.8 g
- Cholesterol: 23 mg
- Sodium: 218 mg
- Total Carbohydrate: 9.1 g
- Protein: 4.5 g

15. Tex Mex Shark and Shrimp

"This is a great spicy recipe for shark and shrimp. You can probably get non-seafood eaters to enjoy this! I did!"

Serving: 6 | Prep: 15 m | Cook: 23 m | Ready in: 40 m

Ingredients

- 1 (16 ounce) package uncooked wide egg noodles
- 1 teaspoon olive oil
- 1 pound shark steaks, cut into chunks
- 1 pound frozen medium shrimp
- 1 (14.5 ounce) can diced tomatoes and green chiles
- 2 cups shredded mozzarella cheese
- ground black pepper to taste

Direction

- Bring a large pot of lightly salted water to a boil. Add egg noodles, cook for 6 to 8 minutes, until al dente, and drain.
- Heat the olive oil in a skillet over medium heat. Mix in the shark, shrimp, and tomatoes with green chiles. Cover, and cook 15 minutes, or until shark is easily flaked with a fork.
- Serve the shark mixture over the cooked egg noodles. Sprinkle with mozzarella cheese, and season with pepper.

Nutrition Information

- Calories: 528 calories
- Total Fat: 14.8 g
- Cholesterol: 232 mg
- Sodium: 706 mg
- Total Carbohydrate: 50.6 g
- Protein: 46.3 g

16. Texas Smoked Flounder

"Nothing tastes better on a summers day then smoked fish. This can be adapted for trout etc., but the flounder cooks quick. It might take a couple tries for the novice smoker to time it right, but the effort is worth it. These are great as a main course, or a snack during all day grilling sessions. We don't just fry fish down here, we smoke 'em! Besides, aren't you tired of flipping burgers like the rest of suburbia?"

Serving: 2 | Prep: 10 m | Cook: 30 m | Ready in: 40 m

Ingredients

- 1 whole flounder
- 1 lemon, halved
- ground black pepper to taste
- 2 tablespoons chopped fresh dill
- 1 tablespoon olive oil
- 1 cup wood chips, soaked

Direction

- Preheat a smoker for high heat, about 350 degrees F (175 degrees C). If you do not have a smoker, prepare a grill for indirect heat. If you have a gas grill, stop here and find another recipe!
- Clean and scale a fresh flounder. I leave the head on for dramatic appearance, but most people panic at the sight. Use a sharp knife to make 3 or 4 diagonal slits on the body big enough for lemon slices. Slice half of the lemon into thin slices. Rub a light coating of olive oil over the fish, then squeeze the other half of the lemon over it, and rub in some black pepper. Rub or press 1 tablespoon of dill into the slits on the body, and insert lemon slices firmly. Place the flounder on a large piece of aluminum foil, and fold the sides up high around the fish. There should be enough foil to seal into a packet, although you want it open for now.
- Place the fish onto the grill or smoker, and throw a couple of handfuls of soaked wood chips onto the coals. Close the lid and smoke thoroughly for about 10 minutes. Once the fish has been flavored by the smoke, you can seal up the foil and move to direct heat if you like, but I prefer to smoke it until done. When the fish is done, the flesh should flake easily with a fork.
- Remove the fish from the grill using the foil as a handle, and garnish with remaining fresh dill.

Nutrition Information

- Calories: 385 calories
- Total Fat: 11 g
- Cholesterol: 181 mg
- Sodium: 284 mg
- Total Carbohydrate: 6.4 g
- Protein: 65.1 g

17. TexMex Corn Chowder

"I like things that are a little unexpected and unusual. But easy. Everyone raves about the full flavors and textures of this chowder. For the adventuresome--enjoy!"

Serving: 6 | Prep: 10 m | Cook: 30 m | Ready in: 40 m

Ingredients

- 1 1/2 cups chopped onion
- 2 tablespoons margarine
- 1 tablespoon all-purpose flour
- 1 tablespoon chili powder
- 1 teaspoon ground cumin
- 1 (16 ounce) package frozen corn kernels, thawed
- 2 cups medium salsa
- 1 (14.5 ounce) can chicken broth
- 8 ounces cream cheese, softened
- 1 cup milk

Direction

- In a large saucepan, sauté onions in margarine. Stir in flour, chili powder, and cumin. Add corn, picante sauce, and broth. Bring to boil; remove from heat.
- Gradually add 1/4 cup hot mixture to cream cheese in a small bowl. Stir until blended.

- Add cream cheese mixture and milk to saucepan, stirring until well blended. Heat through but do not boil. Serve immediately.

Nutrition Information

- Calories: 299 calories
- Total Fat: 18.6 g
- Cholesterol: 45 mg
- Sodium: 706 mg
- Total Carbohydrate: 29.5 g
- Protein: 8.6 g

18. Ultimate Gulf Coast Gumbo

"Gumbo filled with shrimp, crab, chicken, sausage, vegetables, and Cajun spices. I've also included crab and/or scallops in this recipe. Serve over rice, accompanied with garlic bread. Also have salt, red pepper flakes, and additional file powder on the table. Great with cold beer."

Serving: 20 | Prep: 1 h 30 m | Cook: 2 h 20 m | Ready in: 3 h 50 m

Ingredients

- 4 pounds medium shrimp - peeled and deveined
- 1/2 cup corn oil
- 1/2 cup all-purpose flour
- 1 cup chicken broth
- 1 (3 pound) whole chicken
- 2 onions, chopped
- 5 stalks celery, chopped
- 1 green bell pepper, chopped
- 5 large tomatoes, chopped
- 4 cloves garlic, minced
- 2 bay leaves
- 1 tablespoon salt
- 2 tablespoons Old Bay Seasoning TM
- 1 tablespoon ground cayenne pepper
- 3 (6 ounce) cans crab meat, drained
- 1 pound andouille sausage, diced
- 2 tablespoons file powder

Direction

- Peel and devein the shrimp. Refrigerate shrimp meat. Place the shrimp heads and shells in a large pot, and cover with 2 quarts of water. Cover, and simmer over medium low heat until liquid is reduced by half. Strain out the shrimp heads and shells.
- Select a large stock pot capable of holding all the ingredients. Add oil to the pot, and heat over medium high heat. Using a long handled spoon, stir in flour; cook and stir for several minutes until dark brown. At that point, the flour suddenly puffs and absorbs the oil. Slowly stir in chicken broth and an equal amount of water. Place chicken in the pot. Add onions, celery, bell pepper, tomatoes, garlic, bay leaves, red pepper flakes, Old Bay seasoning, and salt. Boil for about 1 1/2 hours, or until chicken meat is no longer pink and the juices run clear.
- Remove chicken from the pot, and set aside until cool enough to handle. Remove bones, and chop the chicken into about one inch pieces.
- Add chicken meat, shrimp broth, crab meat, sausage, and shrimp to. Add the file powder, and stir from the bottom of the pot. When the gumbo comes to a boil, remove from heat. Continue to stir from the bottom for 1 minute. Serve.

Nutrition Information

- Calories: 333 calories
- Total Fat: 18.3 g
- Cholesterol: 204 mg
- Sodium: 999 mg
- Total Carbohydrate: 7.3 g
- Protein: 33.3 g

Chapter 2: Dallas Recipes

***

19. Baby Doe's Cheese Soup with Beer

"Baby Doe's Cheese Soup came from a famous steak place in Dallas, Texas."

Serving: 12 | Cook: 35 m | Ready in: 35 m

Ingredients

- 2 quarts milk
- 1 1/2 tablespoons chicken bouillon powder
- 1 tablespoon Worcestershire sauce
- 1 tablespoon hot pepper sauce
- 1/2 tablespoon salt
- 6 tablespoons cornstarch
- 1/2 cup water
- 12 fluid ounces dark beer
- 1 (16 ounce) jar processed cheese sauce

Direction

- In a large pot over medium heat, combine the milk, bouillon, Worcestershire sauce, hot pepper sauce and salt. Bring close to a boil.
- In a small bowl, dissolve the cornstarch in the water and add to the soup, stirring well. Add the beer and the cheese sauce, reduce heat to low and mix well. Allow to heat through before serving.

Nutrition Information

- Calories: 217 calories
- Total Fat: 11.2 g
- Cholesterol: 41 mg
- Sodium: 1284 mg
- Total Carbohydrate: 16.4 g
- Protein: 10.3 g

20. Baked Chicken Reuben

"This is a great make-ahead dish from Marcia C. Adams of Fort Wayne, Indiana. It took the top $10,000 prize in the National Chicken Cooking Contest in Dallas, Texas. It sounds weird, but it is good."

Serving: 6 | Prep: 5 m | Cook: 1 h 30 m | Ready in: 1 h 35 m

Ingredients

- 6 skinless, boneless chicken breast halves
- 1/4 teaspoon salt
- 1/8 teaspoon ground black pepper
- 1 (16 ounce) can sauerkraut, drained and pressed
- 4 slices Swiss cheese
- 1 1/4 cups thousand island salad dressing
- 1 tablespoon chopped fresh parsley

Direction

- Preheat oven to 325 degrees F (165 degrees C).
- Place chicken in a lightly greased 9x13 inch baking dish. Sprinkle with salt and pepper. Place sauerkraut over chicken and top with cheese slices. Pour dressing over all and cover dish with aluminum foil.
- Bake in preheated oven for 90 minutes, or until chicken is cooked through (fork can be easily inserted and juices run clear). Sprinkle with chopped parsley and serve.

Nutrition Information

- Calories: 446 calories
- Total Fat: 28.1 g
- Cholesterol: 104 mg
- Sodium: 1306 mg
- Total Carbohydrate: 16.7 g
- Protein: 33 g

21. Best Ever Cowboy Caviar

"Every time I make this I get asked for the recipe. I keep it on a file in my computer so I can print and email it easily. To add heat it is also good with jalapenos. Serve with tortilla chips."

Serving: 8 | Prep: 15 m | Ready in: 1 d 15 m

Ingredients

- 1/2 cup olive oil
- 1/2 cup vegetable oil
- 1/2 cup cider vinegar
- 1/2 cup white sugar
- 1 (14 ounce) can pinto beans, rinsed and drained
- 1 (14 ounce) can black-eyed peas, rinsed and drained
- 1 (11 ounce) can white shoepeg corn, drained
- 1 red onion, chopped
- 2 stalks celery, chopped
- 1 red bell pepper, chopped
- 1/2 cup chopped cilantro

Direction

- Combine olive oil, vegetable oil, cider vinegar, and sugar in a saucepan; bring to a boil, remove from heat, and cool to room temperature.
- Stir pinto beans, black-eyed peas, corn, onion, celery, red bell pepper, and cilantro together in a large bowl. Pour cooled oil mixture over bean mixture and toss to coat. Cover the bowl with plastic wrap and refrigerate, stirring occasionally, for 24 hours. Drain excess dressing before serving.

Nutrition Information

- Calories: 426 calories
- Total Fat: 28.3 g
- Cholesterol: 0 mg
- Sodium: 415 mg
- Total Carbohydrate: 37.5 g
- Protein: 6.2 g

22. Bethanys Frito Pie

"Fritos® and chili! This was a real favorite when I was a kid, and it still is. With the Frito-Lay® Company being based in Dallas, this dish is about as Texan as you can get."

Serving: 4 | Prep: 10 m | Cook: 15 m | Ready in: 25 m

Ingredients

- 3 cups corn chips (such as Fritos®)
- 1 cup shredded Cheddar cheese
- 3/4 cup chopped onion
- 2 1/2 cups prepared chili

Direction

- Preheat oven to 350 degrees F (175 degrees C).
- Spread about 2 cups corn chips in a baking dish. Sprinkle half the onion and half the Cheddar cheese over chips and top with chili. Spread remaining 1 cup corn chips over the chili, followed by remaining chopped onion and cheese.
- Bake until hot and bubbly, 15 to 20 minutes.

Nutrition Information

- Calories: 422 calories
- Total Fat: 23.1 g
- Cholesterol: 52 mg
- Sodium: 991 mg
- Total Carbohydrate: 35.6 g
- Protein: 20 g

23. Brazilian Grilled Pineapple

"Favorite at a Brazilian steakhouse in Dallas. Not sure if this is the exact recipe they use but it tastes very close. Great side for kabobs and steak."

Serving: 6 | Prep: 10 m | Cook: 10 m | Ready in: 20 m

Ingredients

- 1 cup brown sugar
- 2 teaspoons ground cinnamon
- 1 pineapple - peeled, cored, and cut into 6 wedges

Direction

- Preheat an outdoor grill for medium-high heat and lightly oil the grate.
- Whisk brown sugar and cinnamon together in a bowl. Pour sugar mixture into a large resealable plastic bag. Place pineapple wedges in bag and shake to coat each wedge.
- Grill pineapple wedges on the preheated grill until heated through, 3 to 5 minutes per side.

Nutrition Information

- Calories: 255 calories
- Total Fat: 0.3 g
- Cholesterol: 0 mg
- Sodium: 13 mg
- Total Carbohydrate: 66.4 g
- Protein: 1.3 g

24. Cowboy Bread

"Similar to pita breads, this is a round fried bread which supposedly traces its origins back to the great American West."

Serving: 8 | Prep: 1 h 30 m | Cook: 10 m | Ready in: 1 h 40 m

Ingredients

- 1/2 cup boiling water
- 3/4 cup cold milk
- 1 teaspoon white sugar
- 1 1/2 teaspoons active dry yeast
- 1 egg, beaten
- 2 tablespoons butter, melted and cooled
- 1/4 teaspoon salt
- 1/4 teaspoon ground nutmeg
- 4 cups all-purpose flour

Direction

- In a large bowl, stir together the water, milk, and sugar. Sprinkle the yeast over the top, and let stand for 5 minutes to dissolve.

- Stir the egg and butter into the yeast mixture, then stir in the salt, nutmeg, and 2 cups of the flour. Mix until everything is well blended. Mix in remaining flour, 1/2 cup at a time until the dough pulls away from the side of the bowl. Turn out onto a floured surface, and knead for 10 minutes (no cheating!). Place dough into a greased bowl, and let rise until doubled in size.
- Divide the dough into 8 balls, and let rest for another 20 minutes. Roll each ball out to 8 to 10 inches in diameter.
- Heat a cast-iron skillet over medium-high heat. Fry each of the pieces of bread from 30 to 60 seconds on each side, or until light to medium brown spots appear. Keep covered with a damp cloth, or store in a plastic bag until serving.

Nutrition Information

- Calories: 278 calories
- Total Fat: 4.6 g
- Cholesterol: 33 mg
- Sodium: 113 mg
- Total Carbohydrate: 49.7 g
- Protein: 8.3 g

25. Cowboy Caviar

"Black beans absorb other flavors superbly, so try to leave this for at least 20 minutes before serving to allow the different flavors to blend together."

Serving: 8 | Prep: 20 m | Ready in: 40 m

Ingredients

- 1 (15.5 ounce) can black beans, drained
- 1 (15.5 ounce) can black-eyed peas, drained
- 1 (14.5 ounce) can diced tomatoes, drained
- 2 cups frozen corn kernels, thawed
- 1/2 medium onion, chopped
- 1/4 green bell pepper, finely chopped
- 1/2 cup chopped pickled jalapeno peppers
- 1/2 teaspoon garlic salt
- 1 cup Italian salad dressing
- 3/4 cup chopped cilantro

Direction

- Mix beans, peas, tomatoes, corn, onion, bell pepper, and jalapeno peppers in a large bowl. Season with garlic salt. Add dressing and cilantro; toss to coat. Refrigerate for 20 minutes or until ready to serve.

Nutrition Information

- Calories: 233 calories
- Total Fat: 9.1 g
- Cholesterol: 0 mg
- Sodium: 1255 mg
- Total Carbohydrate: 32.3 g
- Protein: 7.9 g

26. Cowboy Cookie Mix in a Jar

"Cookie mix layered in a jar. They are great for gift-giving or bake sales."

Serving: 18 | Prep: 25 m | Ready in: 25 m

Ingredients

- 1 1/3 cups rolled oats
- 1/2 cup packed brown sugar
- 1/2 cup white sugar
- 1/2 cup chopped pecans
- 1 cup semisweet chocolate chips
- 1 1/3 cups all-purpose flour
- 1 teaspoon baking powder
- 1 teaspoon baking soda
- 1/4 teaspoon salt

Direction

- Layer the ingredients in a 1 quart jar in the order given. Press each layer firmly in place before adding the next layer.
- Include a card with the following instructions: Cowboy Cookie Mix in a Jar 1. Preheat oven to 350 degrees F (175 degrees C). Grease cookie

sheets. 2. In a medium bowl, mix together 1/2 cup melted butter or margarine, 1 egg, and 1 teaspoon of vanilla. Stir in the entire contents of the jar. You may need to use your hands to finish mixing. Shape into walnut sized balls. Place 2 inches apart on prepared cookie sheets. 3. Bake for 11 to 13 minutes in the preheated oven. Transfer from cookie sheets to cool on wire racks.

Nutrition Information

- Calories: 167 calories
- Total Fat: 5.5 g
- Cholesterol: 0 mg
- Sodium: 133 mg
- Total Carbohydrate: 29.1 g
- Protein: 2.4 g

- Combine the melted and cooled butter or margarine with the brown and white sugars. Beat in the eggs at medium speed of an electric mixer. Add the vanilla, oats, corn flakes, flour, baking soda and baking powder; beating well.
- Drop tablespoon sized spoonfuls of the dough on to an ungreased cookie sheet. Bake at 350 degrees F (175 degrees C) for 15 minutes for a soft and chewy cookie.

Nutrition Information

- Calories: 393 calories
- Total Fat: 16.8 g
- Cholesterol: 72 mg
- Sodium: 289 mg
- Total Carbohydrate: 57.4 g
- Protein: 4.4 g

27. Cowboy Cookies Dunkin Platters

"These are great for dunking and are also large and satisfying enough for a man's appetite. Cowboy cookies should be about 2-1/2 inches in diameter. My Grandma makes these cookies and I have enjoyed them since I was a kid."

Serving: 24

Ingredients

- 2 cups butter, melted
- 2 cups packed brown sugar
- 2 cups white sugar
- 4 eggs
- 2 teaspoons vanilla extract
- 2 cups quick cooking oats
- 2 cups cornflakes cereal
- 4 cups all-purpose flour
- 2 teaspoons baking powder
- 2 teaspoons baking soda

Direction

- Preheat oven to 350 degrees F (175 degrees C).

28. Cowboy Cookies II

"We made these cookies in school during the 1950s. They are delicious. May substitute butterscotch chips, peanut butter chips, or raisins for chocolate chips."

Serving: 66

Ingredients

- 2 cups all-purpose flour
- 1 teaspoon baking soda
- 1/2 teaspoon salt
- 1/2 teaspoon baking powder
- 1 cup shortening
- 1 cup white sugar
- 1 cup packed brown sugar
- 2 eggs
- 2 cups rolled oats
- 1 teaspoon vanilla extract
- 2 cups semisweet chocolate chips

Direction

- Blend shortening and sugars together. Add eggs, and beat until fluffy. Whisk together flour, soda, salt, and baking powder; mix into the egg mixture. Stir in oats, vanilla, and

chocolate chips. Drop by teaspoonfuls on ungreased cookie sheets
- Bake at 350 degrees F (175 degrees C) for 15 minutes. Cool on wire racks.

Nutrition Information

- Calories: 102 calories
- Total Fat: 5 g
- Cholesterol: 6 mg
- Sodium: 44 mg
- Total Carbohydrate: 14.1 g
- Protein: 1.1 g

chocolate chips. Drop by rounded teaspoonfuls onto the prepared baking sheets.
- Bake for 8 to 10 minutes in the preheated oven. Allow cookies to cool on baking sheets for 5 minutes before removing.

Nutrition Information

- Calories: 95 calories
- Total Fat: 4.3 g
- Cholesterol: 14 mg
- Sodium: 74 mg
- Total Carbohydrate: 13.7 g
- Protein: 1.1 g

29. Cowboy Cookies III

"These are yummy. If you can manage to get them to cook just the right way, they aren't crunchy, but soft and the tiniest bit chewy, and melt in your mouth!"

Serving: 60 | Prep: 15 m | Cook: 10 m | Ready in: 1 h

Ingredients

- 2 cups all-purpose flour
- 1 teaspoon baking powder
- 1 teaspoon baking soda
- 1/2 teaspoon salt
- 1 cup butter, softened
- 1 cup white sugar
- 1 cup packed brown sugar
- 2 eggs
- 1 teaspoon vanilla extract
- 2 cups rolled oats
- 1 cup semisweet chocolate chips

Direction

- Preheat oven to 350 degrees F (175 degrees C). Grease baking sheets. Sift together the flour, baking powder, baking soda, and salt. Set aside.
- In a large bowl, cream together the butter, white sugar, and brown sugar until light and fluffy. Beat in the eggs one at a time, then stir in the vanilla. Gradually stir in the sifted ingredients. Stir in the rolled oats and

30. Cowboy Dip

"I made up this dip years ago and have found through the years that family and friends request this in football season every year."

Serving: 8 | Prep: 15 m | Ready in: 15 m

Ingredients

- 2 roma (plum) tomatoes, seeded and chopped
- 1 (4 ounce) can chopped black olives
- 1 (4 ounce) can chopped green chilies
- 3 green onions, chopped
- 3 tablespoons olive oil
- 1 1/2 tablespoons red wine vinegar
- 1 teaspoon garlic salt

Direction

- Mix tomatoes, black olives, green chiles, green onions, olive oil, vinegar, and garlic salt in a bowl.

Nutrition Information

- Calories: 70 calories
- Total Fat: 6.6 g
- Cholesterol: 0 mg
- Sodium: 515 mg
- Total Carbohydrate: 2.9 g
- Protein: 0.5 g

31. Cowboy Kale

"The apple, red peppers, and carrots add a nice sweetness to this dish, complemented by the balsamic vinaigrette."

Serving: 6 | Prep: 25 m | Cook: 5 m | Ready in: 30 m

Ingredients

- 1 tablespoon olive oil
- 1 red pepper, thinly sliced
- 1 green pepper, thinly sliced
- 12 white mushrooms, halved
- 4 green onions, sliced
- 1 clove garlic, minced
- 1 teaspoon sea salt
- 1 large bunch kale, stems removed, chopped
- 1 Granny Smith apple, shredded
- 1 carrot, shredded
- 1 teaspoon balsamic vinaigrette, or to taste

Direction

- Heat olive in a skillet over medium heat. Sauté red pepper, green pepper, mushrooms, green onions, garlic, and salt until tender but not soggy, 3 to 5 minutes. Add kale and cook until wilted and tender, 1 to 2 minutes. Add apple and shredded carrot, cook until warmed through, 1 to 2 minutes. Sprinkle with balsamic vinaigrette.

Nutrition Information

- Calories: 63 calories
- Total Fat: 2.8 g
- Cholesterol: 0 mg
- Sodium: 319 mg
- Total Carbohydrate: 8.9 g
- Protein: 2.1 g

32. Cowboy Margaritas

"This is a fun cocktail that will appeal to many different tastes because it balances the tart, sweet, and tangy flavors of the liquors beautifully. This may be served frozen or on the rocks in a sugar-rimmed glass."

Serving: 6 | Prep: 10 m | Ready in: 10 m

Ingredients

- 1 (12 ounce) container frozen limeade concentrate
- 6 fluid ounces tequila
- 3 fluid ounces raspberry-flavored liqueur
- 1 (12 fluid ounce) can or bottle light beer

Direction

- Blend limeade, tequila, and raspberry-flavored liqueur in a blender until well mixed. Slowly stir light beer into limeade mixture.

Nutrition Information

- Calories: 316 calories
- Total Fat: 0 g
- Cholesterol: 0 mg
- Sodium: 4 mg
- Total Carbohydrate: 53 g
- Protein: 0.1 g

33. Cowboy Mashed Potatoes

"Quick, easy and delicious mashed potatoes with corn and carrots."

Serving: 10 | Prep: 20 m | Cook: 20 m | Ready in: 40 m

Ingredients

- 1 pound red potatoes
- 1 pound Yukon Gold (yellow) potatoes
- 1 fresh jalapeno pepper, sliced
- 12 ounces baby carrots
- 4 cloves garlic
- 1 (10 ounce) package frozen white corn, thawed
- 1/4 cup butter

- 1/2 cup shredded Cheddar cheese
- salt and pepper to taste

Direction

- Place red potatoes, yellow potatoes, jalapeno pepper, carrots and garlic cloves in a large pot. Cover with water, and bring to a boil over high heat. Cook 15 to 20 minutes, or until potatoes are tender. Drain water from pot.
- Stir in corn and butter. Mash the mixture with a potato masher until butter is melted and potatoes have reached desired consistency. Mix in cheese, salt, and pepper. Serve hot.

Nutrition Information

- Calories: 175 calories
- Total Fat: 7.3 g
- Cholesterol: 19 mg
- Sodium: 108 mg
- Total Carbohydrate: 24.6 g
- Protein: 4.7 g

34. Cowboy Mexican Dip

"A quick and easy hot dip that's guaranteed to be a hit! I have never seen this recipe anywhere else. I got it when I was in college and it was years before I tried it. Now it is a staple of all my parties."

Serving: 24 | Prep: 10 m | Cook: 30 m | Ready in: 40 m

Ingredients

- 12 beef tamales, husked and mashed
- 1 (15 ounce) can chili without beans
- 1 (14.5 ounce) can diced tomatoes and green chiles
- 1 (1 pound) loaf processed cheese, cubed

Direction

- Place the tamales, chili, diced tomatoes, and processed cheese into a slow cooker. Set heat on high, and cook, stirring occasionally until cheese is melted. Reduce heat to low to keep the dip warm while serving. Serve with corn chips or tortilla chips.

Nutrition Information

- Calories: 117 calories
- Total Fat: 7.5 g
- Cholesterol: 21 mg
- Sodium: 447 mg
- Total Carbohydrate: 7.2 g
- Protein: 5.7 g

35. Cowboy Oatmeal Cookies

"It's a great cookie, one of the kids' favorites. This doesn't call for nuts, but I sometimes add about 1/2 cup of chopped walnuts or pecans."

Serving: 36 | Prep: 15 m | Cook: 10 m | Ready in: 40 m

Ingredients

- 2 cups all-purpose flour
- 1/2 teaspoon baking powder
- 1 teaspoon baking soda
- 1/2 teaspoon salt
- 1/2 cup margarine
- 1/2 cup vegetable oil
- 1 cup packed brown sugar
- 1 cup white sugar
- 2 eggs
- 2 cups quick cooking oats
- 1 cup butterscotch chips

Direction

- Preheat the oven to 350 degrees F (175 degrees C). Sift together flour, baking powder, baking soda, and salt; set aside.
- In a medium bowl, cream margarine, oil, brown sugar, and white sugar until smooth. Beat in eggs one at a time. Gradually stir in the sifted ingredients until well blended. Mix in oats and butterscotch chips. Drop from a teaspoon onto ungreased cookie sheets.
- Bake for 10 to 12 minutes in preheated oven, or until edges are golden. Let set up on the

cookie sheets for a few minutes before transferring to wire racks to cool completely.

Nutrition Information

- Calories: 167 calories
- Total Fat: 7.5 g
- Cholesterol: 10 mg
- Sodium: 114 mg
- Total Carbohydrate: 23 g
- Protein: 1.7 g

36. Cowboy Skillet New Potato Medley Italian Sausage Eggs

"This Cowboy Skillet: New Potato Medley, Italian Sausage and Eggs recipe is courtesy of Sandra's Easy Cooking, a part of Potatoes USA's Potato Lovers Club Program."

Serving: 4 | Prep: 7 m | Cook: 20 m | Ready in: 30 m

Ingredients

- 1 pound new potatoes (red, yellow, purple)
- 3/4 teaspoon kosher salt
- 1/2 teaspoon freshly ground black pepper
- 2 tablespoons vegetable oil
- 1/4 onion, sliced
- 1/2 tablespoon minced fresh rosemary leaves
- 6 ounces ground mild Italian sausage
- 5 large organic eggs
- Garnish:
- Chives or scallions, sliced

Direction

- Place the potatoes in a bowl; toss with the salt and pepper until the potatoes are well coated. Heat the oil in a heavy oven-safe skillet and drop in the potatoes carefully, a few at a time.
- Flip potatoes several times with tongs during cooking to ensure even browning.
- About halfway through cooking, add the onion and mix while cooking. When they're done, the potatoes should be crispy. Sprinkle on the rosemary leaves. Spoon out unwanted oil, if you wish.
- While potatoes are cooking, in a nonstick pan, sauté the Italian sausage over medium-high heat for a few minutes, or until it is no longer pink.
- Add the sausage to the potatoes and onion. Mix it very well and break eggs (sunny side up) into the pan; add few dashes of salt to season eggs. Try to go in between the potatoes, allowing the egg whites to go all around and under potatoes and sausage; try not to break egg yolks. Once the egg whites are getting almost cooked, turn on the broiler to high, and set a baking rack in the middle of the oven.
- Place the pan under the broiler and let it cook for a minute or two, just so the egg whites are completely cooked; the yolks may be still a little runny/soft. If you do not like runny/soft eggs just let them cook under broiler longer. Sprinkle chopped chives or scallions on at the end and dig in!

Nutrition Information

- Calories: 386 calories
- Total Fat: 26.3 g
- Cholesterol: 264 mg
- Sodium: 762 mg
- Total Carbohydrate: 21.5 g
- Protein: 16.3 g

37. Cowboy Stew I

"This is nice and thick and yummy. Sour cream is also good on this."

Serving: 4 | Prep: 5 m | Cook: 45 m | Ready in: 50 m

Ingredients

- 1 1/2 pounds ground beef
- 1 onion, chopped
- 1 (14.75 ounce) can cream-style corn
- 1 (15 ounce) can chili with beans
- 1 (15 ounce) can baked beans with pork

- 1 (15 ounce) can tomato sauce
- 1 (4 ounce) can diced green chiles

Direction

- Crumble the ground beef into a large skillet or Dutch oven over medium-high heat. Add onion; cook and stir until beef is no longer pink. Drain off grease. Reduce heat to medium-low and stir in the corn, chili with beans, baked beans, tomato sauce and green chilies. Cover and simmer for 30 minutes, stirring occasionally.

Nutrition Information

- Calories: 655 calories
- Total Fat: 27.9 g
- Cholesterol: 129 mg
- Sodium: 2176 mg
- Total Carbohydrate: 63.4 g
- Protein: 43.9 g

38. Dallas-Style Sloppy Joes

"These sloppy Joes feature zesty sauces and fresh veggies."

Serving: 5 | Prep: 20 m | Cook: 25 m | Ready in: 45 m

Ingredients

- 1 1/2 pounds lean ground beef
- 1 yellow onion, chopped
- 1 red bell pepper, chopped
- sea salt and ground black pepper to taste
- 1 1/2 cups ketchup
- 3 tablespoons apple cider vinegar
- 3 tablespoons Worcestershire sauce
- 3 tablespoons brown sugar
- 3 tablespoons yellow mustard
- 3 tablespoons hickory flavored barbecue sauce
- 2 tablespoons grated Parmesan cheese
- 5 large hamburger buns, toasted

Direction

- Cook the ground beef in a large skillet over medium heat until completely browned, 5 to 7 minutes. Add the onion and bell pepper, season with sea salt and black pepper, and cook until vegetables soften, about 7 minutes.
- Stir in the ketchup, vinegar, Worcestershire sauce, brown sugar, mustard, and barbeque sauce. Reduce heat to low and simmer the mixture until thickened, about 10 minutes. Add Parmesan cheese and serve on toasted hamburger buns.

Nutrition Information

- Calories: 530 calories
- Total Fat: 19.5 g
- Cholesterol: 85 mg
- Sodium: 1531 mg
- Total Carbohydrate: 59.4 g
- Protein: 29.6 g

39. Easy Cowboy Beans Frijoles Charros

"This is a tasty, zesty side dish that can easily become a main meal. Serve soupy with warm flour tortillas or crusty bread, crumble corn bread on top, or scoop up with tortilla chips. Like mac and cheese, it's a great comfort food. It is easy to make because it doesn't require constant attention and is good for everything from a family meal to a football party. It can easily be doubled. Check flavor before serving and alter seasonings to taste if necessary. Top with more onion and cilantro as desired. If there are any leftovers, they hold up well and taste great the next day."

Serving: 6 | Prep: 10 m | Cook: 1 h | Ready in: 1 h 10 m

Ingredients

- 2 (15.5 ounce) cans pinto beans, undrained
- 1 (10 ounce) can diced tomatoes with green chile peppers (such as RO*TEL®), drained
- 1 cup cubed cooked ham
- 1/4 cup finely chopped fresh cilantro
- 1/4 cup finely chopped red onion

- 2 cloves garlic, minced
- ground black pepper to taste
- 1 dash hot sauce, or to taste

Direction

- Combine pinto beans, tomatoes with green chile peppers, ham, cilantro, red onion, garlic, black pepper, and hot sauce in a saucepan; bring to a boil. Reduce heat and simmer for about 1 hour.

Nutrition Information

- Calories: 194 calories
- Total Fat: 5.4 g
- Cholesterol: 13 mg
- Sodium: 913 mg
- Total Carbohydrate: 25.2 g
- Protein: 11.8 g

40. Grandmas Cowboy Cookies

"A soft cookie with tons of chocolate and flavor."

Serving: 36 | Prep: 30 m | Cook: 9 m | Ready in: 39 m

Ingredients

- 3/4 cup shortening
- 3/4 cup margarine
- 1 cup white sugar
- 1 cup brown sugar
- 1/2 cup peanut butter
- 2 eggs
- 1 teaspoon vanilla extract
- 2 cups all-purpose flour
- 1/3 cup unsweetened cocoa powder
- 1 teaspoon baking powder
- 1 teaspoon baking soda
- 1 teaspoon cream of tartar
- 1 cup rolled oats
- 1 cup flaked coconut
- 1/2 cup chopped walnuts (optional)
- 2 cups miniature semisweet chocolate chips

Direction

- Preheat oven to 350 degrees F (175 degrees C). Grease cookie sheets.
- In a large bowl, cream together the shortening, margarine, white sugar and brown sugar until smooth. Beat in the eggs one at a time, then stir in the peanut butter and vanilla. Combine the flour, cocoa, baking powder, baking soda and cream of tartar; stir into the sugar mixture. Mix in the oats, walnuts (if desired) and chocolate chips. Drop by rounded spoonfuls onto the prepared cookie sheets.
- Bake for 8 to 10 minutes in the preheated oven. Allow cookies to cool on baking sheet for 5 minutes before removing to a wire rack to cool completely.

Nutrition Information

- Calories: 235 calories
- Total Fat: 14.9 g
- Cholesterol: 10 mg
- Sodium: 118 mg
- Total Carbohydrate: 25 g
- Protein: 3.2 g

41. Greek Cowboy Hash and Eggs

"This recipe features one of my all-time favorite vegetables: the sweet potato. The tanginess of the feta (the Greek part) is a strange but tasty complement to the smoky, spicy chipotle chili powder (the cowboy part). This meal is great for brunch and simple to scale down for a quick dinner when you're cooking for yourself."

Serving: 2 | Prep: 20 m | Cook: 15 m | Ready in: 35 m

Ingredients

- 2 tablespoons olive oil
- 1 large sweet potato, peeled and cut into 1/4-inch cubes
- 1 red onion, chopped
- 4 cloves garlic, minced
- 1 tablespoon chipotle chile powder
- 1 teaspoon ground cumin

- 1 teaspoon ground coriander
- salt and ground black pepper to taste
- 2 tablespoons olive oil
- 4 eggs
- 1/4 cup fresh cilantro, chopped
- 1/2 cup crumbled feta cheese
- 1/2 avocado, sliced

Direction

- Heat 2 tablespoons olive oil in a skillet over medium heat. Cook the potatoes in the heated oil until they begin to soften, about 5 minutes. Add the onion and garlic; continue cooking until the onions sweat and begin to caramelize. Season with chipotle chile powder, cumin, coriander, salt, and pepper; stir. Transfer to a bowl and cover with a plate to retain the heat.
- Pour 2 tablespoons olive oil into the skillet and return to medium heat. Crack the eggs into the heated oil and cook until they begin to turn opaque; flip and continue cooking until no clear white remains. (Don't overcook the eggs -- the best part of this meal is the smoothness that the yolk adds to the mix). Place the cooked eggs atop the potato mixture. Top with cilantro, feta cheese, and avocado to serve.

Nutrition Information

- Calories: 769 calories
- Total Fat: 51.6 g
- Cholesterol: 434 mg
- Sodium: 777 mg
- Total Carbohydrate: 56.1 g
- Protein: 24.6 g

42. Harriet and Marlos Cowboy Stew

"Delicious, filling, convenient, and economical - what's not to love? I got this recipe from my good friend Harriet who got it from her daughter-in-law Marlo. It tastes like a light chili, and my children and husband are very fond of it. It makes a bunch, so I always have leftovers for school lunches."

Serving: 6 | Prep: 10 m | Cook: 30 m | Ready in: 40 m

Ingredients

- 1 pound lean ground beef
- 1 medium onion, diced
- 2 (14 ounce) cans diced tomatoes, undrained
- 1 (14 ounce) can pork and beans
- 1 (14 ounce) can creamed corn
- 1 (14 ounce) can whole kernel corn, drained
- 1/4 cup ketchup
- 2 teaspoons ground cumin
- 2 teaspoons chili powder
- 1/2 teaspoon garlic powder

Direction

- Heat a Dutch oven over medium-high heat. Add beef and onion; cook and stir until beef is browned and crumbly, 5 to 7 minutes. Add tomatoes, pork and beans, creamed corn, whole kernel corn, ketchup, cumin, chili powder, and garlic powder. Stir to combine. Bring to a boil, stirring occasionally.
- Reduce heat to medium or medium-low. Cover and cook, stirring occasionally, until stew is hot and flavors meld, about 20 minutes.

Nutrition Information

- Calories: 378 calories
- Total Fat: 11.8 g
- Cholesterol: 56 mg
- Sodium: 974 mg
- Total Carbohydrate: 48 g
- Protein: 23.6 g

43. Holy Hot Mango Daiquiri Batman

"My best friend took me out on the town in Nashville and we ordered a few of these amazing drinks. Then... a few weeks later I had something similar in Dallas! I became obsessed with figuring out how to throw one together and this is as close as it comes to heaven in a glass with a splash of burning as it goes down!"

Serving: 4 | Prep: 10 m | Ready in: 1 h 10 m

Ingredients

- 2 cups mango-flavored rum (such as Malibu®)
- 1/2 jalapeno pepper, coarsely chopped, or more to taste
- 2 cups orange-peach-mango juice (such as Dole®)
- 3 tablespoons orange-flavored liqueur (such as Grand Marnier® or Cointreau®), or to taste
- 1 1/2 limes, juiced
- crushed ice
- 4 thin slices jalapeno pepper

Direction

- Combine mango-flavored rum and chopped jalapeno pepper in a large glass container. Let infuse, at least 1 hour. Strain out jalapeno pepper and discard.
- Mix infused rum with orange-peach-mango juice, orange-flavored liqueur, and lime juice together in a bowl.
- Fill a cocktail shaker with ice and add rum mixture, working in batches. Cover shaker and shake until outside of the cocktail shaker is frosted; pour into serving glasses. Garnish with jalapeno pepper slices.

Nutrition Information

- Calories: 356 calories
- Total Fat: 0.1 g
- Cholesterol: 0 mg
- Sodium: 21 mg
- Total Carbohydrate: 19.3 g
- Protein: 0.6 g

44. Rich Mexican Corn

"This recipe came from my step-mom in Dallas, Texas. They like it hot so they put in a few extra jalapenos."

Serving: 8 | Prep: 15 m | Cook: 45 m | Ready in: 1 h

Ingredients

- 1 (8 ounce) package cream cheese
- 1/2 cup butter
- 1/2 cup milk
- 1 (16 ounce) package frozen corn
- 1 red bell pepper, diced
- 8 fresh jalapeno peppers, diced

Direction

- Preheat oven to 350 degrees F (175 degrees C).
- In a saucepan over medium-low heat, melt the cream cheese and butter, and mix with the milk until smooth and bubbly.
- In a medium casserole dish, mix the frozen corn, red bell pepper, and jalapeno peppers. Pour in the cream cheese mixture, and toss to coat.
- Bake 35 to 45 minutes in the preheated oven, until bubbly and lightly brown.

Nutrition Information

- Calories: 265 calories
- Total Fat: 22.1 g
- Cholesterol: 63 mg
- Sodium: 173 mg
- Total Carbohydrate: 14.8 g
- Protein: 4.8 g

45. Tangy Cowboy Caviar

"This sugar-free variation is sweet and tangy and great as a dip, on chicken or pork, or as a salad topping or side dish."

Serving: 8 | Prep: 30 m | Ready in: 8 h 30 m

Ingredients

- 3 (11 ounce) cans white shoepeg corn, drained
- 1 (15 ounce) can black beans, rinsed and drained
- 1 (15 ounce) can pinto beans, rinsed and drained
- 1 (15 ounce) can black-eyed peas, rinsed and drained
- 1 red bell pepper, diced
- 1 yellow bell pepper, diced
- 1 orange bell pepper, diced
- 1/2 red onion, diced
- 2 tablespoons vegetable oil
- 1/2 cup granular sweetener (such as Equal®)
- 1/2 cup apple cider vinegar
- 2 cups water

Direction

- Mix corn, black beans, pinto beans, black-eyed peas, red bell pepper, yellow bell pepper, orange bell pepper, and red onion together in a large bowl; stir in vegetable oil.
- Put granular sweetener into a bowl; stir vinegar into sweetener. Mix water into sweetener-vinegar mixture until sweetener is dissolved. Pour mixture over corn-bean mixture; toss to coat. Cover bowl with plastic wrap and refrigerate 8 hours to overnight. Drain liquid from mixture in a colander before serving.

Nutrition Information

- Calories: 300 calories
- Total Fat: 4.9 g
- Cholesterol: 0 mg
- Sodium: 725 mg
- Total Carbohydrate: 43 g
- Protein: 24.5 g

46. Texas Cowboy Stew

"Hearty, filling and man-pleasing describes this stew. Link sausage, cumin, chilies, and chili powder is what gives this soup its Southwest flavor. This dish is quick, easy, and tastes best when it simmers in a slow cooker or even on the stove all day. Bake some Mexican cornbread, toss a simple green salad, and you have a great meal."

Serving: 10 | Prep: 30 m | Cook: 1 h | Ready in: 1 h 30 m

Ingredients

- 2 pounds ground beef
- 2 (16 ounce) packages kielbasa sausage, sliced into 1/2 inch pieces
- 2 cloves garlic, chopped
- 1 onion, chopped
- 2 (14.5 ounce) cans peeled and diced tomatoes, drained
- 4 medium baking potatoes, peeled and diced
- 2 (15 ounce) cans pinto beans, with liquid
- 2 (15.2 ounce) cans whole kernel corn, with liquid
- 1 (14.5 ounce) can diced tomatoes with green chile peppers, with liquid
- 1 (10 ounce) package frozen mixed vegetables
- 4 cups water
- 2 teaspoons ground cumin
- 2 teaspoons chili powder
- salt and pepper to taste

Direction

- Crumble the ground beef into a large skillet over medium-high heat. Add the sausage, garlic and onion; cook and stir until the meat is no longer pink. Drain off grease, and transfer the contents of the skillet to a large pot.
- Pour the tomatoes into the pot with the meat, and stir in the potatoes, pinto beans, corn, diced tomatoes with chilies, mixed vegetables and water. Season with cumin, chili powder, salt and pepper. Cover, and simmer over medium-low heat for at least 1 hour. Stir

occasionally. The longer this stew cooks, the better it gets.

Nutrition Information

- Calories: 677 calories
- Total Fat: 37.1 g
- Cholesterol: 115 mg
- Sodium: 1620 mg
- Total Carbohydrate: 52.2 g
- Protein: 35.3 g

47. Uptown Cowboy Caviar

"Colorful, delicious bean salsa."

Serving: 10 | Prep: 20 m | Cook: 5 m | Ready in: 2 h 25 m

Ingredients

- 1 (15 ounce) can black beans, rinsed and drained
- 1 (15 ounce) can black-eyed peas, rinsed and drained
- 1 (15 ounce) can pinto beans, rinsed and drained
- 1 (11 ounce) can yellow shoepeg corn, drained
- 1 cup diced celery
- 1 small bunch cilantro leaves, chopped
- 1/2 red bell pepper, diced
- 1/2 yellow bell pepper, diced
- 1/2 cup chopped green onion
- 1 (2 ounce) jar chopped pimento peppers
- 2 tablespoons minced jalapeno pepper
- 1 tablespoon minced garlic
- 1/2 cup rice vinegar
- 1/2 cup extra virgin olive oil
- 1/3 cup white sugar
- 1 teaspoon salt
- 1/2 teaspoon ground black pepper

Direction

- Combine the black beans, black-eyed peas, pinto beans, shoepeg corn, celery, cilantro, red and yellow bell peppers, green onion, pimento peppers, jalapeno pepper, and garlic in a large bowl. Set aside.
- Bring the rice vinegar, olive oil, sugar, salt, and black pepper to a boil in a saucepan over medium-high heat until sugar is dissolved, about 5 minutes. All to cool to room temperature, then pour over the bean mixture. Cover and refrigerate for 2 hours or overnight. Drain before serving.

Nutrition Information

- Calories: 266 calories
- Total Fat: 12.1 g
- Cholesterol: 0 mg
- Sodium: 710 mg
- Total Carbohydrate: 32.6 g
- Protein: 7.2 g

48. Vincents Famous Garlic Coleslaw

"Tired of all the super sweet coleslaw dressings out there? Look no further! Caution - must LOVE garlic!

This is a copycat recipe for the famous garlic coleslaw served at Vincent's seafood restaurant, a Dallas legend since 1968. Growing up, we had an Easter tradition of dinner at Vincent's every year. The coleslaw was my dad's favorite and became mine too! We still go there for Easter but I love being able to recreate this unique recipe at home anytime. Goes great with barbecue ribs, burgers, seafood steam pot, or just as a cool crisp snack. The longer it cures, the better it gets!"

Serving: 8 | Prep: 15 m | Ready in: 1 h 15 m

Ingredients

- 1 medium head green cabbage, finely shredded
- 3 tablespoons finely chopped garlic
- 1 1/2 teaspoons kosher salt
- 1/3 cup grapeseed oil
- 1/3 cup mayonnaise
- 1/3 cup apple cider vinegar

- 1/4 teaspoon ground paprika
- 1/4 teaspoon ground white pepper
- 1/8 teaspoon white sugar
- 1/8 teaspoon celery seed

Direction

- Place shredded cabbage into a large bowl.
- Gather chopped garlic into a mound on a cutting board and pour salt over top. Using the flat side of a chef's knife, smash the garlic and salt together and transfer to a bowl. Whisk grapeseed oil, mayonnaise, apple cider vinegar, ground paprika, ground white pepper, sugar, and celery seed together with garlic mixture until dressing reaches a uniform consistency.
- Pour dressing over shredded cabbage and toss to evenly coat. Press coleslaw down into the bowl using the back of a spoon or place another bowl on top. Cover and refrigerate for at least 1 hour. Stir before serving.

Nutrition Information

- Calories: 182 calories
- Total Fat: 16.5 g
- Cholesterol: 3 mg
- Sodium: 434 mg
- Total Carbohydrate: 8.2 g
- Protein: 1.8 g

49. Winter Blossoms Often Requested Ham Salad

"I have been making this salad for years and recently traveled from NJ to Oklahoma to make a batch for one of my friends. I have also Overnighted this salad to a friend in Dallas who simply loves it. Of course, I pack it in dry ice. It's fast, simple and great for a cocktail party on party rye, on toast or a bagel for breakfast, on rye with lettuce, thinly sliced onions and dill (or sweet)pickles and mayo for lunch or with pea soup and sandwich for dinner. It's down right Yummy!!! And make no changes to the ingredients because the salad will not taste the same."

Serving: 12 | Prep: 15 m | Ready in: 2 h 15 m

Ingredients

- 1 1/2 pounds cooked ham, chopped
- 3/4 cup mayonnaise, or as needed
- 1/3 cup dried minced onion
- 1/3 cup dill pickle relish
- 1/4 cup brown mustard

Direction

- Process the ham in a food processor until finely chopped but not pasty, about 6 or 7 pulses. You may need to do this in batches. Place the finely chopped ham in a large bowl and continue processing the remaining ham.
- Add the mayonnaise, onions, relish, and mustard to the processed ham. Mix well and, if the mixture is too dry, add more mayonnaise. Refrigerate until serving. The dried onions absorb some of the moisture from the mayonnaise and relish so you may need to add more mayonnaise before serving.

Nutrition Information

- Calories: 249 calories
- Total Fat: 21.8 g
- Cholesterol: 37 mg
- Sodium: 930 mg
- Total Carbohydrate: 2.2 g
- Protein: 11.1 g

Chapter 3: Amazing Texas Recipes

***

50. Addictive Texas Trash

"I make this as yearly tradition at holiday time in my home. I also make a batch of this to send to my brother for his care package that I send him when he is deployed. I will warn you, it is very spicy and addictive. There should be a 12 step recovery program for this stuff."

Serving: 48 | Prep: 30 m | Cook: 2 h | Ready in: 3 h 30 m

Ingredients

- 1 (14 ounce) package bite-size corn square cereal (such as Corn Chex®)
- 1 (14 ounce) package crispy rice cereal squares (such as Rice Chex ®)
- 1 (14 ounce) package bite-size wheat square cereal (such as Wheat Chex®)
- 1 (8.9 ounce) box toasted oat cereal rings (such as Cheerios®)
- 3 cups salted mixed nuts
- 1 (15 ounce) package mini pretzel twists
- 2 (6 ounce) packages goldfish crackers
- 1 (12 ounce) package sesame snack sticks (optional)
- 1 cup warm (liquid) bacon drippings
- 1 cup unsalted butter, melted
- 1/4 cup Worcestershire sauce
- 2 tablespoons monosodium glutamate (MSG)
- 2 tablespoons liquid smoke flavoring
- 1 tablespoon cayenne pepper
- 4 teaspoons seasoned salt
- 4 teaspoons chili powder
- 4 teaspoons garlic powder
- 4 teaspoons hot pepper sauce (such as Tabasco®)

Direction

- Preheat oven to 250 degrees F (120 degrees C).
- Gently mix corn, rice, and wheat squares, oat rings, mixed nuts, mini pretzels, goldfish crackers, and sesame snacks in two 13x24-inch aluminum roasting pans, taking care not to break cereal.
- Stir bacon drippings, unsalted butter, Worcestershire sauce, MSG, liquid smoke, cayenne pepper, seasoned salt, chili powder,

garlic powder, and hot pepper sauce together in a microwave-safe bowl. Cook on high in microwave for 3 or 4 30-second intervals, stirring each time, until mixture is warm, liquid, and fully combined.
- Stir seasoning sauce continuously as you pour half over the cereal mixture in each pan. Gently stir the snack mix and seasonings with a slotted spoon until thoroughly coated; do not crush cereal.
- Bake in the preheated oven until sauce is completely absorbed and the snack mix is crisp, about 2 hours; stir gently every 15 minutes. Cool completely and store in airtight containers. The snack mix stores well in freezer in airtight freezer bags, if it makes it that long.

Nutrition Information

- Calories: 355 calories
- Total Fat: 18.6 g
- Cholesterol: 15 mg
- Sodium: 790 mg
- Total Carbohydrate: 42.3 g
- Protein: 6.4 g

51. Aunt Blanches Blueberry Muffins

"These are delicious and cake-like. I always double the recipe and make huge Texas-style muffins."

Serving: 12

Ingredients

- 1/2 cup butter
- 2 cups all-purpose flour
- 1 1/4 cups white sugar
- 2 eggs
- 1/2 cup milk
- 2 teaspoons baking powder
- 1/2 teaspoon salt
- 1 1/2 cups fresh blueberries

Direction

- Preheat oven to 350 degrees F (175 degrees C). Grease and flour muffin pan or use paper liners. Sift flour, baking powder and salt together and set aside.
- Cream butter and sugar until light and fluffy. Add eggs and beat well. Add milk and flour mixture. Beat until combined. Stir in blueberries.
- Fill muffin cups 2/3 full. Bake at 350 degrees F (175 degrees C) for 25 to 30 minutes.

Nutrition Information

- Calories: 252 calories
- Total Fat: 9 g
- Cholesterol: 52 mg
- Sodium: 249 mg
- Total Carbohydrate: 40.1 g
- Protein: 3.8 g

52. Baked Beans Texas Ranger

"Want to wow everyone at the bar-b-que? Then this is the recipe. This is one of my most requested recipes!"

Serving: 6 | Prep: 15 m | Cook: 1 h | Ready in: 1 h 15 m

Ingredients

- 1 (28 ounce) can baked beans with pork
- 1 medium onion, diced
- 1 medium bell pepper, diced
- 4 links spicy pork sausage, cut into chunks
- 2 tablespoons chili powder
- 3 tablespoons Worcestershire sauce
- 4 tablespoons vinegar
- 1/2 cup packed brown sugar
- 1/2 cup ketchup
- 1 teaspoon garlic powder
- salt to taste
- 1 dash cayenne pepper (optional)

Direction

- Preheat the oven to 350 degrees F (175 degrees C).
- In a Dutch oven, combine the baked beans, onion, bell pepper, and sausage. Season with chili powder, Worcestershire sauce, vinegar, brown sugar, ketchup, garlic powder and salt. Add a dash of cayenne if desired.
- Cover and bake for one hour in the preheated oven.

Nutrition Information

- Calories: 301 calories
- Total Fat: 6.1 g
- Cholesterol: 23 mg
- Sodium: 1031 mg
- Total Carbohydrate: 55.7 g
- Protein: 10.8 g

53. Beaumont Ranch Potato Salad

"I have kept this recipe a ranch secret, but I have decided to share it. This is my variation of a French classic garlic potato salad. It is different than the dish that inspired it, but very good and easy as well."

Serving: 20 | Prep: 20 m | Cook: 20 m | Ready in: 1 h 40 m

Ingredients

- 5 pounds red potatoes
- 1 (.7 ounce) package dry Italian salad dressing mix (such as Good Seasons®)
- 1/4 cup tarragon vinegar
- 1/4 cup water
- 1 cup extra-virgin olive oil
- 1/2 cup chopped celery
- 1 cup real bacon bits
- 1/4 cup chopped dill pickle (optional)
- 1/4 cup chopped green onion
- 3 cups mayonnaise

Direction

- Place the potatoes into a large pot and cover with water. Bring to a boil over high heat, then reduce heat to medium-low, cover, and simmer until tender, about 20 minutes. Drain and allow to steam dry for a minute or two.
- In a bowl, whisk together the dry Italian dressing mix, tarragon vinegar, water, and olive oil until thoroughly blended. Set aside.
- Place the hot potatoes into a large bowl, and roughly but thoroughly slice them with a table knife until the potatoes are in chunks. Pour the dressing mixture over the hot potatoes, toss to coat, and let the potatoes cool. Add the celery, bacon bits, dill pickle, and green onion to the potatoes; lightly stir in mayonnaise until all ingredients are well combined, and serve.

Nutrition Information

- Calories: 441 calories
- Total Fat: 38.8 g
- Cholesterol: 17 mg
- Sodium: 555 mg
- Total Carbohydrate: 19.8 g
- Protein: 4.9 g

54. Beer Can Chicken Texas Style

"A great way to cook whole fryer chickens. I added my mopping sauce to keep the birds from drying out."

Serving: 6 | Prep: 20 m | Cook: 2 h 10 m | Ready in: 8 h 30 m

Ingredients

- 1 (3 pound) whole fryer chicken
- 2 lemons, quartered
- 2 limes, quartered
- 1/2 teaspoon garlic salt, or to taste
- 1/4 teaspoon ground allspice, or to taste
- salt and ground black pepper to taste
- 6 tablespoons minced garlic, divided
- 3/4 (12 ounce) can beer

- 4 cups water
- 1 (12 fluid ounce) can or bottle beer
- 1 cup vinegar
- 6 tablespoons Worcestershire sauce
- 1 red onion, chopped
- 1 red bell pepper, chopped
- 3 tablespoons minced garlic
- 1 tablespoon salt
- 1 tablespoon ground black pepper

Direction

- Rinse chicken and pat dry with paper towels. Squeeze lemon and lime quarters over the chicken. Mix garlic salt and allspice with salt and black pepper to taste in a bowl and rub the spices over the chicken skin; place squeezed lemon and lime quarters inside the chicken cavity. Place 3 tablespoons minced garlic into cavity. Wrap chicken in plastic wrap and refrigerate 6 to 8 hours.
- Preheat grill for medium-low heat; a grill thermometer should read 275 degrees F (135 degrees C) with the lid closed.
- Place remaining 3 tablespoons garlic into the partially full can of beer and sit chicken upright on the beer can, taking care not to lose any lemon and lime quarters and garlic.
- Pour water, 1 12-ounce can of beer, vinegar, and Worcestershire sauce into a saucepan over medium heat; stir in red onion, red bell pepper, 3 tablespoons minced garlic, salt, and black pepper. Bring the mopping sauce to a boil, reduce heat, and simmer for 10 minutes. Set sauce aside.
- Place chicken upright with beer can onto the preheated grill and cook until the skin is browned and the meat is no longer pink inside, about 2 hours. An instant-read meat thermometer inserted into the thickest part of a breast should read at least 160 degrees F (70 degrees C). Use a brush to spread mopping sauce on the chicken every 30 minutes as it cooks. Discard leftover sauce.

Nutrition Information

- Calories: 393 calories
- Total Fat: 17.4 g
- Cholesterol: 97 mg
- Sodium: 1588 mg
- Total Carbohydrate: 21.2 g
- Protein: 33 g

55. BestEver Texas Caviar

"This is a yummy Texas caviar made with black beans and pinto beans instead of black-eyed peas. Serve with scoop-style tortilla chips as a great party appetizer."

Serving: 10 | Prep: 35 m | Ready in: 35 m

Ingredients

- 2 (15 ounce) cans black beans, rinsed and drained
- 2 (15 ounce) cans pinto beans, rinsed and drained
- 2 (15 ounce) cans white corn, rinsed and drained
- 1 (4 ounce) can chopped green chiles, undrained
- 1 jalapeno chile pepper, seeded and finely chopped (optional)
- 1 red bell pepper - cored, seeded and finely chopped
- 1 green bell pepper - cored, seeded and finely chopped
- 1 small red onion, finely chopped
- 1 bunch cilantro leaves, finely chopped
- 1/2 cup rice vinegar
- 1/2 cup olive oil
- 1/3 cup white sugar
- 1/2 teaspoon garlic powder

Direction

- Mix the black beans, pinto beans, white corn, green chiles, jalapeno pepper, red and green bell peppers, red onion, and cilantro together in a large bowl.
- To make the dressing, stir the rice vinegar, olive oil, sugar, and garlic powder together in a pan. Bring to a boil, then remove from heat,

and cool. Pour dressing over bean mixture, and toss to mix evenly.

Nutrition Information

- Calories: 262 calories
- Total Fat: 12 g
- Cholesterol: 0 mg
- Sodium: 564 mg
- Total Carbohydrate: 35.5 g
- Protein: 6.3 g

56. Big Kevs Texas Style Long Island Iced Tea

"This Long Island Iced Tea Recipe is sure to make you party like you are from Texas!"

Serving: 1 | Prep: 5 m | Ready in: 5 m

Ingredients

- 1 fluid ounce vodka
- 1 fluid ounce dry gin
- 1 fluid ounce triple sec (orange-flavored liqueur)
- 1 fluid ounce rum
- 1 fluid ounce tequila
- 1 (12 fluid ounce) can or bottle cola-flavored carbonated beverage
- 1 wedge lemon
- 1 wedge lime

Direction

- Pour vodka, gin, triple sec, rum, and tequila into a tall glass with ice. Top off with cola. Stir gently. Garnish with lemon and lime wedges.

57. Boudreauxs Zydeco Stomp Gumbo

"Dis is da toe curlin Texicajun hybrid of a classic dish. This will put a smile on everyone's face that's eatin it. Throw on some Zydeco music and serve on a bed of rice with corn bread and a cold beer. Whew doggie...be thankful to be alive and toast all us Texicajuns!!!"

Serving: 10 | Prep: 1 h | Cook: 1 h | Ready in: 2 h

Ingredients

- 1 tablespoon olive oil
- 1 cup skinless, boneless chicken breast halves - chopped
- 1/2 pound pork sausage links, thinly sliced
- 1 cup olive oil
- 1 cup all-purpose flour
- 2 tablespoons minced garlic
- 3 quarts chicken broth
- 1 (12 fluid ounce) can or bottle beer
- 6 stalks celery, diced
- 4 roma (plum) tomatoes, diced
- 1 sweet onion, sliced
- 1 (10 ounce) can diced tomatoes with green chile peppers, with liquid
- 2 tablespoons chopped fresh red chile peppers
- 1 bunch fresh parsley, chopped
- 1/4 cup Cajun seasoning
- 1 pound shrimp, peeled and deveined

Direction

- Heat oil in a medium skillet over medium high heat, and cook chicken until no longer pink and juices run clear. Stir in sausage, and cook until evenly browned. Drain chicken and sausage, and set aside.
- In a large, heavy saucepan over medium heat, blend olive oil and flour to create a roux. Stir constantly until browned and bubbly. Mix in garlic, and cook about 1 minute.
- Gradually stir chicken broth and beer into the roux mixture. Bring to a boil, and mix in celery, tomatoes, sweet onion, diced tomatoes with green chile peppers, red chile peppers, parsley, and Cajun seasoning. Reduce heat,

- cover, and simmer about 40 minutes, stirring often.
- Mix chicken, sausage, and shrimp into the broth mixture. Cook, stirring frequently, about 20 minutes.

Nutrition Information

- Calories: 437 calories
- Total Fat: 29.3 g
- Cholesterol: 105 mg
- Sodium: 2052 mg
- Total Carbohydrate: 18.5 g
- Protein: 21.7 g

58. Brisket with BBQ Sauce

"After growing up in West Texas for 30 years where barbecue is the best, I found this recipe which is so tender and absolutely delicious. Leftovers, if you have any, make really great sandwiches. You can increase the liquid smoke to 4 tablespoons for really smoky flavor."

Serving: 10 | Prep: 10 m | Cook: 6 h | Ready in: 14 h 10 m

Ingredients

- 4 pounds lean beef brisket
- 2 tablespoons liquid smoke flavoring
- 1 tablespoon onion salt
- 1 tablespoon garlic salt
- 1 1/2 tablespoons brown sugar
- 1 cup ketchup
- 3 tablespoons butter
- 1/4 cup water
- 1/2 teaspoon celery salt
- 1 tablespoon liquid smoke flavoring
- 2 tablespoons Worcestershire sauce
- 1 1/2 teaspoons mustard powder
- salt and pepper to taste

Direction

- Pour liquid smoke over brisket. Rub with onion salt and garlic salt. Roll brisket in foil and refrigerate overnight.
- Preheat oven to 300 degrees F (150 degrees C). Place brisket in a large roasting pan. Cover and bake for 5 to 6 hours. Remove from oven, cool, and then slice. Put slices back into pan.
- In a medium saucepan, combine brown sugar, ketchup, butter, water, celery salt, liquid smoke, Worcestershire sauce, mustard, salt and pepper. Stir, and cook until boiling.
- Pour sauce over meat slices in pan. Cover and bake for 1 more hour.

Nutrition Information

- Calories: 560 calories
- Total Fat: 42.3 g
- Cholesterol: 133 mg
- Sodium: 1613 mg
- Total Carbohydrate: 9.3 g
- Protein: 34.1 g

59. Capidotada Mexican Bread Pudding

"Several varieties of this dessert exist, depending upon which region of Mexico or Texas it's made in. The biggest difference being the nut used. My own preference is to use pecans."

Serving: 8 | Prep: 45 m | Cook: 30 m | Ready in: 1 h 15 m

Ingredients

- 2 cups water
- 3 (3 inch) cinnamon sticks
- 2 cups white sugar
- 2 cups vegetable oil for frying
- 1 (1 pound) loaf French bread, cut into 1/2 inch thick slices
- 1 cup raisins
- 1 cup chopped pecans
- 1 small onion, finely chopped
- 6 ounces sliced mild Cheddar cheese

Direction

- Preheat an oven to 350 degrees F (175 degrees C). Grease a 2 quart casserole dish.
- Combine the water, cinnamon sticks, and sugar in a large saucepan and bring to a boil over high heat. Reduce the heat to medium-low, cover, and simmer until the cinnamon turns the water dark brown, about 15 minutes. Remove cinnamon sticks and reserve the water.
- Heat the vegetable oil in a large skillet to 350 degrees F (175 degrees C). Fry the slices of French bread in oil until light brown, turning if necessary, about 1 minute per side. Remove toasted bread from the oil and place on paper towels to drain.
- Arrange half of the toasted bread in a single layer in the greased casserole dish. Sprinkle bread with half of the raisins, pecans, and onion. Arrange a layer of Cheddar cheese on top. Repeat with another layer of bread, raisins, pecans, onions, and cheese.
- Slowly pour the reserved cinnamon water over the casserole, allowing the bread to absorb as much of the liquid as possible. Do not allow the dish to overflow.
- Cover dish with aluminum foil and place in the center of the preheated oven. Bake until lightly browned and puffed, about 30 minutes. Remove from oven and allow to rest for 15 minutes before serving.

Nutrition Information

- Calories: 661 calories
- Total Fat: 24.4 g
- Cholesterol: 22 mg
- Sodium: 499 mg
- Total Carbohydrate: 102.3 g
- Protein: 14 g

60. Cattlemans Beans

"Fantastic recipe given to me by a Texas rancher. Pinto or red beans are cooked with pork sausage. Great blend of spices and flavorings and doubly yummy with a little Jamaican rum and sour cream. Easy and the best beans ever to serve as your main dish with cornbread. You can substitute red beans for the pinto beans."

Serving: 8 | Prep: 20 m | Cook: 4 h 5 m | Ready in: 12 h 25 m

Ingredients

- 6 cups cold water
- 2 1/4 cups dried pinto beans
- 2 tablespoons butter
- 1/2 pound bulk pork sausage
- 2 cups peeled tart apple slices
- 1 1/2 cups tomato juice
- 1 cup chopped onion
- 1/4 cup brown sugar
- 2 cloves garlic, mashed
- 2 teaspoons salt
- 1 teaspoon chili powder
- 1 teaspoon dry mustard
- 1/4 teaspoon coarse black pepper
- 1/4 cup Jamaican rum
- 1/4 cup sour cream, for topping

Direction

- Combine cold water and beans in a pot; let stand 8 hours to overnight.
- Stir butter into the pot with the beans and water; bring to a boil, reduce heat to low, cover the pot, and simmer until beans are tender, about 2 hours.
- Heat a large skillet over medium-high heat. Cook and stir pork sausage in the hot skillet until browned and crumbly, 5 to 7 minutes; drain and reserve 2 tablespoons sausage drippings.
- Stir sausage and reserved drippings, apple slices, tomato juice, onion, brown sugar, garlic, salt, chili powder, mustard, and black pepper into beans. Bring bean mixture to a boil, reduce heat to low, cover the pot, and simmer until flavors blend, about 2 hours.

- Stir rum into beans, ladle beans into bowls, and top with sour cream.

Nutrition Information

- Calories: 380 calories
- Total Fat: 11.4 g
- Cholesterol: 27 mg
- Sodium: 999 mg
- Total Carbohydrate: 49.9 g
- Protein: 16.6 g

61. Cheapskate Stew

"A hearty beef vegetable stew from leftovers you have on hand. I love this recipe on a cold Texas winter nights."

Serving: 6 | Prep: 15 m | Cook: 45 m | Ready in: 1 h

Ingredients

- 1 1/2 pounds lean ground beef
- 1/2 onion, chopped
- 3 stalks celery, chopped
- 2 cups frozen mixed vegetables
- 2 cups water
- 3 carrots, chopped
- 2 cups cooked elbow macaroni
- 1 (15 ounce) can tomato sauce
- 1 1/2 teaspoons Italian seasoning
- salt to taste
- ground black pepper to taste

Direction

- Brown the hamburger meat with onion and celery. Drain (if it is fatty hamburger meat).
- Add water and carrots, then cook 'til carrots are beginning to get tender. The carrots will be crunchy unless you cook them a fairly long time.
- Add leftover vegetables, macaroni, tomato sauce, Italian spices, and salt and pepper to taste, and simmer until the flavors blend and all ingredients are warm through.

Nutrition Information

- Calories: 448 calories
- Total Fat: 24.5 g
- Cholesterol: 85 mg
- Sodium: 512 mg
- Total Carbohydrate: 30.6 g
- Protein: 26.1 g

62. Cheesy Chicken Toast Sandwich

"Chicken is baked in four-cheese pasta sauce, covered in a four-cheese blend and served in between two pieces of Texas cheese toast."

Serving: 4 | Prep: 10 m | Cook: 50 m | Ready in: 1 h

Ingredients

- 1 (24 ounce) jar four-cheese pasta sauce (such as Classico®)
- 4 skinless, boneless chicken breast halves
- 2 cups fiesta-style four-cheese blend
- 8 slices Texas-style cheese toast

Direction

- Preheat oven to 400 degrees F (200 degrees C).
- Pour enough four-cheese pasta sauce into the bottom of a casserole dish to cover in a light layer. Arrange chicken breasts into the casserole dish. Pour remaining sauce over the chicken breasts to cover. Cover dish with aluminum foil.
- Bake in preheated oven until no longer pink in the center and the juices run clear, 30 to 40 minutes. An instant-read thermometer inserted into the center should read at least 165 degrees F (74 degrees C).
- Cover chicken breasts with a layer of cheese and continue baking uncovered until the cheese melts, about 10 minutes more.
- Arrange cheese toast onto a baking sheet.

- Bake cheese toast in preheated oven until cheese is melted and the toast is browned around the edges, about 10 minutes.
- Sandwich each chicken breast between two slices of the toast with the cheesy sides touching the chicken.

Nutrition Information

- Calories: 630 calories
- Total Fat: 30.6 g
- Cholesterol: 135 mg
- Sodium: 1477 mg
- Total Carbohydrate: 43.3 g
- Protein: 45.4 g

63. Chilled Vegetable Salad

"This is a simple salad using raw zucchini and yellow squash that goes wonderfully with a good ole Texas backyard barbeque."

Serving: 6 | Prep: 25 m | Ready in: 1 h 25 m

Ingredients

- 2 tomatoes, cut into chunks
- 1 large zucchini, cut into chunks
- 1 large yellow squash, cut into chunks
- 1/2 green bell pepper, diced
- 1/2 sweet red onion, chopped
- 2 cloves garlic, minced
- 1 teaspoon dried basil
- 1/2 teaspoon salt, or to taste
- 1/2 teaspoon ground black pepper, or to taste
- 1/4 cup olive oil
- 1/4 cup red wine vinegar
- 3 tablespoons water

Direction

- Place tomatoes, zucchini, yellow squash, green bell pepper, red onion, garlic, basil, salt, and black pepper in a large bowl; add olive oil, vinegar, and water. Toss to coat. Refrigerate for about 1 hour before serving.

Nutrition Information

- Calories: 113 calories
- Total Fat: 9.3 g
- Cholesterol: 0 mg
- Sodium: 203 mg
- Total Carbohydrate: 7.5 g
- Protein: 1.7 g

64. ChoriQueso

"YUMMY. I am from a border town in Texas, this is really simple. I can't think of any other way they serve cheese in Mexican restaurants. This is also good with avocado, salsa, and fajitas."

Serving: 16 | Prep: 5 m | Cook: 20 m | Ready in: 25 m

Ingredients

- 2 tablespoons corn oil
- 8 ounces chorizo sausage
- 8 ounces sliced mozzarella cheese
- 1 (12 ounce) package corn tortillas

Direction

- Preheat the oven to 400 degrees F (200 degrees C).
- Heat the corn oil in a large skillet over medium heat. Crumble in the chorizo sausage; cook and stir until evenly browned, about 5 minutes. Remove from the pan, and set aside. Place slices of cheese in a single layer to cover the bottom of the pan. It is okay if they overlap a little bit. When cheese melts, quickly pour into a nice casserole dish, or oven-proof bowl. Sprinkle the chorizo on top.
- Bake for 5 minutes in the preheated oven, or until cheese is fully melted. Remove from the oven, stick a fork in it and load your tortilla.

Nutrition Information

- Calories: 161 calories
- Total Fat: 10 g
- Cholesterol: 22 mg

- Sodium: 272 mg
- Total Carbohydrate: 10 g
- Protein: 8.1 g

65. Cinnamon Brown Sugar Butter

"On a hurried school day, my kids love this on toast or muffins. I always keep on batch on hand. They tell me it tastes like Texas Roadhouse® butter."

Serving: 8 | Prep: 5 m | Ready in: 5 m

Ingredients

- 1/2 cup butter, softened
- 4 teaspoons packed brown sugar
- 1/4 teaspoon ground nutmeg
- 1/4 teaspoon ground cinnamon

Direction

- Beat butter, brown sugar, nutmeg, and cinnamon together until fluffy. Store in the refrigerator.

Nutrition Information

- Calories: 111 calories
- Total Fat: 11.5 g
- Cholesterol: 31 mg
- Sodium: 82 mg
- Total Carbohydrate: 2.4 g
- Protein: 0.1 g

66. Classic Texas Caviar

"Don't bother with soaking and cooking beans for Classic Texas Caviar - the canned variety works well. But skip the bottled dressing, and take a little extra time to measure your own vinegar, oil and spices."

Serving: 40

Ingredients

- 2 (15.8 ounce) cans black-eyed peas, drained
- 1 (14.5 ounce) can petite diced tomatoes, drained
- 2 fresh medium jalapenos, stemmed, seeded and minced
- 1 small onion, cut into small dice
- 1/2 yellow bell pepper, stemmed, seeded and cut into small dice
- 1/4 cup chopped fresh cilantro
- 6 tablespoons red wine vinegar
- 6 tablespoons olive oil (not extra virgin)
- 1/2 teaspoon salt
- 1/2 teaspoon ground black pepper
- 1/2 teaspoon garlic powder
- 1 teaspoon dried oregano
- 1 1/2 teaspoons ground cumin

Direction

- Mix all ingredients in a medium bowl; cover and refrigerate 2 hours or up to 2 days. Before serving, adjust seasonings to taste, adding extra vinegar, salt and pepper. Transfer to a serving bowl.

Nutrition Information

- Calories: 40 calories
- Total Fat: 2.2 g
- Cholesterol: 0 mg
- Sodium: 112 mg
- Total Carbohydrate: 4 g
- Protein: 1.2 g

67. Cowboy Jacks Beer Bread

"This rich and tasty beer bread recipe is from a 200-year-old horse ranch in West Texas."

Serving: 8 | Prep: 10 m | Cook: 50 m | Ready in: 1 h 15 m

Ingredients

- 2/3 cup brown sugar
- 1 (12 fluid ounce) can beer
- 1/2 teaspoon baking powder

- 3 cups flour
- 1/2 cup butter, melted

Direction

- Preheat oven to 375 degrees F (190 degrees C). Lightly grease a 9x5 inch loaf pan.
- Beat the beer and brown sugar together in a mixing bowl to make a smooth mixture. Add the baking powder, and gradually stir in the flour to make a smooth dough. Pour the batter into the prepared pan.
- Bake in preheated oven for 40 minutes.
- Remove the bread from the oven, and pour melted butter over the top. Return to the oven, and continue baking until a knife inserted in the center comes out clean, about 10 minutes more. Cool in pan 5 minutes before turning out onto a rack. Cool bread 10 minutes more before slicing.

Nutrition Information

- Calories: 338 calories
- Total Fat: 12 g
- Cholesterol: 31 mg
- Sodium: 118 mg
- Total Carbohydrate: 49.3 g
- Protein: 5.2 g

68. Crispy French Toast

"I first ate this French toast in a coffee shop in Galveston, Texas. After I'd tried it I couldn't wait to come up with my own version. It's great for a late brunch; especially when topped with syrup, fresh strawberries and whipped cream"

Serving: 6 | Prep: 10 m | Cook: 10 m | Ready in: 30 m

Ingredients

- 8 cups vegetable oil for deep-frying
- 6 thick slices white bread
- 2 eggs
- 1 cup milk
- 1 tablespoon white sugar
- 1 teaspoon ground cinnamon
- 1 teaspoon vanilla extract
- 2 cups cornflakes cereal

Direction

- Heat deep-fryer to 375 degrees F (190 degrees C).
- In a large bowl combine eggs, milk, sugar, cinnamon and vanilla; beat well. Place cornflakes in a separate bowl. Dip bread slices in egg mixture and press into cornflakes.
- Carefully slide coated bread slices into hot oil. Fry on each side until golden brown. Drain on paper towels and serve hot.

Nutrition Information

- Calories: 428 calories
- Total Fat: 32.8 g
- Cholesterol: 65 mg
- Sodium: 312 mg
- Total Carbohydrate: 27.8 g
- Protein: 6.4 g

69. Critter Fritter Casserole

"This year at the Texas State Fair, I had a treat called a Critter Fritter, which was a deep fried battered, meat-filled jalapeno. The combination of tastes was so great, I decided to try and replicate it in casserole form at home. The following is what I came up with."

Serving: 6 | Prep: 15 m | Cook: 50 m | Ready in: 1 h 5 m

Ingredients

- 2 pounds ground beef
- 1/2 onion, chopped
- 1/4 teaspoon garlic powder
- 1 teaspoon salt
- 1/2 teaspoon ground black pepper
- 1 teaspoon ground cumin
- 1/2 teaspoon chili powder
- 1/2 teaspoon dried oregano
- 1/4 cup canned jalapeno slices, drained and chopped

- 1 (8.5 ounce) package corn muffin and bread mix
- 2 tablespoons unsalted butter, melted
- 3/4 cup milk
- 1 egg
- 2 cups shredded extra-sharp Cheddar cheese

Direction

- Preheat the oven to 375 degrees F (190 degrees C).
- Heat a large skillet over medium-high heat. Add ground beef, and cook, stirring to crumble, until no longer pink, about 10 minutes. Remove meat with a slotted spoon and set aside. Drain off most of the fat, leaving enough to coat the bottom of the pan. Add onions to the fat in the pan; cook and stir until tender, about 5 minutes. Return the meat to the skillet and season with garlic powder, salt, pepper, cumin, chili powder and oregano. Mix in jalapeno slices and cook until heated through. Transfer this mixture to an 8 inch square baking dish.
- Meanwhile, in a medium bowl, stir together the cornbread mix, butter, milk and egg. This can be done while the meat is cooking. Spoon over the top of the meat mixture in the baking dish, then top with shredded cheese.
- Bake in the preheated oven until the top is golden brown and a knife inserted into the center comes out clean, about 40 minutes. Cool slightly, then cut into squares to serve.

Nutrition Information

- Calories: 838 calories
- Total Fat: 61.4 g
- Cholesterol: 213 mg
- Sodium: 1491 mg
- Total Carbohydrate: 31 g
- Protein: 40 g

70. Daddys If Theyda had This at the Alamo we wouldha WON Texas Chili

"My Daddy, 'born and bred' in Texas, came up with this recipe and the name for it. It took some convincing, but I got him to allow me to share the recipe. We love it and hope you do to. Enjoy!!"

Serving: 20 | Prep: 30 m | Cook: 2 h | Ready in: 2 h 30 m

Ingredients

- 3 tablespoons bacon drippings
- 2 large onions, chopped
- 8 pounds beef stew meat, or coarse ground chili beef
- 5 cloves garlic, finely chopped
- 4 tablespoons ground red chile pepper
- 4 tablespoons mild chili powder
- 1 tablespoon ground cumin
- 1/4 cup sweet Hungarian paprika
- 1 teaspoon dried Mexican oregano
- 3 (10 ounce) cans tomato sauce
- 1 (6 ounce) can tomato paste
- 3 cups water
- 2 tablespoons salt
- 1/4 cup dried parsley (optional)
- 1 fresh jalapeno peppers
- 1 cup masa harina flour

Direction

- Melt the bacon drippings in a large heavy pot over medium heat. Add the onions and cook until they are translucent.
- Combine the beef with the garlic, ground chile, chili powder and cumin. Add this meat-and-spices to the onions in the pot. Break up any meat that sticks together as you cook, stirring occasionally, about 30 minutes, until meat is evenly browned (very browned, not just gray). Sprinkle in Hungarian paprika and oregano.
- Pour in the tomato sauce, tomato paste, water, salt, parsley and jalapeno. Bring to a boil, then lower the heat and simmer, uncovered, for 1 hour. NOTE: True Texans DO NOT add beans to their chili, but my husband loves them, so

- this is the point where you can add as many cans of drained and rinsed pinto beans as you wish (I add 2 cans, but shhhhhh don't tell my Daddy!!!).
- During cooking you may squeeze the jalapeno as it softens against the sides of the pot to release more heat if desired.
- Mix in the masa harina, and cook while stirring for 30 minutes longer, or until desired consistency is achieved. Taste and adjust seasonings.

Nutrition Information

- Calories: 538 calories
- Total Fat: 38.1 g
- Cholesterol: 124 mg
- Sodium: 1109 mg
- Total Carbohydrate: 12.9 g
- Protein: 35.6 g

71. Dakotas Texas Style Chili

"A spicy Texas-style chili: no beans, tomatoes or ground beef. Great on a cold winter day and goes especially well with Golden Sweet Cornbread (which can also be found on Allrecipes). If you don't want to use beer in the chili, simply replace it with the same amount of water."

Serving: 8 | Prep: 20 m | Cook: 3 h | Ready in: 3 h 20 m

Ingredients

- 4 slices bacon, chopped
- 2 onions, chopped
- 8 cloves garlic, chopped
- 2 teaspoons dried oregano
- 1 teaspoon cayenne pepper
- 3 tablespoons paprika
- 1/3 cup chili powder
- 1 tablespoon cumin
- 4 pounds boneless beef chuck or rump, cut into 1/2-inch cubes
- 4 3/4 cups water
- 1 (12 fluid ounce) can beer
- 4 canned Chipotle peppers in adobo sauce, seeded and minced
- 2 tablespoons cornmeal

Direction

- In a heavy pot or Dutch oven, cook bacon over medium heat until crispy, stirring occasionally. Drain off excess grease, leaving enough to coat the bottom of the pan. Add onions and garlic; cook and stir until the onions are tender. Season with oregano, cayenne pepper, paprika, chili powder and cumin. Cook and stir for about 30 seconds to toast the spices.
- Stir in the beef, water, beer, chipotle peppers, and cornmeal; bring to a boil. Reduce heat to low and simmer, uncovered, until beef is tender, 2 1/2 to 3 hours.

Nutrition Information

- Calories: 675 calories
- Total Fat: 49.1 g
- Cholesterol: 168 mg
- Sodium: 351 mg
- Total Carbohydrate: 12.4 g
- Protein: 42.4 g

72. Davids Mesquite Smoked Texas Brisket

"My husband David gets raves for his South Texas Dilly Digs Brisket. Please read the whole recipe thoroughly before you start."

Serving: 16 | Prep: 10 m | Cook: 4 h 30 m | Ready in: 4 h 40 m

Ingredients

- 8 pounds beef brisket
- 15 cloves garlic, peeled
- 1/4 cup Greek-style seasoning

Direction

- Make deep cuts into the brisket with a paring knife. Place cloves all the way into the cuts. Liberally sprinkle brisket with Greek seasoning.
- Place mesquite wood over gray/hot charcoals.
- Put brisket fat side down on the grill. Smoke for 2 hours and do not turn the meat.
- Take the meat out and wrap tightly 2 times in extra heavy aluminum foil. Put in the oven for 2 hours on a cookie sheet at 250 degrees F.
- Remove from oven and let sit (still wrapped in foil) 30 minutes to 1 hour before serving to let the meat "firm up" and the juice to be absorbed.

Nutrition Information

- Calories: 717 calories
- Total Fat: 60.3 g
- Cholesterol: 166 mg
- Sodium: 498 mg
- Total Carbohydrate: 1.8 g
- Protein: 38.7 g

73. Dinner Rolls Made With Healthy Coconut Oil

"I grew up in my family's restaurant. I revamped this recipe to make it a little healthier. The original recipe was one of my dad's, who was a master chef. People came from all over West Texas to eat 'Stanton's Hot Rolls' and cake doughnuts. I had gained almost 200 pounds and decided to make some changes. At 75 pounds lighter, I'm changing the recipes. Took out the bad cholesterol and added the good. I took out the eggs and cut the salt in half."

Serving: 24 | Prep: 30 m | Cook: 22 m | Ready in: 1 h 52 m

Ingredients

- 5 cups bread flour, divided
- 1/4 cup white sugar
- 4 (.25 ounce) packages instant yeast
- 1 1/2 teaspoons salt
- 1 1/2 cups milk
- 1 cup water
- 1/3 cup coconut oil
- 1 tablespoon coconut oil

Direction

- Combine 2 1/2 cups flour, sugar, yeast, and salt in the bowl of a stand mixer fitted with a paddle attachment.
- Heat milk, water, and 1/3 cup coconut oil in a saucepan until a thermometer inserted into the mixture reads 120 degrees F (49 degrees C), 2 to 3 minutes.
- Pour milk mixture over flour; beat together on high speed until combined, about 2 minutes. Stir in remaining 2 1/2 cups flour until a soft, sticky dough forms.
- Turn dough out onto a lightly floured surface and knead until smooth and elastic, about 10 minutes.
- Place dough in a bowl; cover with a towel and let rise in a warm place until doubled in volume, about 30 minutes.
- Grease 24 muffin cups. Divide dough into 48 equal-sized balls; place 2 balls into each prepared muffin cup. Cover with a towel and let rise in a warm place until doubled in volume, about 30 minutes.
- Preheat oven to 375 degrees F (190 degrees C).
- Bake in the preheated oven until golden brown, about 20 minutes. Brush tops with 1 tablespoon coconut oil.

Nutrition Information

- Calories: 153 calories
- Total Fat: 4.4 g
- Cholesterol: 1 mg
- Sodium: 153 mg
- Total Carbohydrate: 23.9 g
- Protein: 4.4 g

74. Ds Famous Salsa

"This is a Texas recipe I've developed and refined over many years. It's very fast, easy, and I usually have everything on hand. I often give it as gifts to my family back East."

Serving: 16 | Prep: 10 m | Ready in: 10 m

Ingredients

- 2 (14.5 ounce) cans stewed tomatoes
- 1/2 onion, finely diced
- 1 teaspoon minced garlic
- 1/2 lime, juiced
- 1 teaspoon salt
- 1/4 cup canned sliced green chiles, or to taste
- 3 tablespoons chopped fresh cilantro

Direction

- Place the tomatoes, onion, garlic, lime juice, salt, green chiles, and cilantro in a blender or food processor. Blend on low to desired consistency.

Nutrition Information

- Calories: 16 calories
- Total Fat: 0.1 g
- Cholesterol: 0 mg
- Sodium: 283 mg
- Total Carbohydrate: 3.9 g
- Protein: 0.6 g

75. Easy Armadillo Eggs

"A quick and easy version of this spicy Texas favorite. Be sure to have something to drink close by!"

Serving: 8 | Prep: 20 m | Cook: 25 m | Ready in: 45 m

Ingredients

- 1 (8 ounce) package cream cheese, softened
- 1/4 cup bacon bits
- 1 tablespoon chopped fresh chives
- 1 teaspoon hot sauce
- 1 pound pork sausage
- 1 cup shredded Cheddar cheese
- 1 (5.5 ounce) package seasoned coating mix
- 1/8 teaspoon ground cumin
- 1/8 teaspoon chili powder
- 16 fresh jalapeno peppers

Direction

- Preheat oven to 350 degrees F (175 degrees C).
- In a bowl, mix the cream cheese, bacon bits, chives, and hot sauce. In a separate bowl, mix the uncooked sausage and Cheddar cheese. On a flat surface, mix the seasoned coating mix, cumin, and chili powder.
- Cut a slit lengthwise into each jalapeno pepper, and remove the seeds. Stuff the peppers with the cream cheese mixture. Press the sausage mixture around the stuffed jalapenos, and roll in the seasoned coating mix to coat.
- Arrange the coated jalapenos on a baking sheet in a single layer. Bake 25 minutes in the preheated oven, until the sausage is evenly brown.

Nutrition Information

- Calories: 397 calories
- Total Fat: 29.5 g
- Cholesterol: 81 mg
- Sodium: 1227 mg
- Total Carbohydrate: 16.5 g
- Protein: 17.2 g

76. Easy Texas Caviar

"Super simple classic dish. Keeps very well in refrigerator and flavors best when allowed to sit overnight."

Serving: 8 | Prep: 5 m | Ready in: 5 m

Ingredients

- 2 (15 ounce) cans black-eyed peas, rinsed and drained

- 1 (10 ounce) can diced tomatoes and green chiles (such as RO*TEL® Chunky), partially drained
- 1/3 (12 ounce) jar banana peppers, drained and sliced
- 1 tablespoon balsamic vinaigrette salad dressing

Direction

- Stir black-eyed peas, diced tomatoes and green chiles, banana peppers, and balsamic vinaigrette salad dressing together in a bowl.

Nutrition Information

- Calories: 96 calories
- Total Fat: 1.3 g
- Cholesterol: 0 mg
- Sodium: 713 mg
- Total Carbohydrate: 16.4 g
- Protein: 5.3 g

77. Easy Texas Chili

"This is a simple recipe for Texas chili I learned from my mother. I like my chili with a little fire to it, but you can adjust this recipe to your liking. This is a chili that only gets better the second day so don't worry about using a large pot and having more than your family can eat the first night because you can have it a couple of nights later. ENJOY. I know I do every time I make this chili."

Serving: 20 | Prep: 30 m | Cook: 30 m | Ready in: 1 h

Ingredients

- 2 pounds lean ground beef
- 1 large onion, diced
- 1 large bell pepper, minced
- 3 (15 ounce) cans pinto beans
- 2 (28 ounce) cans diced tomatoes
- 4 (8 ounce) cans tomato sauce
- 3 jalapeno peppers, minced (optional)
- 1/2 cup chili powder
- 1 teaspoon crushed red pepper flakes
- 1 teaspoon ground black pepper
- 1/2 teaspoon salt
- 1/4 teaspoon garlic powder

Direction

- Cook and stir the beef, onion, and bell pepper in a large pot over medium heat until the beef is brown and onion and pepper are tender, about 10 minutes. Drain grease from beef.
- Stir in beans, tomatoes, tomato sauce, jalapenos (if using), chili powder, red pepper flakes, black pepper, salt, and garlic powder. Bring mixture to a slow boil; cover and reduce heat. Simmer chili at least 30 minutes, stirring occasionally so that it does not stick. This chili can be simmered for several hours; the longer you simmer, the more flavor you will get.

Nutrition Information

- Calories: 171 calories
- Total Fat: 7.3 g
- Cholesterol: 27 mg
- Sodium: 605 mg
- Total Carbohydrate: 14.9 g
- Protein: 11.9 g

78. Embarrassingly Easy Barbecue Chicken

"This chicken is as good as it is easy. It is a real family favorite even in Texas."

Serving: 4

Ingredients

- 1 (3 pound) whole chicken, cut into pieces
- 1 (12 fluid ounce) can cola-flavored carbonated beverage
- 14 ounces ketchup

Direction

- Preheat oven to 350 degrees F (175 degrees C).
- Mix the cola and ketchup in a 9x13 inch baking dish. Add the chicken pieces, turning to coat

well. Bake skin side down for 30 minutes. Turn and bake for an additional 30 minutes. Let cool for 10 minutes and serve!

Nutrition Information

- Calories: 865 calories
- Total Fat: 51.6 g
- Cholesterol: 255 mg
- Sodium: 1334 mg
- Total Carbohydrate: 34.3 g
- Protein: 65 g

79. Fiesta Grilled Chicken

"This main dish stars chicken marinated in tequila that's then grilled, and topped with Texas Bean Salsa and splashed with lime juice. Apple juice can be substituted for the tequila if you choose, and the chicken can also be broiled."

Serving: 6 | Prep: 25 m | Cook: 10 m | Ready in: 6 h 35 m

Ingredients

- Texas Bean Salsa:
- 1 (15.5 ounce) can black beans, rinsed and drained
- 1 (15.5 ounce) can black-eyed peas, rinsed and drained
- 1 (15.5 ounce) can whole kernel corn, drained
- 1 small red onion, chopped
- 1/2 cup chopped green bell pepper
- 1 (4.5 ounce) can diced green chilies, drained
- 2 ripe tomatoes, diced and drained
- 1 cup Italian-style salad dressing
- 2 tablespoons chopped fresh cilantro
- 2 cloves garlic, minced
- 1/2 teaspoon garlic salt
- Chicken:
- 6 skinless, boneless chicken breast halves
- 3 limes, juiced
- 1/3 cup tequila
- 3 teaspoons paprika
- 2 teaspoons salt
- 1 teaspoon pepper
- 6 Romaine lettuce leaves
- 6 sprigs cilantro leaves, for garnish (optional)
- 6 lime wedges, for garnish (optional)

Direction

- To make the salsa, mix the black beans, black-eyed peas, corn, red onion, bell pepper, chiles, and tomatoes together in a bowl. Toss vegetables with the Italian dressing, cilantro, garlic, and garlic salt until evenly blended. Cover, and refrigerate 6 hours or overnight.
- Preheat a grill for medium-high heat.
- About 45 minutes before serving time, place the chicken breasts in a baking dish and drizzle with lime juice and tequila. Sprinkle evenly with paprika, salt, and pepper. Cover the dish, refrigerate, and allow to marinate 10 minutes.
- Remove chicken breasts from the marinade, and discard remaining marinade.
- Cook the chicken breasts on the preheated grill until the juices run clear and the meat is no longer pink, 10 to 12 minutes.
- To serve, place a lettuce leaf on each plate. Top with a chicken breast, and spoon Texas Bean Salsa over each, dividing evenly among servings. If desired, garnish with additional cilantro leaves and lime wedges.

Nutrition Information

- Calories: 512 calories
- Total Fat: 15.8 g
- Cholesterol: 67 mg
- Sodium: 2600 mg
- Total Carbohydrate: 56.4 g
- Protein: 36.4 g

80. Fort Worth Fish Tacos

"Yes, I live in Fort Worth, and yes, I love fish tacos!"

Serving: 8 | Prep: 40 m | Cook: 20 m | Ready in: 1 h

Ingredients

- Fish:

- 8 (3 ounce) fillets tilapia
- 2 teaspoons salt
- 2 teaspoons hot pepper sauce
- Cilantro Cream Sauce:
- 4 ounces cream cheese, softened
- 2 tablespoons chopped fresh cilantro
- 1/2 cup mayonnaise
- 1 (5.3 ounce) container plain Greek yogurt
- 1 tablespoon lime juice
- Beer Batter:
- 1 cup flour
- 1 teaspoon salt
- 1 teaspoon garlic powder
- cayenne pepper to taste
- 1/4 teaspoon ground black pepper
- 1 cup dark beer
- 3 cups peanut oil for frying
- For the Tacos:
- 8 (8 inch) flour tortillas
- 1/4 medium head cabbage, finely shredded
- 1 (8 ounce) jar prepared salsa
- 1/4 cup chopped fresh cilantro
- 2 small limes, quartered

Direction

- Place tilapia fillets on plate and sprinkle with salt and hot sauce; cover and refrigerate while making cilantro cream sauce.
- Combine cream cheese, 2 tablespoons cilantro, mayonnaise, and yogurt in a small bowl or large measuring cup; mix well. Stir lime juice into cream sauce. Cover and refrigerate.
- Whisk flour, salt, garlic powder, cayenne, and pepper in a bowl until thoroughly combined; whisk in beer to make a smooth batter.
- Heat oil in a large, deep frying pan to 375 degrees F (190 degrees C).
- Remove fish from refrigerator; dip in beer batter and fry fillets 3 at a time in the hot oil, turning when golden (approximately 2 minutes on each side, depending on the thickness). Transfer to paper towels to drain; set fish on a covered plate to keep warm. Repeat with remaining fillets.
- Wrap tortillas in a clean kitchen towel and heat in the microwave until warm, about 20 seconds. Assemble tacos by placing a fish fillet on a warm tortilla. Top with shredded cabbage, a dollop of cilantro cream sauce, a spoonful of salsa, and a sprinkle of chopped cilantro. Serve each taco with a lime quarter for squeezing.

Nutrition Information

- Calories: 589 calories
- Total Fat: 31.5 g
- Cholesterol: 56 mg
- Sodium: 1591 mg
- Total Carbohydrate: 47.8 g
- Protein: 27 g

81. Fried Cabbage Texas Style

"This cabbage is sauteed with onion and jalapeno, and gets an added kick from a pinch of cayenne pepper. A little spicy , but works well with any Southern meal!"

Serving: 4 | Prep: 10 m | Cook: 20 m | Ready in: 30 m

Ingredients

- 1 small head cabbage, thinly sliced
- 1 teaspoon white sugar
- 6 slices bacon
- 5 tablespoons corn bread mix
- 1/4 teaspoon cayenne pepper
- 1/2 cup chopped onion
- 2 fresh jalapeno peppers, seeded and julienned
- salt and pepper to taste

Direction

- Place the shredded cabbage into a large bowl, and sprinkle the sugar over it. This will remove the excess water from the cabbage. Place bacon in a large, deep skillet. Cook over medium high heat until evenly brown. Drain, crumble and set aside, reserving grease in skillet.
- In a small bowl, mix together the cornbread mix and cayenne pepper. Stir into the cabbage until well blended. In the skillet the bacon was

cooked in, sauté onion and jalapeno in the hot bacon grease until tender. Stir in cabbage, and season with salt and pepper to taste. Cook until the cabbage wilts, about 15 minutes. Stir in crumbled bacon, and serve immediately.

Nutrition Information

- Calories: 300 calories
- Total Fat: 20.4 g
- Cholesterol: 29 mg
- Sodium: 584 mg
- Total Carbohydrate: 22.5 g
- Protein: 8.5 g

82. German Texas Chili

"Fred is German and I am Texan! This creation is a blend of the two! Have a different ethnic background? You can easily add spices and other ingredients to make it your own, although, we have to say - it's quite good the way it is. This can easily be prepared the day before or put into the freezer for later use. Serve over baked potato or corn chips with 'fixins' such as sour cream, grated cheese, onions, etc. For a richer flavor, you are able to make this dish the night before and keep in refrigerator until the next day. Enjoy!
"

Serving: 12 | Prep: 25 m | Cook: 6 h 20 m | Ready in: 6 h 45 m

Ingredients

- 1/4 cup olive oil
- 4 red onions, chopped
- 6 chipotle peppers in adobo sauce, chopped, or to taste
- 1 pound hot pork sausage (such as Jimmy Dean®)
- 2 1/2 pounds ground turkey
- 2 (28 ounce) cans crushed tomatoes with juice (such as Hunt's®)
- 1 (28 ounce) can Italian-style diced tomatoes (such as Hunt's® Diced Tomatoes with Basil, Garlic and Oregano)
- 1 (12 fluid ounce) can or bottle beer
- 1 tablespoon garlic powder
- 1 1/2 teaspoons kosher salt
- 1 tablespoon ground black pepper
- 3 tablespoons ground cumin
- 1 tablespoon chili powder
- 1/4 cup paprika
- 1/4 cup brown sugar
- 4 cinnamon sticks
- 12 whole cloves

Direction

- Heat the olive oil in a very large skillet over medium heat, and cook the onions and chipotle peppers until the onions are translucent, about 10 minutes. Place the hot sausage and turkey into the skillet and cook until brown, chopping the meat up with a spoon into crumbles as it cooks, 10 to 15 more minutes. Spoon the meat mixture into a large slow cooker, leaving excess grease behind in the skillet. Stir the crushed tomatoes, Italian-style diced tomatoes, beer, garlic powder, kosher salt, black pepper, cumin, chili powder, paprika, and brown sugar into the meat mixture until thoroughly combined.
- Tie the cinnamon sticks and cloves into a piece of cheesecloth, and drop the bundle into the slow cooker. Set the cooker to Low, and cook 6 to 8 hours. Remove the cheesecloth spice bundle before serving.

Nutrition Information

- Calories: 402 calories
- Total Fat: 21.1 g
- Cholesterol: 92 mg
- Sodium: 956 mg
- Total Carbohydrate: 26 g
- Protein: 28.1 g

83. Grampa Daves Texas Chainsaw BarBQue Sauce

"A spicy-sweet sauce that has won rave reviews from all who have tried it."

Serving: 40 | Prep: 15 m | Cook: 45 m | Ready in: 1 h

Ingredients

- 2 tablespoons butter
- 1 medium onion, finely chopped
- 2 garlic, minced
- 1/2 cup orange juice
- 1 cup cider vinegar
- 2 tablespoons fresh lemon juice
- 2 slices lemon
- 1 cup real maple syrup
- 1/4 cup Worcestershire sauce
- 2 cups ketchup
- 1/4 cup molasses
- 1/4 cup brown sugar
- 2 tablespoons dry mustard
- 1 teaspoon salt
- 1/2 teaspoon red pepper flakes
- 1/2 teaspoon ground cumin
- 1/2 teaspoon paprika

Direction

- Melt butter in a large saucepan over medium heat. Add the onion and garlic; cook and stir until tender, about 5 minutes. Stir in the orange juice, cider vinegar, lemon juice, lemon slices, maple syrup, Worcestershire sauce, ketchup, molasses, and brown sugar. Season with dry mustard, salt, red pepper flakes, cumin and paprika. Simmer for 45 minutes to 1 hour. Remove lemon slices before using.

Nutrition Information

- Calories: 57 calories
- Total Fat: 0.8 g
- Cholesterol: 2 mg
- Sodium: 215 mg
- Total Carbohydrate: 12.5 g
- Protein: 0.4 g

84. Grand Margarita

"This is my husband's secret recipe from Austin Texas. We always serve this to our favorite friends. A very straightforward margarita with no added sugar."

Serving: 6 | Prep: 10 m | Ready in: 10 m

Ingredients

- 3 cups water
- 1 1/2 cups fresh lime juice
- 1 1/2 cups cointreau
- 1 1/2 cups silver tequila
- 1 lime, cut into 8 wedges
- coarse salt

Direction

- Combine the water, lime juice, tequila, and cointreau in a half-gallon pitcher. Stir to mix.
- To serve, rub the rim of a margarita glass with lime, and dip in salt. Fill the glass with ice, and top with the tequila mixture. Garnish with a slice of lime.

85. Healthy Turkey Tex Mex Chili

"Thick chili made with black beans, tomatoes, ground turkey, corn, and spices. Quick and easy. Perfect for a cool day. Serve with hot jasmine rice. Adjust the amount of black beans as desired."

Serving: 4 | Prep: 15 m | Cook: 1 h | Ready in: 1 h 15 m

Ingredients

- 1 1/2 cups dry black beans
- 2 tablespoons olive oil
- 1 pound ground turkey
- 1 large sweet onion, chopped
- 1 (28 ounce) can diced tomatoes
- 3 ears corn, kernels cut from cob
- 1 tablespoon maple syrup
- 1 tablespoon molasses
- 1 tablespoon Hungarian paprika

- 1 tablespoon chili powder
- 1 tablespoon garlic powder
- 1/2 teaspoon chipotle chile powder
- 1/4 teaspoon cayenne pepper
- sea salt to taste
- 1 (8 ounce) container plain yogurt (optional)
- 1 bunch green onions, diced (optional)

Direction

- Put black beans in a large pot with water to cover; bring to a boil. Reduce heat to medium-low and cook at a simmer until tender, 30 to 40 minutes; drain. Return beans to the pot.
- Heat olive oil in a large cast-iron skillet over medium heat. Cook and stir turkey in the hot oil until completely browned, about 10 minutes; add sweet onion and continue cooking and stirring until the onion is translucent, about 10 minutes more. Add to the black beans.
- Stir tomatoes, corn kernels, maple syrup, molasses, Hungarian paprika, chili powder, garlic powder, chipotle chile powder, cayenne pepper, and sea salt into the black bean mixture; bring to a simmer and cook until heated through, 15 to 20 minutes. Top servings of chili with yogurt and green onions.

Nutrition Information

- Calories: 657 calories
- Total Fat: 18.3 g
- Cholesterol: 87 mg
- Sodium: 541 mg
- Total Carbohydrate: 82.4 g
- Protein: 45.2 g

86. Hearty Meat Sauce

"My grandmother fixed this for us growing up and I love it. It is a thick and hearty sauce for spaghetti or your favorite noodle! Of course the bread of choice would have to be Texas garlic bread!"

Serving: 4 | Prep: 15 m | Cook: 30 m | Ready in: 45 m

Ingredients

- 1/2 pound ground beef
- 2 (16 ounce) jars spaghetti sauce
- 1 diced yellow pepper
- 1 diced red bell pepper
- 1 (14.5 ounce) can peeled and diced tomatoes, drained
- 6 fresh mushrooms, coarsely chopped

Direction

- In a skillet over medium heat, brown the ground beef until no pink shows; drain.
- In a large pot combine browned beef and spaghetti sauce over medium heat for 5 or 10 minutes. Add yellow peppers, red peppers, canned tomatoes and mushrooms. Lower heat and simmer covered for 30 minutes, stirring every once in a while.

Nutrition Information

- Calories: 351 calories
- Total Fat: 14 g
- Cholesterol: 39 mg
- Sodium: 1111 mg
- Total Carbohydrate: 39.3 g
- Protein: 15.8 g

87. Hill Country Turkey Chili with Beans

"Created from memory of a recipe I once used, this is the best chili I've ever made. It makes a hearty, healthy, and flavorful chili. Difficult to tell that beef was not used. Top as desired with cheese, sour cream, jalapenos, etc."

Serving: 8 | Prep: 10 m | Cook: 1 h 35 m | Ready in: 1 h 45 m

Ingredients

- 3 tablespoons olive oil
- 1 pound ground turkey
- 3 cloves garlic, minced
- 1 (14 ounce) can beef broth
- 1 (28 ounce) can crushed tomatoes
- 1 onion, chopped
- 1 (15 ounce) can tomato paste
- 1 (10 ounce) can diced tomatoes and green chiles (such as RO*TEL®)
- 1 (15 ounce) can black beans, rinsed and drained

Direction

- Heat olive oil in a large pot over medium heat; cook and stir ground turkey and garlic in hot oil until browned completely, 5 to 7 minutes.
- Pour beef broth over browned turkey mixture, bring to a boil, reduce heat to medium-low, and cook for 20 minutes.
- Stir crushed tomatoes, onion, tomato paste, and diced tomatoes and green chiles with the turkey mixture; bring to a boil, reduce heat to medium-low, and cook at a simmer until thick, about 1 hour.
- Stir black beans into the chili; cook until the beans are heated through, about 10 minutes more.

Nutrition Information

- Calories: 273 calories
- Total Fat: 10.2 g
- Cholesterol: 42 mg
- Sodium: 1089 mg
- Total Carbohydrate: 30.3 g
- Protein: 19.5 g

88. Hollys Texas Brisket

"Season your next beef brisket roast with this flavorful spice rub. Slow roasting makes a tender and juicy brisket. This is not a quick fix recipe. It takes time and planning to make this a success. Follow the directions and make sure that the brisket is sealed tightly so that juices do not evaporate. It is well worth the time and trouble. You won't be sorry, it is awesome!"

Serving: 28 | Prep: 30 m | Cook: 12 h | Ready in: 12 h 30 m

Ingredients

- 2 tablespoons chili powder
- 2 tablespoons brown sugar
- 1 tablespoon salt
- 1 tablespoon garlic powder
- 1 tablespoon onion powder
- 1 tablespoon ground black pepper
- 2 teaspoons dry mustard
- 14 pounds beef brisket

Direction

- Preheat grill for medium-low heat or 270 degrees F (132 degrees C), and lightly oil the grate.
- Whisk chili powder, brown sugar, salt, garlic powder, onion powder, ground black pepper, and dry mustard together in a small bowl to create the dry rub.
- Pierce fatty side of the brisket with a knife about 50 times. Sprinkle 1/2 the dry rub generously over the lean side of the brisket. Turn meat over and sprinkle remaining 1/2 the dry rub over the fatty side, rubbing into the pierced fat.
- Cook brisket, uncovered and fatty-side up, on the preheated grill for 4 hours. Transfer brisket to a roasting pan and cover pan tightly with aluminum foil.
- Preheat oven to 270 degrees F (132 degrees C).
- Cook in the preheated oven until meat is tender and pulls easily away from the side of

the brisket, about 8 more hours. Let meat rest 30 minutes before slicing.

Nutrition Information

- Calories: 391 calories
- Total Fat: 31.5 g
- Cholesterol: 93 mg
- Sodium: 316 mg
- Total Carbohydrate: 1.9 g
- Protein: 23.5 g

89. Honey Smoked Turkey

"Sweet and light, this is the easiest way to cook a big bird! It will be the best turkey you have ever had. The breast is moist and juicy, and the honey makes a great thin sauce. I hope you enjoy it as much as my friends and family do when I make it. I never have any leftovers! Enjoy!"

Serving: 16 | Prep: 30 m | Cook: 3 h 15 m | Ready in: 3 h 45 m

Ingredients

- 1 (12 pound) whole turkey
- 2 tablespoons chopped fresh sage
- 2 tablespoons ground black pepper
- 2 tablespoons celery salt
- 2 tablespoons chopped fresh basil
- 2 tablespoons vegetable oil
- 1 (12 ounce) jar honey
- 1/2 pound mesquite wood chips

Direction

- Preheat grill for high heat. If you are using a charcoal grill, use about twice the normal amount of charcoal. Soak wood chips in a pan of water, and set next to the grill.
- Remove neck and giblets from turkey. Rinse the bird and pat dry. Place in a large disposable roasting pan.
- In a medium bowl, mix together sage, ground black pepper, celery salt, basil, and vegetable oil. Pour mixture evenly over the turkey. Turn the turkey breast side down in the pan, and tent loosely with aluminum foil.
- Place the roasting pan on the preheated grill. Throw a handful of the wood chips onto the coals. Close the lid, and cook for 1 hour.
- Throw about 2 more handfuls of soaked wood chips on the fire. Drizzle 1/2 the honey over the bird, and replace the foil. Close the lid of the grill, and continue cooking 1 1/2 to 2 hours, or until internal temperature reaches 180 degrees F (80 degrees C) in the thickest part of the thigh.
- Uncover turkey, and carefully turn it breast side up in the roasting pan. Baste with remaining honey. Leave the turkey uncovered, and cook 15 minutes. The cooked honey will be very dark.

Nutrition Information

- Calories: 647 calories
- Total Fat: 28.8 g
- Cholesterol: 228 mg
- Sodium: 776 mg
- Total Carbohydrate: 25.3 g
- Protein: 68.9 g

90. Jalapeno Ranch Salad Dressing

"Cool, creamy, and spicy. Crazy good salad dressing you could also use as a dip. This recipe is a lot like the dip they serve at Chuy's, which is a restaurant we have in Texas."

Serving: 12 | Prep: 15 m | Ready in: 15 m

Ingredients

- 3 tomatillos, husked and quartered
- 1/2 bunch cilantro
- 2 pickled jalapeno peppers
- 1 (16 ounce) container fat-free sour cream
- 2 (1 ounce) packages ranch dressing mix

Direction

- Place tomatillos, cilantro, and jalapenos in a food processor or blender. Blend until smooth and set aside.
- Combine the sour cream and ranch dressing mix in a medium bowl. Whisk in about 3/4 of the green sauce; taste and adjust the heat level by adding more green sauce.

Nutrition Information

- Calories: 49 calories
- Total Fat: 0.1 g
- Cholesterol: 7 mg
- Sodium: 405 mg
- Total Carbohydrate: 8.4 g
- Protein: 2.8 g

91. Jamoncillo de Leche Mexican Fudge

"If you have ever been in Texas or any of the Southwest border cities you will be familiar with this candy. If you are Mexican-American, good food is a part of our tradition. This candy resembles a type of fudge."

Serving: 24 | Prep: 10 m | Cook: 45 m | Ready in: 55 m

Ingredients

- 1 quart whole milk
- 1 3/4 cups white sugar
- 2 teaspoons vanilla extract
- 1 teaspoon baking soda
- 1 cinnamon stick
- 1 cup chopped pecans
- 24 pecan halves for garnish

Direction

- Combine milk, sugar, vanilla, baking soda, and cinnamon stick in a large heavy saucepan. Bring to a boil over medium heat and cook, stirring continuously. After about 20 minutes remove the cinnamon stick. Place a candy thermometer in the pan and cook until the thermometer reaches soft-ball stage 240 degrees F (115 degrees C) or until you can see the bottom of the pan when you stir.
- Remove the candy from the heat and add the chopped pecans. Beat the candy with a mixer for about 5 minutes. Pour the candy into a buttered 9x9-inch pan. Press pecan halves onto the top of the warm candy. Cool, then cut into pieces. Store candy in an airtight container.

Nutrition Information

- Calories: 124 calories
- Total Fat: 5.7 g
- Cholesterol: 4 mg
- Sodium: 69 mg
- Total Carbohydrate: 17.4 g
- Protein: 1.9 g

92. Jesses Hot Sauce

"I'm a chile pepper nut from South Carolina. This is an awesome recipe I adapted from a Chilihead in East Texas; it's great if you like fresh salsa. This can be eaten with tortilla chips or as a soup!"

Serving: 24 | Prep: 50 m | Cook: 45 m | Ready in: 1 h 35 m

Ingredients

- 1 pound bacon, diced
- 1 red onion, diced
- 1 tablespoon minced garlic
- 1 bunch green onions, sliced
- 2 green bell peppers, chopped
- 2 yellow bell peppers chopped
- 8 jalapeno or serrano peppers, chopped
- 2 poblano peppers, chopped
- 1/2 cup sliced mushrooms (optional)
- 8 roma tomatoes, diced
- 2 (10 ounce) cans diced tomatoes with green chile peppers, drained
- 1 teaspoon lime juice
- 3/4 cup chopped cilantro
- 2 teaspoons salt
- 2 teaspoons black pepper

Direction

- Cook bacon in a large skillet over medium heat until it releases its oil and begins to crisp. Strain out bacon, and pour off all but 1 tablespoon of bacon grease.
- Stir in the red onion, garlic, green onions, green bell peppers, yellow bell peppers, jalapeno peppers, poblano peppers, mushrooms, and roma tomatoes. Pour in the canned tomatoes and lime juice. Season with cilantro, salt, and black pepper. Bring to a boil, and then reduce heat to medium-low; simmer until the sauce reaches desired consistency.

Nutrition Information

- Calories: 107 calories
- Total Fat: 8.7 g
- Cholesterol: 13 mg
- Sodium: 450 mg
- Total Carbohydrate: 4.8 g
- Protein: 3.2 g

93. KCs Smoked Brisket

"Beef brisket slowly smoked with mesquite, Texas-style. Time-consuming but very tasty."

Serving: 12 | Prep: 10 m | Cook: 6 h 15 m | Ready in: 14 h 55 m

Ingredients

- 5 pounds beef brisket, trimmed of fat
- 3 tablespoons mustard, or as needed
- 2 tablespoons brisket rub (such as Fiesta®), or as needed

Direction

- Coat beef brisket with mustard. Cover with brisket rub. Let marinate in the refrigerate, 8 hours to overnight.
- Remove brisket from the refrigerator and bring to room temperature.
- Preheat a smoker to 220 degrees F (104 degrees F) according to manufacturer's instructions.
- Place beef brisket in the smoker and smoke until easily pierced with a knife and an instant-read thermometer inserted into the center reads 190 degrees F (88 degrees C), 6 1/4 to 7 1/2 hours.
- Wrap brisket with aluminum foil and let rest for 30 minutes before slicing.

Nutrition Information

- Calories: 245 calories
- Total Fat: 16.3 g
- Cholesterol: 77 mg
- Sodium: 556 mg
- Total Carbohydrate: 0.7 g
- Protein: 22.4 g

94. Kens Texas Chili

"This is a Texas style chili recipe with beans. It also uses hamburger rather than chuck. Leaving behind a small amount of the hamburger fat gives it that unique Texas chili taste."

Serving: 8 | Prep: 20 m | Cook: 45 m | Ready in: 1 h 5 m

Ingredients

- 2 pounds ground beef
- 1/2 teaspoon garlic powder
- 3 tablespoons chili powder
- 2 teaspoons ground cumin
- 3 tablespoons all-purpose flour
- 1 tablespoon dried oregano
- 2 (14 ounce) cans beef broth
- 1 teaspoon salt
- 1/4 teaspoon black pepper
- 3 (15.5 ounce) cans pinto beans, drained

Direction

- In a stockpot over medium heat, brown the ground beef until no longer pink. Drain off grease, reserving 2 tablespoons to remain in the pan. In a small bowl, stir together the

garlic powder, chili powder, cumin, and flour. Sprinkle the mixture over the meat, and stir until the meat is evenly coated.
- Stir the oregano into the meat mixture, then pour in the 2 cans of beef broth. Season with salt and pepper. Bring to a boil, then add the cans of beans. If you like your chili soupy, add only 2 cans of beans, but if you like thick chili, use all three. Reduce heat to low, and simmer for 30 minutes to blend flavors.

Nutrition Information

- Calories: 525 calories
- Total Fat: 32.4 g
- Cholesterol: 96 mg
- Sodium: 1208 mg
- Total Carbohydrate: 29.8 g
- Protein: 28.9 g

95. King Beef Oven Brisket

"Grady calls supper at Perini Ranch Steakhouse in Texas one of life's great pleasures. Here he's adapted their brisket recipe so you can make it at home in the oven."

Serving: 8 | Prep: 15 m | Cook: 4 h | Ready in: 4 h 15 m

Ingredients

- 2 tablespoons chili powder
- 2 tablespoons salt
- 1 tablespoon garlic powder
- 1 tablespoon onion powder
- 1 tablespoon freshly ground black pepper
- 1 tablespoon white sugar
- 2 teaspoons dry mustard
- 1 bay leaf, crushed
- 1 (4 pound) beef brisket
- 1 1/2 cups beef stock

Direction

- Preheat oven to 350 degrees F (175 degrees C).
- Mix chili powder, salt, garlic powder, onion powder, black pepper, sugar, mustard, and bay leaf together in a small bowl; season

brisket with spice mixture. Arrange beef in a roasting pan or Dutch oven. Do not cover.
- Bake in the preheated oven for 1 hour. Fill pan with enough beef stock to cover by 1/2 inch. Cover pan with lid or aluminum foil and reduce heat to 300 degrees F (150 degrees C).
- Continue baking until beef is very tender, about 3 hours more. Slice beef thinly, across the grain and serve with juices from the pan.

Nutrition Information

- Calories: 165 calories
- Total Fat: 5.2 g
- Cholesterol: 46 mg
- Sodium: 3029 mg
- Total Carbohydrate: 7.3 g
- Protein: 21.6 g

96. King Ranch Chicken Casserole

"From what I hear, it's impossible to go to any sort of potluck in Texas and not see one of these."

Serving: 8 | Prep: 30 m | Cook: 45 m | Ready in: 1 h 15 m

Ingredients

- 1 tablespoon vegetable oil
- 1 white onion, diced
- 1 red bell pepper, diced
- 1 green bell pepper, diced
- 1 (10.75 ounce) can condensed cream of mushroom soup
- 1 (10.75 ounce) can condensed cream of chicken soup
- 1 (10 ounce) can diced tomatoes with green chile peppers (such as RO*TEL®)
- 1 cup chicken broth
- 2 tablespoons sour cream
- 2 teaspoons ground cumin
- 1 teaspoon ancho chile powder
- 1/2 teaspoon dried oregano
- 1/4 teaspoon chipotle chile powder

- 1 cooked chicken, torn into shreds or cut into chunks
- 8 ounces shredded Cheddar cheese
- 10 corn tortillas, cut into quarters

Direction

- Preheat oven to 350 degrees F (175 degrees C).
- Heat oil in a large skillet over high heat. Sauté onion, red bell pepper, and green bell pepper in hot oil until warmed through, about 2 minutes.
- Combine onion-pepper mixture, cream of mushroom soup, cream of chicken soup, diced tomatoes, chicken broth, sour cream, cumin, ancho chile powder, oregano, and chipotle chile powder together in a large bowl and stir until sauce is well-combined.
- Spread a few tablespoons of the sauce in the bottom of a 9x13-inch baking dish. Spread 1/2 the chicken over the sauce. Spread about half the sauce over the chicken and top with 1/3 the cheese. Spread a layer of tortillas over the cheese. Spread remaining 1/2 the chicken over the tortillas, and top with almost all of the remaining sauce, reserving 1/2 cup sauce. Top with 1/3 the cheese, remaining tortillas, the reserved 1/2 cup sauce, and remaining 1/3 cheese.
- Bake casserole in the preheated oven until bubbling, about 40 minutes. Increase the oven temperature to broil. Broil the casserole until top is golden, 2 to 3 minutes more.

Nutrition Information

- Calories: 481 calories
- Total Fat: 28.1 g
- Cholesterol: 100 mg
- Sodium: 1010 mg
- Total Carbohydrate: 25.1 g
- Protein: 32.1 g

97. Kristins Turkey Butternut Squash Casserole

"I got this recipes from Allrecipes.com member Mildred Sherrer, Fort Worth, Texas. This is my very tweaked version that cuts some of the fat and calories. I think this is a great recipe for a family."

Serving: 6 | Prep: 15 m | Cook: 35 m | Ready in: 50 m

Ingredients

- 1 tablespoon olive oil
- 1 pound lean ground turkey
- 2 cups cubed butternut squash
- 1 onion, chopped
- 1 cup 1% milk
- 1 cup shredded mozzarella cheese
- 1/4 cup butter, melted
- 2 eggs
- 1/2 teaspoon salt
- 1/4 teaspoon ground black pepper
- 1 cup crushed buttery round crackers (such as Ritz®)

Direction

- Preheat oven to 375 degrees F (190 degrees C). Grease a 9-inch square baking dish.
- Heat olive oil in a skillet over medium heat; cook and stir ground turkey until crumbly and browned, 5 to 10 minutes. Add butternut squash and onion to ground turkey; cook and stir until squash is slightly tender, 5 to 10 minutes. Drain any excess grease from skillet.
- Whisk milk, mozzarella cheese, butter, eggs, salt, and pepper together in a bowl; stir into turkey mixture. Transfer squash-turkey mixture to the prepared baking dish. Sprinkle crackers over squash-turkey mixture.
- Bake in the preheated oven until cooked through and bubbling, 25 to 30 minutes.

Nutrition Information

- Calories: 509 calories
- Total Fat: 31.2 g
- Cholesterol: 152 mg
- Sodium: 793 mg
- Total Carbohydrate: 31.9 g

- Protein: 26 g

98. Lemon Butter Chicken

"I love lemons on everything and created this quick and easy recipe one night. You can reduce the lemon juice for a less lemony taste. I use tenderloins for a shorter cooking time. It is even better if you have the time to marinate. The leftover juice is great served with rice or to dip with Texas Toast or rolls."

Serving: 4 | Prep: 15 m | Cook: 25 m | Ready in: 40 m

Ingredients

- 1 tablespoon butter
- 1/3 cup Italian salad dressing
- 1 lemon, zested and juiced
- 1 tablespoon Worcestershire sauce
- 8 chicken tenderloins
- lemon pepper to taste
- garlic salt to taste
- onion powder to taste

Direction

- Preheat oven to 350 degrees F (175 degrees C). Place the butter in a 9x9 inch baking dish, and melt in the oven. Remove from heat, and mix in Italian salad dressing, lemon juice, and Worcestershire sauce.
- Arrange the chicken tenderloins in the baking dish, coating with the melted butter mixture. Season both sides of chicken with lemon pepper, garlic salt, and onion powder. Sprinkle with lemon zest.
- Bake 25 minutes in the preheated oven, or until chicken juices run clear.

Nutrition Information

- Calories: 214 calories
- Total Fat: 11.2 g
- Cholesterol: 70 mg
- Sodium: 581 mg
- Total Carbohydrate: 6 g
- Protein: 23.3 g

99. Mamas TexasStyle Peach Cobbler

"This is very traditional southern comfort food always cooked in a big bowl. My grandmother passed down her 'cobbler bowl' to me that she got from her grandmother."

Serving: 6 | Prep: 10 m | Cook: 50 m | Ready in: 1 h

Ingredients

- 1 cup self-rising flour
- 1 cup white sugar
- 1 cup milk
- 1 cup butter, melted
- 1 (28 ounce) can sliced cling peaches in heavy syrup

Direction

- Preheat oven to 350 degrees F (175 degrees C).
- Mix self-rising flour and sugar in a bowl. Stir milk into the flour mixture.
- Pour melted butter in an oven-safe bowl. Pour flour mixture over melted butter. Layer peaches in heavy syrup atop flour mixture. Do not stir!
- Bake in preheated oven until peaches are bubbly and crust is lightly browned, 50 to 60 minutes.

Nutrition Information

- Calories: 553 calories
- Total Fat: 31.7 g
- Cholesterol: 85 mg
- Sodium: 504 mg
- Total Carbohydrate: 66 g
- Protein: 4.6 g

100. Margarita Balls II

"This is a great old Texas recipe. Everyone seems to like it, but it's obviously only for grown-ups."

Serving: 48

Ingredients

- 1 (12 ounce) package vanilla wafers
- 2 cups small pretzel twists
- 6 ounces cream cheese
- 1 pound confectioners' sugar
- 3/4 cup frozen margarita mix, thawed
- 2 tablespoons tequila
- 2 tablespoons brandy-based orange liqueur (such as Grand Marnier®)
- 1 tablespoon grated lime zest
- 2/3 cup white sugar
- 4 drops green food coloring

Direction

- Using a food processor or blender, process all of the vanilla wafers and pretzels to fine crumbs.
- In a medium bowl, combine all of the crumbs with the confectioners' sugar. In another bowl, mix together the cream cheese, margarita mix, tequila and Grand Marnier, stir into the crumb mixture. Divide dough into two pieces, wrap and refrigerate for at least 2 hours.
- Divide the white sugar into two small bowls. Add the zest of 1 lime to each bowl. Stir the food coloring into one of the bowls. Unwrap dough and roll into walnut sized balls. Roll half of the balls in the green sugar, and the other half in the white sugar. Store in the refrigerator in the unlikely event that there are any left!

Nutrition Information

- Calories: 106 calories
- Total Fat: 2.7 g
- Cholesterol: 4 mg
- Sodium: 62 mg
- Total Carbohydrate: 19.6 g
- Protein: 0.7 g

101. Marks Surprise Meatloaf

"Not your grandma's meatloaf! I asked my husband to make a meatloaf for dinner using my Tex Mex recipe basics. I came home to the best meatloaf I ever tasted! He took my recipe and added extra ingredients to get an incredible flavor. We ate for dinner and had pan-fried meatloaf sandwiches the next day. Awesome!"

Serving: 8 | Prep: 15 m | Cook: 1 h | Ready in: 1 h 15 m

Ingredients

- 1 1/2 pounds ground beef
- 1/2 cup minced onion
- 1/2 cup minced green bell pepper
- 2 cloves garlic, minced
- 1 cup seasoned bread crumbs
- 1 egg, lightly beaten
- 1 teaspoon cayenne pepper
- 1 1/2 teaspoons salt
- 1/2 teaspoon freshly ground black pepper
- 2 tablespoons Dijon mustard
- 2 tablespoons Worcestershire sauce
- 2 tablespoons olive oil

Direction

- Preheat oven to 350 degrees F (175 degrees C).
- Mix ground beef, onion, bell pepper, and garlic together in a large bowl; add bread crumbs, egg, cayenne pepper, salt, and black pepper and mix.
- Stir mustard and Worcestershire sauce together in a small bowl; add to meat mixture and mix. Shape the meat mixture into an 8x4-inch loaf and place on a rimmed baking sheet. Spread olive oil over the top and sides of the loaf.
- Bake in the preheated oven until no longer pink in the center, about 1 hour. An instant-read thermometer inserted into the center should read at least 160 degrees F (70 degrees C). Transfer meatloaf to a platter and cut into 8 slices.

Nutrition Information

- Calories: 261 calories
- Total Fat: 15 g
- Cholesterol: 77 mg
- Sodium: 729 mg
- Total Carbohydrate: 13.2 g
- Protein: 17.2 g

102. Mexican Corn

"This recipe was given to me by my aunt in Texas, where they like everything hot! Now, my family wants it for holidays, barbeques, or just by itself."

Serving: 6 | Prep: 10 m | Cook: 10 m | Ready in: 20 m

Ingredients

- 2 (15.25 ounce) cans whole kernel corn, drained
- 1 (8 ounce) package cream cheese
- 1/4 cup butter
- 10 jalapeno peppers, chopped
- 1 teaspoon garlic salt

Direction

- In a medium saucepan combine corn, cream cheese, butter, jalapeno peppers and garlic salt. Cook over medium heat for about 10 minutes or until heated through, stirring constantly after cream cheese begins to melt.

Nutrition Information

- Calories: 359 calories
- Total Fat: 22.7 g
- Cholesterol: 61 mg
- Sodium: 491 mg
- Total Carbohydrate: 38.2 g
- Protein: 8 g

103. Mexican Rice

"This flavored rice is a local favorite in San Antonio."

Serving: 8 | Prep: 20 m | Cook: 30 m | Ready in: 50 m

Ingredients

- 3 tablespoons vegetable oil
- 2/3 cup diced onion
- 1 1/2 cups uncooked white rice
- 1 cup chopped green bell pepper
- 1 teaspoon ground cumin
- 1 teaspoon chili powder
- 1 1/2 (8 ounce) cans tomato sauce
- 2 teaspoons salt
- 1 clove garlic, minced
- 1/8 teaspoon powdered saffron
- 3 cups water

Direction

- In a large saucepan, heat vegetable oil over a medium-low heat. Place the onions in the pan, and sauté until golden.
- Add rice to pan, and stir to coat grains with oil. Mix in green bell pepper, cumin, chili powder, tomato sauce, salt, garlic, saffron, and water. Cover, bring to a boil, and then reduce heat to simmer. Cook for 30 to 40 minutes, or until rice is tender. Stir occasionally.

Nutrition Information

- Calories: 199 calories
- Total Fat: 5.6 g
- Cholesterol: 0 mg
- Sodium: 809 mg
- Total Carbohydrate: 33.8 g
- Protein: 3.4 g

104. Mock Chicken Patties

"For years I've endured paying $1 for a patty at the store feeling like I could figure out the recipe, but never could until now. Eureka! Mock chicken patties that taste marvelous on a bun with fixin's or slathered in gravy, Texas-style. Very good stuff."

Serving: 12 | Prep: 25 m | Cook: 13 m | Ready in: 38 m

Ingredients

- 3/4 cup minced onion (optional)
- 3/4 cup minced celery (optional)
- 1 (12 ounce) package extra-firm tofu
- 1 cup water
- 2 cubes vegetable bouillon (such as Knorr®)
- 1 tablespoon vegetable soup base
- 3 cups rolled oats
- 1 cup finely chopped raw cashews
- 1 tablespoon olive oil

Direction

- Place a steamer insert into a saucepan and fill with water to just below the bottom of the steamer. Bring water to a boil. Add onion and celery, cover, and steam until tender, 2 to 3 minutes.
- Place tofu and water in a blender or food processor. Pulse briefly. Add bouillon cubes and vegetable base. Pulse until completely combined. Stir in onion, celery, oats, and cashews until evenly distributed.
- Form tofu mixture into patties.
- Heat oil in a skillet over medium heat. Cook tofu patties until golden brown, about 3 minutes per side.

Nutrition Information

- Calories: 179 calories
- Total Fat: 9.1 g
- Cholesterol: < 1 mg
- Sodium: 90 mg
- Total Carbohydrate: 19.2 g
- Protein: 6.8 g

105. Moms Chili

"Quick, easy, yummy chili from Texas."

Serving: 4 | Prep: 10 m | Cook: 2 h | Ready in: 2 h 10 m

Ingredients

- 1 pound ground beef
- 1 large onion, chopped
- 1 (15 ounce) can ranch-style beans
- 1 (10 ounce) can diced tomatoes with green chile peppers
- 1 (1.25 ounce) package chili seasoning mix
- salt and pepper to taste
- 2 teaspoons chili powder, or to taste
- 1 cup water, or as needed

Direction

- In a large saucepan over medium-high heat, cook beef and onion until meat is brown. Stir in beans, diced tomatoes, chili seasoning, salt, pepper, chili powder and water. Reduce heat and simmer 2 hours.

Nutrition Information

- Calories: 382 calories
- Total Fat: 18.7 g
- Cholesterol: 70 mg
- Sodium: 1701 mg
- Total Carbohydrate: 26.8 g
- Protein: 27 g

106. Moms Favorite Baked Mac and Cheese

"This is a macaroni and cheese I first made 3 years ago when I was in California. When I got back to Texas I made it for my mom. This is now her favorite baked macaroni and cheese. She begs me to make it when I come to visit."

Serving: 6 | Prep: 10 m | Cook: 45 m | Ready in: 1 h 5 m

Ingredients

- 2 tablespoons butter

- 1/4 cup finely chopped onion
- 2 tablespoons all-purpose flour
- 2 cups milk
- 3/4 teaspoon salt
- 1/2 teaspoon dry mustard
- 1/4 teaspoon ground black pepper
- 1 (8 ounce) package elbow macaroni
- 2 cups shredded sharp Cheddar cheese
- 1 (8 ounce) package processed American cheese, cut into strips

Direction

- Preheat oven to 350 degrees F (175 degrees C).
- Melt butter in a medium saucepan over medium heat. Sauté onion for 2 minutes. Stir in flour and cook 1 minute, stirring constantly. Stir in milk, salt, mustard and pepper; cook, stirring frequently, until mixture boils and thickens.
- Meanwhile, bring a pot of lightly salted water to a boil. Add macaroni and cook for 8 to 10 minutes or until al dente; drain.
- To the milk mixture add the Cheddar and American cheeses; stir until cheese melts. Combine macaroni and cheese sauce in a 2 quart baking dish; mix well.
- Bake in preheated oven for 30 minutes, or until hot and bubbly. Let cool 10 minutes before serving.

Nutrition Information

- Calories: 561 calories
- Total Fat: 33.3 g
- Cholesterol: 100 mg
- Sodium: 1194 mg
- Total Carbohydrate: 36.5 g
- Protein: 28.3 g

107. Moms Texas Hash

"This is a quick recipe my mother made a lot when I was growing up. It has a great flavor! Serve over rice."

Serving: 6 | Prep: 5 m | Cook: 20 m | Ready in: 25 m

Ingredients

- 1 1/2 pounds ground beef
- 1 medium onion, chopped
- 1 (28 ounce) can diced tomatoes with juice, pureed
- 2 tablespoons chili powder, or to taste
- 1 tablespoon Worcestershire sauce, or to taste
- salt and ground black pepper to taste

Direction

- In a skillet over medium heat, brown the ground beef with the onion, until the meat is no longer pink, and the onion is soft; drain fat.
- In a Dutch oven or large saucepan, combine the ground beef mixture, and pureed tomatoes. Season with Worcestershire sauce, chili powder, salt and pepper. I just keep adding stuff until it tastes good. Bring to a boil, and let simmer for 15 to 20 minutes to blend flavors. Serve over rice.

Nutrition Information

- Calories: 397 calories
- Total Fat: 30.6 g
- Cholesterol: 96 mg
- Sodium: 434 mg
- Total Carbohydrate: 8 g
- Protein: 20.5 g

108. Mr Goodbar Frosting

"This is just like the frosting used on Texas sheet cakes except it has crunchy peanut butter in it, making it taste just like a Mr.Goodbar candy bar."

Serving: 15

Ingredients

- 2 cups white sugar
- 2 tablespoons unsweetened cocoa powder
- 3/4 cup evaporated milk
- 1 teaspoon vanilla extract
- 2 cups crunchy peanut butter

Direction

- Combine the sugar, cocoa, and milk in a medium saucepan. Bring to a boil, and cook for 3 minutes. Stir in the vanilla and peanut butter. Mix well. Spread over hot cake while frosting is also still hot. Let frosted cake cool before cutting.

Nutrition Information

- Calories: 325 calories
- Total Fat: 18.2 g
- Cholesterol: 4 mg
- Sodium: 181 mg
- Total Carbohydrate: 35.8 g
- Protein: 9.3 g

109. Ninas Texas Chili

"This is the best chili you will ever have! It's not your ordinary chili with chopped meat! I make this and let it cook in a slow cooker. It's great for parties or cold winter nights."

Serving: 12 | Prep: 30 m | Cook: 2 h 15 m | Ready in: 2 h 45 m

Ingredients

- 2 teaspoons cooking oil
- 3 pounds beef top sirloin, thinly sliced
- 2 pounds sweet Italian sausage, casings removed
- 1 onion, chopped
- 1 green bell pepper, chopped
- 1 red bell pepper, chopped
- 1 yellow bell pepper, chopped
- 2 cloves garlic, minced
- 20 ounces diced tomatoes
- 3 (8 ounce) cans tomato sauce
- 2 teaspoons chicken bouillon granules
- 1/2 cup honey
- 1 (15 ounce) can kidney beans, rinsed and drained
- 2 tablespoons cayenne pepper
- 6 tablespoons chili powder
- 3 tablespoons dried oregano
- 1 teaspoon ground black pepper
- 2 teaspoons salt
- 1/3 cup white sugar
- 1 cup shredded Cheddar cheese
- 1/4 cup masa (corn flour)

Direction

- Heat the oil in a large pot over medium heat; cook the steak, sausage, onion, green pepper, red, pepper, yellow pepper, and garlic in the pot until the onions and peppers are soft, about 5 minutes. Add the diced tomatoes, tomato sauce, chicken bouillon, honey, and kidney beans; bring to a boil. One at a time, stir in the cayenne pepper, chili powder, oregano, black pepper, salt, and sugar. Sprinkle the Cheddar cheese into the chili in small batches and stir to melt. Reduce heat to low and slow cook about 2 hours. Thicken by stirring the masa through the chili, and simmering for 10 minutes.

Nutrition Information

- Calories: 675 calories
- Total Fat: 37 g
- Cholesterol: 142 mg
- Sodium: 1695 mg
- Total Carbohydrate: 37.6 g
- Protein: 48.3 g

110. OnePot Texas Borracho Beans

"I got this recipe from a coworker whose wife made borracho beans for a work function. They are easy to make and go great as a side dish with BBQ or Mexican food."

Serving: 6 | Prep: 15 m | Cook: 35 m | Ready in: 50 m

Ingredients

- 6 ounces bacon, roughly chopped
- 1 yellow onion, chopped
- 1 jalapeno pepper, seeded and chopped
- 2 cups chicken stock
- 1 (15 ounce) can pinto beans, rinsed and drained
- 1 (14.5 ounce) can diced tomatoes
- 1 cup water
- 1 green onion, chopped
- 2 tablespoons chopped fresh cilantro, or more to taste
- 1/2 teaspoon salt
- 1/2 teaspoon garlic powder
- 1/4 teaspoon ground dried chipotle pepper

Direction

- Place bacon in a 2-quart pot. Cook over medium-high heat, turning occasionally, until evenly browned, 5 to 7 minutes. Remove some bacon grease, as needed, to keep from boiling the bacon. Drain bacon slices on paper towels.
- Add onion to the pot; sauté in the remaining bacon grease until translucent, about 5 minutes. Add chopped jalapeno; sauté until starting to soften, about 2 minutes.
- Add the bacon, pinto beans, tomatoes, water, green onion, cilantro, salt, garlic powder, and chipotle to the onion mixture. Bring to a slow boil; reduce heat to medium. Cook, stirring occasionally, until mixture is hot and flavors meld, about 15 minutes.

Nutrition Information

- Calories: 120 calories
- Total Fat: 4.5 g
- Cholesterol: 11 mg
- Sodium: 892 mg
- Total Carbohydrate: 12.5 g
- Protein: 7 g

111. Peanut Butter Sheet Cake

"Texas Sheet Cake made with peanut butter instead of chocolate! Wonderfully moist with a delicious peanut butter frosting!"

Serving: 20 | Prep: 20 m | Cook: 25 m | Ready in: 45 m

Ingredients

- 2 cups all-purpose flour
- 2 cups white sugar
- 1/2 teaspoon baking soda
- 1/4 teaspoon salt
- 1 cup water
- 3/4 cup butter or margarine, softened
- 1/2 cup peanut butter
- 1/4 cup vegetable oil
- 2 eggs
- 1/2 cup buttermilk
- 1 teaspoon vanilla extract
- 2/3 cup white sugar
- 1/3 cup evaporated milk
- 1 tablespoon butter or margarine
- 1/3 cup chunky peanut butter
- 1/3 cup miniature marshmallows
- 1/2 teaspoon vanilla extract

Direction

- Preheat the oven to 350 degrees F (175 degrees C). Grease a 10x15x1 inch jellyroll pan.
- In a large bowl, stir together the flour, 2 cups sugar, baking soda and salt. Set aside. Combine the water and 3/4 cup of butter in a saucepan, and bring to a boil. Remove from the heat and stir in 1/2 cup peanut butter and

vegetable oil until well blended. Stir this mixture into the dry ingredients. Combine the eggs, buttermilk and vanilla; stir into the peanut butter mixture until well blended. Spread the batter evenly in the prepared pan.
- Bake for 18 to 26 minutes in the preheated oven, or until a toothpick inserted near the center comes out clean.
- While the cake bakes, place 2/3 cup sugar, evaporated milk, and butter in a saucepan. Bring to a boil, stirring constantly. Cook stirring for 2 minutes. Remove from heat and stir in the peanut butter, marshmallows and vanilla until marshmallows are melted and the mixture is smooth.
- Spoon the frosting over the warm cake and spread in an even layer. Allow to cool before cutting and serving.

Nutrition Information

- Calories: 321 calories
- Total Fat: 16.6 g
- Cholesterol: 40 mg
- Sodium: 184 mg
- Total Carbohydrate: 39.9 g
- Protein: 5.1 g

112. Pecan Pie I

"Down-home Texas pecan pie that's not overly sweet. Easy to make, and great served warm with a scoop of vanilla ice cream and a few lines of chocolate syrup."

Serving: 8 | Prep: 10 m | Cook: 55 m | Ready in: 1 h 5 m

Ingredients

- 3 eggs
- 1 cup dark corn syrup
- 1 cup white sugar
- 2 tablespoons sifted all-purpose flour
- 1 teaspoon vanilla extract
- 1 1/2 cups chopped pecans
- 1 (9 inch) deep dish pie crust

Direction

- Preheat the oven to 350 degree F (175 degree C).
- In a medium bowl, mix together the sugar and flour until flour is blended in. Stir in the eggs, corn syrup and vanilla. Mix in the pecans and pour the filling into the pie crust.
- Bake for 50 to 55 minutes in the preheated oven, until a knife inserted halfway between center and edge comes out clean. Cool.

Nutrition Information

- Calories: 508 calories
- Total Fat: 24.1 g
- Cholesterol: 70 mg
- Sodium: 237 mg
- Total Carbohydrate: 72.6 g
- Protein: 5.4 g

113. Pineapple and Basil Sorbet

"I had an ice pop with this combination at the Pecan Street Festival in Austin, Texas, and thought it was the most amazing flavor! I recreated the recipe at home--who knew basil paired so well with pineapple?! An alternative is after blending everything, pour into ice pop molds and enjoy!"

Serving: 16 | Prep: 20 m | Ready in: 9 h 20 m

Ingredients

- 1 pineapple - peeled, cored, and cut into chunks
- 1/2 cup white sugar
- 1/2 cup pineapple juice
- 1/4 cup basil leaves

Direction

- Blend the pineapple, sugar, pineapple juice, and basil in a blender until smooth; chill in refrigerate for 1 hour.
- Place mixture in an ice cream maker and mix according to manufacturer's instructions; pour

into an airtight container, and freeze 8 hours or overnight.

Nutrition Information

- Calories: 43 calories
- Total Fat: 0 g
- Cholesterol: 0 mg
- Sodium: < 1 mg
- Total Carbohydrate: 11.1 g
- Protein: 0.2 g

114. Port Wine Jelly

"Fredricksburg Texas has some of the best Texas wineries close by. While experimenting with a great port I found there, I came up with this beautiful, jeweled jelly. It's easy to make for a gift basket."

Serving: 40 | Prep: 10 m | Cook: 20 m | Ready in: 4 h 30 m

Ingredients

- 4 cups port wine
- 1 (2 ounce) package powdered fruit pectin
- 4 1/2 cups white sugar
- 1/2 teaspoon butter
- 5 half pint canning jars with lids and rings

Direction

- Pour the port into a large saucepan, and sprinkle in the pectin. Bring to a boil over high heat, stirring frequently. Once boiling, pour in the sugar, and stir until dissolved. Return the mixture to a boil, and stir in the butter until melted. Continue boiling for 1 minute, skimming and discarding any foam the forms on the surface.
- Sterilize the jars and lids in boiling water for at least 5 minutes. Pour the jelly into the hot, sterilized jars, filling the jars to within 1/2 inch of the top. Wipe the rims of the jars with a moist paper towel to remove any food residue. Top with lids, and screw on rings.
- Place a rack in the bottom of a large stockpot and fill halfway with water. Bring to a boil over high heat, then carefully lower the jars into the pot using a holder. Leave a 2 inch space between the jars. Pour in more boiling water if necessary until the water level is at least 1 inch above the tops of the jars. Bring the water to a full boil, cover the pot, and process for 10 minutes.
- Remove the jars from the stockpot and place onto a cloth-covered or wood surface, several inches apart, until cool. Once cool, press the top of each lid with a finger, ensuring that the seal is tight (lid does not move up or down at all). Store in a cool, dark area.

Nutrition Information

- Calories: 107 calories
- Total Fat: 0.1 g
- Cholesterol: < 1 mg
- Sodium: 2 mg
- Total Carbohydrate: 23.1 g
- Protein: 0 g

115. Potato and Bean Enchiladas

"A great vegetarian main dish that can be spiced up with the addition of jalapenos to either or both sauce and filling."

Serving: 12 | Prep: 1 h | Cook: 45 m | Ready in: 1 h 45 m

Ingredients

- 1 pound potatoes, peeled and diced
- 1 teaspoon cumin
- 1 teaspoon chili powder
- 1 teaspoon salt
- 1 tablespoon ketchup
- 1 pound fresh tomatillos, husks removed
- 1 large onion, chopped
- 1 bunch fresh cilantro, coarsely chopped, divided
- 2 (12 ounce) packages corn tortilla
- 1 (15.5 ounce) can pinto beans, drained

- 1 (12 ounce) package queso fresco
- oil for frying

Direction

- Preheat oven to 400 degrees F (205 degrees C). In a bowl, toss diced potatoes together with cumin, chili powder, salt, and ketchup, and place in an oiled baking dish. Bake in the preheated oven for 20 to 25 minutes, or until tender.
- Meanwhile, boil tomatillos and chopped onion in water to cover for 10 minutes. Set aside to cool. Once cooled, puree with half of the cilantro until smooth.
- Fry tortillas individually in a small amount of hot oil until soft.
- Mix potatoes together with pinto beans, 1/2 cheese, and 1/2 cilantro. Fill tortillas with potato mixture, and roll up. Place seam side down in an oiled 9x13 inch baking dish. Spoon tomatillo sauce over enchiladas, and spread remaining cheese over sauce. Bake for 20 minutes, or until hot and bubbly.

Nutrition Information

- Calories: 247 calories
- Total Fat: 5.7 g
- Cholesterol: 9 mg
- Sodium: 385 mg
- Total Carbohydrate: 41.5 g
- Protein: 9.5 g

116. Queso Cheese Dip

"This is the best queso dip! Being from Texas, I know my queso, and I think this is the one that beats them all! It's full of flavor and all fresh ingredients. You can substitute half-and-half for the heavy whipping cream, if desired. Serve with tortilla chips."

Serving: 12 | Prep: 20 m | Cook: 35 m | Ready in: 1 h 15 m

Ingredients

- 2 poblano peppers, halved lengthwise and seeded
- 2 Anaheim peppers, halved lengthwise and seeded
- 1 fresh jalapeno pepper, halved lengthwise and seeded
- 2 pounds processed cheese food (such as Velveeta ®), cut into cubes
- 3 large roma (plum) tomatoes, diced
- 1 large white onion, diced
- 1 tablespoon butter
- 2 teaspoons ground cumin
- 1/4 cup heavy whipping cream

Direction

- Set oven rack about 6 inches from the heat source and preheat the oven's broiler. Line a baking sheet with aluminum foil.
- Place poblano peppers, Anaheim peppers, and jalapeno pepper, cut-sides down, on the prepared baking sheet.
- Cook peppers under the preheated broiler until the skin of the peppers has blackened and blistered, 5 to 8 minutes. Place the blackened peppers into a bowl and tightly seal with plastic wrap. Allow the peppers to steam as they cool, about 20 minutes. Remove and discard skins; dice peppers.
- Combine diced peppers, cheese food cubes, tomatoes, onion, butter, and cumin in a slow cooker.
- Cook on Low, gradually adding cream, until cheese melts and dip is heated through, about 30 minutes.

Nutrition Information

- Calories: 293 calories
- Total Fat: 21.5 g
- Cholesterol: 58 mg
- Sodium: 744 mg
- Total Carbohydrate: 9.9 g
- Protein: 15.7 g

117. Quick Texas Stew

"A delicious Tex-Mex Chili even the non-cooks will enjoy. Serve with picante sauce and tortilla chips OR you can put some picante sauce right in the bowl, if you like."

Serving: 4

Ingredients

- 1 pound ground beef
- 1 (10 ounce) can diced tomatoes with green chile peppers
- 1 (16 ounce) can ranch style chili beans
- 1 (15.25 ounce) can whole kernel corn
- 1 (19 ounce) can minestrone soup
- salt and pepper to taste

Direction

- In Dutch oven, over medium heat brown and drain 1 pound ground beef.
- Mix in diced tomatoes, ranch style chili beans, corn with liquid, minestrone soup. Season with salt and pepper to taste.
- Cover and simmer 30 minutes.

Nutrition Information

- Calories: 617 calories
- Total Fat: 33.6 g
- Cholesterol: 99 mg
- Sodium: 1593 mg
- Total Carbohydrate: 51.9 g
- Protein: 30.3 g

118. Randys Texas Tea

"On a hot day in Texas, nothing is more refreshing than this sweet, fruity, non-alcoholic summer iced tea."

Serving: 8 | Prep: 10 m | Ready in: 10 m

Ingredients

- 1 cup white sugar
- 1/4 teaspoon salt
- 1 cup hot water
- 6 cups brewed black tea, cold
- 2 cups orange juice
- 1/2 cup lemon juice
- 1 orange, sliced into rounds
- 1 lemon, sliced into rounds
- 1 lime, sliced into rounds

Direction

- In a large pitcher, combine sugar, salt and hot water. Stir until completely dissolved. Sir in the tea, orange juice and lemon juice. Serve in tall glasses with ice and slices of citrus fruit.

Nutrition Information

- Calories: 145 calories
- Total Fat: 0.2 g
- Cholesterol: 0 mg
- Sodium: 79 mg
- Total Carbohydrate: 38.1 g
- Protein: 0.9 g

119. Razors Carne Guizida

"A true Texas favorite! This is a Mexican type stew that is generally served on hot flour tortillas. It is considered a main dish. Best served with guacamole salad over beef flautas with lettuce and tomato chopped, and topped with sour cream. Corn tortillas may be substituted for flour if desired."

Serving: 10 | Prep: 1 h | Cook: 1 h 20 m | Ready in: 2 h 20 m

Ingredients

- 3 pounds lean ground beef
- 1/2 large onion, finely chopped
- 3 green bell peppers, seeded and thinly sliced
- 3 cloves garlic, pressed
- 2 (10 ounce) cans diced tomatoes and green chiles
- 1 pinch monosodium glutamate
- salt and pepper to taste

Direction

- In a Dutch oven or stock pot over medium-high heat, brown the ground beef. As the meat begins to brown, add the onion, green peppers, garlic, and meat tenderizer. Reduce heat to low, and cover. Cook for 30 to 45 minutes, stirring occasionally.
- Stir in the diced tomatoes, season with salt and pepper to taste, and cover. Cook for 45 minutes, or until the meat is the desired tenderness.

Nutrition Information

- Calories: 380 calories
- Total Fat: 28.3 g
- Cholesterol: 102 mg
- Sodium: 391 mg
- Total Carbohydrate: 4.7 g
- Protein: 24.9 g

120. Real Deal TexMex Queso

"This is a real Tex-Mex queso. It has been passed down for many years. If you are looking for restaurant-quality queso then you have found it. Serve queso dip with tortilla chips."

Serving: 18 | Prep: 35 m | Cook: 15 m | Ready in: 50 m

Ingredients

- 2 tablespoons butter
- 1 onion, diced
- 1 green bell pepper, seeded and diced
- 3 stalks celery, diced
- 3 jalapeno peppers, seeded and diced
- 3 green onions, diced
- 2 tablespoons all-purpose flour
- 1 pound Mexican-style processed cheese food (such as Mexican Velveeta®), cut into 1/2-inch cubes
- 1 (8 ounce) package pepper Jack cheese, cut into 1/2-inch cubes
- 1 cup whole milk
- 1 cup heavy whipping cream

Direction

- Melt butter in a saucepan over medium heat and add onion, green bell pepper, celery, jalapeno peppers, and green onions. Cook, stirring occasionally, until soft and slightly brown, about 5 minutes. Stir in flour until combined.
- Reduce heat to low and add processed cheese food, pepper Jack cheese, milk, and heavy cream to the saucepan. Stir continuously until cheese is melted, about 10 minutes.

Nutrition Information

- Calories: 210 calories
- Total Fat: 17 g
- Cholesterol: 57 mg
- Sodium: 462 mg
- Total Carbohydrate: 6.2 g
- Protein: 9.4 g

121. Red Cabbage Slow Slaw

"This slaw takes days to make, so it's hard to keep up with having it ready for my family! We eat this several times a week! This goes great with my husband's Texas BBQ!"

Serving: 8 | Prep: 15 m | Ready in: 2 d s1 h 15 m

Ingredients

- 1 head red cabbage, cored and sliced as thinly as possible
- 3/4 cup red wine vinegar
- 5 tablespoons white sugar
- 2 tablespoons balsamic vinegar
- 1 tablespoon salt
- 1 1/2 teaspoons onion powder
- 1 teaspoon seasoned salt (such as LAWRY'S®)
- 1/2 teaspoon ground black pepper
- 1/2 cup olive oil

Direction

- Put sliced cabbage into a large sealable plastic bag.
- Whisk red wine vinegar, sugar, balsamic vinegar, salt, onion powder, seasoned salt, and black pepper together in a bowl; pour into bag with the cabbage. Massage the bag to ensure cabbage is completely coated with liquid. Squeeze as much air from the bag as possible and seal.
- Marinate cabbage in refrigerator, massaging the bag several times a day, until the cabbage is softened and the marinade is deep purple in color, at least 2 days.
- Pour olive oil into the bag and mix with the cabbage mixture. Seal bag and refrigerate 1 hour more before serving.

Nutrition Information

- Calories: 193 calories
- Total Fat: 13.7 g
- Cholesterol: 0 mg
- Sodium: 1017 mg
- Total Carbohydrate: 18.3 g
- Protein: 1.6 g

122. San Antonio Salad

"A wonderful 'Heart of Texas' salad that makes a great meal! Seasoned ground beef, iceberg lettuce, tomatoes, pinto beans are just starters!"

Serving: 6 | Prep: 15 m | Cook: 10 m | Ready in: 25 m

Ingredients

- 1 pound lean ground beef
- 2 tablespoons chili powder
- 1/2 teaspoon ground cumin
- salt and pepper to taste
- 1 head iceberg lettuce, shredded
- 1 (15.5 ounce) can pinto beans
- 2 tomatoes, cubed
- 1 cup shredded Cheddar cheese
- 1/4 cup chopped fresh cilantro
- 1 (12 ounce) package corn tortilla chips, broken
- 1 jalapeno pepper, seeded and chopped (optional)
- 1/2 cup chopped green onion (optional)
- 1 cup salsa (optional)

Direction

- In a large skillet over medium-high heat, brown the ground beef. Season with chili powder, cumin, salt and pepper. Remove from heat when beef is cooked through.
- In a large salad bowl, toss together the lettuce, tomato, Cheddar cheese, cilantro and pinto beans with their juice. Mix in the ground beef and corn chips. Toss in the jalapeno, green onion, and salsa, if desired.

Nutrition Information

- Calories: 674 calories
- Total Fat: 37.7 g
- Cholesterol: 81 mg
- Sodium: 1043 mg
- Total Carbohydrate: 57.5 g
- Protein: 29.5 g

123. Sangria White

"Red sangria is refreshing, but white just seems even better for those ridiculously hot Texas summer days!"

Serving: 8 | Prep: 15 m | Ready in: 15 m

Ingredients

- 1 (750 milliliter) bottle white wine
- 3/4 cup rum
- 1/2 cup orange juice
- 1/3 cup white sugar
- 1 lemon, sliced
- 1 lime, sliced
- 1 green apple, cored and sliced
- 1 (12 fluid ounce) can or bottle lemon-lime soda
- 1 cup seedless green grapes, or to taste, frozen

Direction

- Stir white wine, rum, orange juice, and sugar together in a large pitcher until the sugar is dissolved; add apple, lemon, and lime slices. Gently stir lemon-lime soda into the wine mixture.
- Put frozen grapes into serving glasses and pour sangria over the grapes.

Nutrition Information

- Calories: 210 calories
- Total Fat: 0.2 g
- Cholesterol: 0 mg
- Sodium: 11 mg
- Total Carbohydrate: 25.2 g
- Protein: 0.6 g

124. Sautéed Patty Pan Squash

"Rarely can you find patty pan (aka scalloped) squash in the grocery store. However, many farmers markets have them. In Texas, it seems that every farmers market is overflowing with squash come June. However, if you can't find them, any summer squash will do. I also have made this recipe using yellow squash and zucchini and it was quite delicious. The freshness of the ingredients scream "summer"."

Serving: 4 | Prep: 15 m | Cook: 10 m | Ready in: 25 m

Ingredients

- 1 tablespoon olive oil
- 1 tablespoon butter
- 1/2 sweet yellow onion (such as Vidalia®), thinly sliced
- 4 patty pan squash, sliced to 1/2-inch-thick pieces
- 3 cloves garlic, crushed, or more to taste
- 1 dash lemon pepper
- 1 1/2 cups packed fresh spinach (optional)
- 1/4 cup chopped fresh parsley
- 1 tablespoon chopped fresh basil
- 1/2 lemon, juiced
- 1 1/2 teaspoons grated Parmesan cheese
- salt and ground black pepper to taste

Direction

- Heat olive oil and butter in a skillet over medium-high heat until foaming, 1 to 2 minutes. Sauté onion in the olive oil-butter until tender and translucent, about 3 minutes. Add squash and garlic; season with lemon pepper. Sauté mixture until squash is easily pierced with a fork, 5 to 6 minutes.
- Mix spinach, parsley, and basil into squash mixture; sauté until spinach wilts, about 1 minute. Squeeze lemon juice over mixture and sprinkle in Parmesan cheese; stir well. Season mixture with salt and black pepper.

Nutrition Information

- Calories: 79 calories
- Total Fat: 6.6 g
- Cholesterol: 8 mg

- Sodium: 141 mg
- Total Carbohydrate: 4.4 g
- Protein: 1.5 g

125. Seven Layer Tex Mex Dip

"This is a great, easy recipe people love. Our family has made it for gatherings for as long as I can remember. Refried beans are layered with guacamole, a seasoned sour cream mixture, cheese and vegetables. Serve it with tortilla chips. Enjoy!"

Serving: 56 | Prep: 15 m | Ready in: 15 m

Ingredients

- 1 (16 ounce) can refried beans
- 1 cup guacamole
- 1/4 cup mayonnaise
- 1 (8 ounce) container sour cream
- 1 (1 ounce) package taco seasoning mix
- 2 cups shredded Cheddar cheese
- 1 tomato, chopped
- 1/4 cup chopped green onions
- 1/4 cup black olives, drained

Direction

- In a large serving dish, spread the refried beans. Layer the guacamole on top of the beans.
- In a medium bowl, mix the mayonnaise, sour cream and taco seasoning mix. Spread over the layer of guacamole.
- Sprinkle a layer of Cheddar cheese over the mayonnaise mixture layer. Sprinkle tomato, green onions and black olives over the cheese.

Nutrition Information

- Calories: 47 calories
- Total Fat: 3.6 g
- Cholesterol: 7 mg
- Sodium: 100 mg
- Total Carbohydrate: 2.3 g
- Protein: 1.7 g

126. Simple Texas Salsa

"This is the most delicious salsa that doesn't require any cooking!"

Serving: 12 | Prep: 5 m | Ready in: 5 m

Ingredients

- 3 tablespoons chopped fresh chives
- 1/2 bunch fresh cilantro
- 2 cloves garlic, chopped
- 2 (14 ounce) cans stewed tomatoes
- 2 serrano chilis, seeded and chopped
- salt and pepper to taste

Direction

- Combine chives, cilantro, garlic, tomatoes, peppers, salt and pepper to taste in an electric blender. Pulse until the salsa is to your desired consistency.

Nutrition Information

- Calories: 21 calories
- Total Fat: 0.2 g
- Cholesterol: 0 mg
- Sodium: 146 mg
- Total Carbohydrate: 5 g
- Protein: 0.8 g

127. Slow Cooker Carolina BBQ

"Miss the tarheel tradition of a pig pickin'? Then find yourself a crock pot, a big pork shoulder, some cider vinegar and get cooking! While ground and crushed red pepper will provide the basic heat - go the extra mile and find some Texas Pete (or Trappey's) pepper sauce to bring the taste of Carolina to your kitchen."

Serving: 10 | Prep: 15 m | Cook: 12 h | Ready in: 12 h 15 m

Ingredients

- 1 (5 pound) bone-in pork shoulder roast
- 1 tablespoon salt
- ground black pepper
- 1 1/2 cups apple cider vinegar
- 2 tablespoons brown sugar
- 1 1/2 tablespoons hot pepper sauce
- 2 teaspoons cayenne pepper
- 2 teaspoons crushed red pepper flakes

Direction

- Place the pork shoulder into a slow cooker and season with salt and pepper. Pour the vinegar around the pork. Cover, and cook on Low for 12 hours. Pork should easily pull apart into strands.
- Remove the pork from the slow cooker and discard any bones. Strain out the liquid, and save 2 cups. Discard any extra. Shred the pork using tongs or two forks, and return to the slow cooker. Stir the brown sugar, hot pepper sauce, cayenne pepper, and red pepper flakes into the reserved sauce. Mix into the pork in the slow cooker. Cover and keep on Low setting until serving.

Nutrition Information

- Calories: 293 calories
- Total Fat: 17.3 g
- Cholesterol: 90 mg
- Sodium: 776 mg
- Total Carbohydrate: 3.6 g
- Protein: 27.6 g

128. Slow Cooker Texas Pulled Pork

"Slow cooked, Texas-style pulled pork that is served on a buttered and toasted roll. My family's favorite."

Serving: 8 | Prep: 15 m | Cook: 5 h | Ready in: 5 h 15 m

Ingredients

- 1 teaspoon vegetable oil
- 1 (4 pound) pork shoulder roast
- 1 cup barbeque sauce
- 1/2 cup apple cider vinegar
- 1/2 cup chicken broth
- 1/4 cup light brown sugar
- 1 tablespoon prepared yellow mustard
- 1 tablespoon Worcestershire sauce
- 1 tablespoon chili powder
- 1 extra large onion, chopped
- 2 large cloves garlic, crushed
- 1 1/2 teaspoons dried thyme
- 8 hamburger buns, split
- 2 tablespoons butter, or as needed

Direction

- Pour the vegetable oil into the bottom of a slow cooker. Place the pork roast into the slow cooker; pour in the barbecue sauce, apple cider vinegar, and chicken broth. Stir in the brown sugar, yellow mustard, Worcestershire sauce, chili powder, onion, garlic, and thyme. Cover and cook on High until the roast shreds easily with a fork, 5 to 6 hours.
- Remove the roast from the slow cooker, and shred the meat using two forks. Return the shredded pork to the slow cooker, and stir the meat into the juices.
- Spread the inside of both halves of hamburger buns with butter. Toast the buns, butter side down, in a skillet over medium heat until golden brown. Spoon pork into the toasted buns.

Nutrition Information

- Calories: 527 calories

- Total Fat: 23.1 g
- Cholesterol: 98 mg
- Sodium: 730 mg
- Total Carbohydrate: 45.5 g
- Protein: 31.9 g

129. SlowCooked TexasStyle Beef Brisket

"This slow-cooker recipe comes directly from the heart of a wonderful Texas cook who makes the best brisket in the world! Yay, Papa Louis! He shared it with me years ago, via my sister (his daughter-in-law). I change it from time to time by adding ingredients to make it more Mexican (serve it with tortillas), or leave it as is and serve it with fresh rolls."

Serving: 20 | Prep: 15 m | Cook: 1 d 1 h | Ready in: 1 d 1 h 15 m

Ingredients

- 8 pounds untrimmed beef brisket
- 1 cup strong black coffee
- 1 (14 ounce) bottle ketchup
- 1 (12 fluid ounce) can cola carbonated beverage
- 3 tablespoons Worcestershire sauce
- 3 tablespoons prepared yellow mustard
- 2 tablespoons liquid smoke flavoring
- 2 tablespoons brown sugar, packed

Direction

- Place the beef brisket in a large slow cooker with the fat side up. Pour the coffee over the meat. Cook the brisket on LOW for 24 hours.
- Meanwhile, stir together the ketchup, cola beverage, Worcestershire sauce, mustard, liquid smoke, and brown sugar in a bowl until well blended. Refrigerate until needed.
- After 24 hours, remove and discard any fat from the brisket. Use a fork to pull apart and shred the meat. Pour the sauce over the meat, stirring to coat evenly, and cook 1 hour longer.

Nutrition Information

- Calories: 353 calories
- Total Fat: 26.6 g
- Cholesterol: 75 mg
- Sodium: 322 mg
- Total Carbohydrate: 8.9 g
- Protein: 19.1 g

130. South Texas Borracho Beans

"These are my favorite Borracho-style beans. I've made them for tailgating and as part of a BBQ menu."

Serving: 6 | Prep: 15 m | Cook: 1 h 45 m | Ready in: 10 h

Ingredients

- 1 pound dried pinto beans
- 1/2 pound bacon
- 1/2 teaspoon salt
- 1/2 teaspoon garlic powder
- 1 (12 fluid ounce) bottle dark lager-style beer (such as Shiner Bock®)
- 1 bunch cilantro, chopped
- 1 bunch green onions, chopped
- 1 (14.5 ounce) can diced tomatoes
- 1 fresh jalapeno pepper

Direction

- Place pinto beans into a large container and cover with several inches of cool water. Soak beans 8 hours to overnight.
- Cook bacon in a large skillet over medium-high heat until crispy, about 10 minutes. Remove bacon slices to a plate lined with paper towel to drain, reserving the bacon drippings. Chop the bacon.
- Drain and rinse pinto beans; transfer to a large pot. Pour enough water over the beans to cover by several inches Stir salt and garlic powder into the water; bring to a boil and reduce heat to medium-low. Add bacon, reserved bacon drippings, beer, cilantro, green onions, diced tomatoes, and jalapeno pepper

to the water; bring mixture to a simmer and cook until the beans are completely tender, 90 minutes to 2 hours.

Nutrition Information

- Calories: 363 calories
- Total Fat: 6.4 g
- Cholesterol: 14 mg
- Sodium: 1012 mg
- Total Carbohydrate: 52.4 g
- Protein: 21.9 g

131. South Texas Carne Guisada

"In this recipe, chunks of lean beef are simmered with fresh tomatoes, bell pepper, onion, garlic, and Mexican seasonings to make a rich spicy gravy (guisada). Serve with warm tortillas and garnish with guacamole, sour cream, and/or cheddar cheese for awesome guisada tacos. If your gravy is too thin, whisk a 1/2 cup of the gravy with 1 tablespoon of flour and stir it back into the meat mixture; cook until the sauce thickens, about 10 minutes."

Serving: 6 | Prep: 25 m | Cook: 45 m | Ready in: 1 h 10 m

Ingredients

- 1 tablespoon vegetable oil
- 2 pounds beef sirloin, cut into 1/2-inch cubes
- 1 large onion, chopped
- 1 large red bell pepper, chopped
- 4 large tomatoes, chopped
- 5 cloves garlic, minced
- 2 tablespoons ground cumin
- 1 teaspoon dried, crushed Mexican oregano
- 1 tablespoon garlic powder
- 1 teaspoon salt
- 1/2 teaspoon ground black pepper
- 1/2 teaspoon paprika
- 1/3 cup water

Direction

- Heat vegetable oil in a Dutch oven over medium-high heat. Place the beef sirloin in the Dutch oven and cook until the cubes are brown on all sides, about 10 minutes. Reduce the heat to medium and add the onion, red bell pepper, tomatoes, garlic, cumin, oregano, garlic powder, salt, black pepper, paprika, and water.
- Continue cooking, stirring often, until the meat is tender, about 30 minutes.

Nutrition Information

- Calories: 309 calories
- Total Fat: 16.9 g
- Cholesterol: 81 mg
- Sodium: 457 mg
- Total Carbohydrate: 11.8 g
- Protein: 27.4 g

132. South Texas Tartar Sauce

"This delicious tartar sauce, vegetable dip is similar to that served at the famous King's Inn restaurant on Baffin Bay in South Texas."

Serving: 25 | Prep: 30 m | Cook: 30 m | Ready in: 1 h

Ingredients

- 1 medium onion, chopped
- 1/4 cup pimento-stuffed green olives
- 1 clove garlic
- 2 tablespoons pickled jalapeno slices
- 1 cup sweet green pickle relish
- 1 cup mayonnaise
- 25 buttery round crackers, crushed
- 5 saltine crackers, crushed
- 1 pinch curry powder

Direction

- Place the onion, olives, garlic and jalapenos into the container of a food processor. Pulse until finely chopped. In a bowl, stir together the mayonnaise, relish, buttery round crackers and saltine crackers. Mix in the contents of the food processor and season with curry powder.

Chill overnight before serving with seafood or vegetables.

Nutrition Information

- Calories: 101 calories
- Total Fat: 8.3 g
- Cholesterol: 3 mg
- Sodium: 230 mg
- Total Carbohydrate: 6.8 g
- Protein: 0.5 g

133. Southern TexasStyle Beef Barbacoa

"This tender, slow-cooked beef tastes great on burritos and tacos. My family of 8 goes nuts over it, and 5 lbs. of this meat isn't enough to satisfy them. It takes a long time to prepare, but the wait is worth the effort."

Serving: 12 | Prep: 15 m | Cook: 3 h | Ready in: 3 h 15 m

Ingredients

- 1 1/2 teaspoons ground black pepper
- 1 tablespoon dried oregano
- 1 1/2 teaspoons cayenne pepper
- 1 1/2 teaspoons chili powder
- 1 1/2 teaspoons garlic powder
- 1 teaspoon ground cumin
- 1 teaspoon salt
- 1 teaspoon seasoned salt
- 1 (3 pound) boneless beef chuck roast

Direction

- Prepare a smoker with dampened hickory wood charcoal. The heat inside your grill or smoker should be around 180 to 200 degrees F (80 to 95 degrees C). Combine the black pepper, oregano, cayenne pepper, chili powder, garlic powder, cumin, salt, and seasoned salt in a small bowl until thoroughly mixed.
- Place the chuck roast into a mixing bowl, and rub all over with the spice mixture. Place the meat into the smoker, and smoke for 1 1/2 hours, turning about every half hour. The meat should be a dark red color, and the edges should be darkened. Place the meat into a roasting pan, and seal tightly with aluminum foil.
- Preheat an oven to 325 degrees F (165 degrees C).
- Bake the barbacoa in the preheated oven for 1 1/2 hours until very tender. Uncover the beef, and shred with two forks while still hot.

Nutrition Information

- Calories: 175 calories
- Total Fat: 12.7 g
- Cholesterol: 52 mg
- Sodium: 307 mg
- Total Carbohydrate: 1.1 g
- Protein: 13.5 g

134. Speedy French Onion Soup

"Warm up with a bowl of this savory soup that's loaded with incredible flavor. Caramelized onions simmer with sweet onion soup and beef consommé. It's topped with cheesy garlic Texas toast and is so good you may want to double the recipe because it will be gone in a flash!"

Serving: 4 | Prep: 5 m | Cook: 25 m | Ready in: 30 m

Ingredients

- 3 tablespoons butter
- 4 large onions, cut in half and thinly sliced
- 1 (14.5 ounce) carton Campbell's® Sweet Onion Soup
- 1 (10.5 ounce) can Campbell's® Condensed Beef Consomme or Campbell's® Condensed Beef Broth
- 4 slices Pepperidge Farm® Garlic Texas Toast, prepared according to package directions

Direction

- Heat the butter in a 4-quart saucepan over medium heat. Add the onions and cook for 15

minutes or until well browned and caramelized, stirring occasionally.
- Stir the soup, consomme and 1 soup can water in the saucepan and heat to a boil. Reduce the heat to low. Cook for 10 minutes, stirring occasionally. Top each serving with 1 toast.

Nutrition Information

- Calories: 341 calories
- Total Fat: 18.4 g
- Cholesterol: 27 mg
- Sodium: 1130 mg
- Total Carbohydrate: 38.2 g
- Protein: 7.7 g

135. Spicy BBQ Chicken

"The traditional BBQ sauce for grilled chicken (or ribs!) that everyone has had at some point -- very tasty with a little extra personality. You will not regret cooking!"

Serving: 6 | Prep: 20 m | Cook: 30 m | Ready in: 50 m

Ingredients

- 2 tablespoons vegetable oil
- 1/4 cup onion, finely chopped
- 1 clove garlic, minced
- 3/4 cup ketchup
- 1/3 cup vinegar
- 1 tablespoon Worcestershire sauce
- 2 teaspoons brown sugar
- 1 teaspoon dry mustard
- 1/2 teaspoon salt
- 1/4 teaspoon black pepper
- 1/4 (5 ounce) bottle hot pepper sauce
- 1 (3 pound) chicken, cut into pieces

Direction

- Heat the oil in a skillet over medium heat and cook the onion and garlic until tender. Mix in ketchup, vinegar, Worcestershire sauce, brown sugar, dry mustard, salt, pepper and hot sauce. Bring to a boil. Reduce heat to low and simmer 10 minutes, stirring occasionally. Remove from heat and set aside.
- Preheat grill for high heat.
- Lightly oil grill grate. Place chicken on grill. Brush constantly with the sauce and cook 8 to 15 minutes on each side, depending on size of piece, until juices run clear. Discard any remaining sauce.

Nutrition Information

- Calories: 364 calories
- Total Fat: 20.9 g
- Cholesterol: 100 mg
- Sodium: 679 mg
- Total Carbohydrate: 10.6 g
- Protein: 32.4 g

136. Spicy Cranberry Pecan Cornbread Stuffing

"This is a cornbread stuffing with jalapenos, cranberries, bacon, and pecans. I cooked up this recipe while living in Texas. I serve it with turkey but I have also stuffed it in apples and cooked them in a crock pot to serve with pork loin for Christmas dinner. This recipe makes the house smell fantastic!"

Serving: 12 | Prep: 25 m | Cook: 45 m | Ready in: 1 h 10 m

Ingredients

- 10 slices bacon
- 1/2 cup butter
- 1 cup chopped celery
- 2 cloves garlic, minced
- 1 small onion, chopped
- 1 cup white wine
- 1 (16 ounce) can whole berry cranberry sauce
- 1 (4 ounce) jar diced jalapeno peppers
- 1 (4 ounce) can diced green chile peppers
- 1 cup chopped toasted pecans
- 2 (14 ounce) packages cornbread stuffing mix
- 1 1/2 cups chicken stock

Direction

- Preheat oven to 375 degrees F (190 degrees C).
- Place a large skillet over medium heat. Cook the bacon in the skillet until crispy. Lie the cooked bacon on a plate lined with paper towels to drain and cool; crumble the bacon.
- Melt the butter in a large skillet over medium-high heat. Cook the celery, garlic, and onion in the hot butter until the onion begins to caramelize; pour the wine into the skillet. When the wine is heated, stir in the cranberry sauce, jalapeno peppers, and green chile peppers. Cover the mixture and cook until boiling. Remove from heat and stir in the bacon and pecans.
- Place the stuffing mix in a large bowl. Pour the liquid mixture and the chicken stock over the stuffing mix; stir until completely moist. Transfer to a 9x13 inch baking dish.
- Bake in preheated oven until browned on top, about 35 minutes.

Nutrition Information

- Calories: 507 calories
- Total Fat: 20.3 g
- Cholesterol: 27 mg
- Sodium: 1404 mg
- Total Carbohydrate: 68.7 g
- Protein: 10.3 g

137. Spicy Fish Soup

"A delicious fish soup that's low in fat! Having grown up on the Texas/Mexico border, I like foods spicy, but you can adjust the seasonings to taste. I also splash in a drop of hot pepper sauce in each bowl."

Serving: 4 | Prep: 10 m | Cook: 30 m | Ready in: 40 m

Ingredients

- 1/2 onion, chopped
- 1 clove garlic, minced
- 1 tablespoon chili powder
- 1 1/2 cups chicken broth
- 1 (4 ounce) can canned green chile peppers, chopped
- 1 teaspoon ground cumin
- 1 1/2 cups canned peeled and diced tomatoes
- 1/2 cup chopped green bell pepper
- 1/2 cup shrimp
- 1/2 pound cod fillets
- 3/4 cup plain nonfat yogurt

Direction

- Spray a large saucepan with the vegetable cooking spray over medium high heat. Add the onions and sauté, stirring often, for about 5 minutes. Add the garlic and chili powder and sauté for 2 more minutes.
- Then add the chicken broth, chile peppers and cumin, stirring well. Bring to a boil, reduce heat to low, cover and simmer for 20 minutes.
- Next, add the tomatoes, green bell pepper, shrimp and cod. Return to a boil, then reduce heat to low, cover and simmer for another 5 minutes. Gradually stir in the yogurt until heated through.

Nutrition Information

- Calories: 146 calories
- Total Fat: 1.7 g
- Cholesterol: 46 mg
- Sodium: 874 mg
- Total Carbohydrate: 12.2 g
- Protein: 19.3 g

138. Spinach Noodle Casserole

"Spinach noodles in a creamy, zesty sauce. Quick, easy and very healthy. It is very yummy as well! If desired, serve with additional sour cream and Texas herb toast!!"

Serving: 8 | Prep: 45 m | Cook: 2 h 30 m | Ready in: 3 h 20 m

Ingredients

- 8 ounces dry spinach noodles
- 2 tablespoons vegetable oil

- 1 1/2 cups sour cream
- 1/3 cup all-purpose flour
- 1 1/2 cups cottage cheese
- 4 green onions, minced
- 2 teaspoons Worcestershire sauce
- 1 dash hot pepper sauce
- 2 teaspoons garlic salt

Direction

- Cook noodles in a large pot of salted boiling water until barely tender. Drain and rinse with cold water. Toss with vegetable oil.
- While noodles are cooking, combine sour cream and flour in a large bowl. Mix well, then stir in cottage cheese, green onions, Worcestershire sauce, hot pepper sauce, and garlic salt. Stir noodles into mixture. Generously grease the inside of a slow cooker and pour in noodle mixture. Cover and cook on high for 1 1/2 to 2 hours.

Nutrition Information

- Calories: 226 calories
- Total Fat: 14.9 g
- Cholesterol: 35 mg
- Sodium: 669 mg
- Total Carbohydrate: 14.7 g
- Protein: 8.8 g

139. Super TexMex Chicken Chop Salad

"This festive dish will have you craving it every night of the week. It's colorful and delicious. It's perfect for those hot summer evenings when you don't really want to cook. This recipe is meant to be chopped into small pieces."

Serving: 2 | Prep: 30 m | Cook: 10 m | Ready in: 40 m

Ingredients

- 1 whole skinless, boneless chicken breast, halved
- 2 tablespoons Montreal steak seasoning
- 2 tablespoons butter
- 1/2 head iceberg lettuce, chopped
- 1 tomato, chopped
- 1/2 green bell pepper, cut into 1/4-inch cubes
- 1/4 cup seeded and chopped jalapeno peppers, 3 tablespoon juice reserved
- 2 tablespoons chopped green chile peppers
- 1/4 cup drained canned corn kernels
- 1/4 cup drained sliced black olives
- 1/4 cup drained and rinsed black beans
- 1/2 cup shredded Cheddar-Monterey Jack cheese blend
- 1 cup ranch dressing
- 1/2 teaspoon ground black pepper
- 1/4 teaspoon garlic powder

Direction

- Sprinkle chicken breast evenly with Montreal steak seasoning.
- Melt butter in a frying pan over medium heat; cook chicken until no longer pink in the center and juices run clear, 5 to 10 minutes per side. Remove chicken from pan and cut into small pieces.
- Mix lettuce, chicken, tomato, green bell pepper, jalapeno peppers, green chile peppers, corn, black olives, black beans, and Cheddar-Monterey Jack cheese blend in a large bowl; gently toss.
- Whisk ranch dressing, reserved 3 tablespoons jalapeno juice, black pepper, and garlic powder together in a bowl; drizzle over salad. Toss to coat.

Nutrition Information

- Calories: 970 calories
- Total Fat: 86 g
- Cholesterol: 122 mg
- Sodium: 3593 mg
- Total Carbohydrate: 26.4 g
- Protein: 25 g

140. Tejano Style Shrimp Cocktail

"For those of you unable to make it to South Texas: a shrimp cocktail made Tex-Mex style to include cilantro and serrano chiles. An authentic flavor that will blow your tastebuds away, without leaving your home! Serve with saltine crackers."

Serving: 8 | Prep: 20 m | Ready in: 20 m

Ingredients

- 1 pound cooked medium shrimp, chilled
- 1/2 large cucumber, cut into 1/2 inch cubes
- 1/2 large tomato, cut into 1/2 inch cubes
- 8 green onions, thinly sliced
- 1 ounce fresh cilantro, finely chopped
- 1 serrano pepper, thinly sliced
- 1 (8 ounce) can tomato sauce
- 2 tablespoons white vinegar
- 1 lime

Direction

- In a large bowl, combine shrimp, cucumber, tomato, green onion, cilantro, and serrano pepper. Stir in tomato sauce, and vinegar. Squeeze lime juice over mixture.

Nutrition Information

- Calories: 76 calories
- Total Fat: 0.8 g
- Cholesterol: 111 mg
- Sodium: 279 mg
- Total Carbohydrate: 4.8 g
- Protein: 12.9 g

141. Terrys Texas Pinto Beans

"An old fashioned 'pot of beans' recipe. It starts with dry pinto beans, onion, and chicken broth. Add green chili salsa, jalapeno and cumin for the spicy kick."

Serving: 8 | Prep: 15 m | Cook: 2 h | Ready in: 2 h 15 m

Ingredients

- 1 pound dry pinto beans
- 1 (29 ounce) can reduced sodium chicken broth
- 1 large onion, chopped
- 1 fresh jalapeno pepper, chopped
- 2 cloves garlic, minced
- 1/2 cup green salsa
- 1 teaspoon cumin
- 1/2 teaspoon ground black pepper
- water, if needed

Direction

- Place the pinto beans in a large pot, and pour in the chicken broth. Stir in onion, jalapeno, garlic, salsa, cumin, and pepper. Bring to a boil, reduce heat to medium-low, and continue cooking 2 hours, stirring often, until beans are tender. Add water as needed to keep the beans moist.

Nutrition Information

- Calories: 210 calories
- Total Fat: 1.1 g
- Cholesterol: 1 mg
- Sodium: 95 mg
- Total Carbohydrate: 37.9 g
- Protein: 13.2 g

142. Tex Mex Black Bean Dip

"This black bean dip is great served with corn or flour tortilla chips. Serve warm or at room temperature."

Serving: 16 | Prep: 10 m | Cook: 10 m | Ready in: 20 m

Ingredients

- 1 (15 ounce) can black beans, rinsed and drained
- 1 teaspoon vegetable oil
- 1/2 cup chopped onion
- 2 cloves garlic, minced
- 1/2 cup fresh corn kernels
- 3/4 cup chopped tomatoes
- 1/2 cup mild picante sauce

- 1 teaspoon ground cumin
- 1 teaspoon chili powder
- 1/2 cup shredded Monterey Jack cheese
- 1/4 cup chopped fresh cilantro
- 1 tablespoon fresh lime juice

Direction

- Place black beans in a medium size mixing bowl, partially mash beans -- beans should remain a little chunky.
- In a medium size frying pan, heat oil over a medium heat. Stir in onion and garlic and sauté for 4 minutes.
- Mix beans, corn, tomato, picante sauce, cumin, and chili powder into the frying pan; cook for 5 minutes or until thickened. Remove the pan from the heat, mix in cheese, cilantro and lime juice; stir until cheese is melted.

Nutrition Information

- Calories: 50 calories
- Total Fat: 1.7 g
- Cholesterol: 3 mg
- Sodium: 149 mg
- Total Carbohydrate: 5.9 g
- Protein: 2.7 g

143. Tex Mex Dip

"This fast, easy dip can be served as a main dish or as an appetizer. Depending on the ingredients, it can be mild to medium. This really needs to be served warm, as it has a layer of cheese that gets firm when cool. It reheats well, but is best when fresh. Serve with plain tortilla chips."

Serving: 12 | Prep: 20 m | Cook: 40 m | Ready in: 1 h

Ingredients

- 1 pound ground beef
- 1 teaspoon chili powder
- 1 (16 ounce) can vegetarian refried beans
- 1 yellow onion, chopped
- 2 (4 ounce) cans chopped green chile peppers, drained

- 1 (16 ounce) jar picante sauce
- 1/2 pound Muenster cheese, cubed
- 1/2 pound Monterey Jack cheese, cubed
- 1 (16 ounce) container sour cream

Direction

- Preheat oven to 350 degrees F (175 degrees C).
- Place ground beef in a large, deep skillet. Cook over medium high heat until evenly brown. Drain well, stir in chili powder and continue cooking 5 minutes.
- In an 8x8 inch baking dish, spread the refried beans. Layer beans with ground beef and chili powder mixture. Top with layers of onion, green chile peppers, picante sauce, Muenster cheese and Monterey Jack cheese.
- Bake in the preheated oven 35 to 45 minutes, until cheese is melted and lightly browned. Top with sour cream before serving.

Nutrition Information

- Calories: 390 calories
- Total Fat: 29.8 g
- Cholesterol: 84 mg
- Sodium: 925 mg
- Total Carbohydrate: 11.5 g
- Protein: 19.1 g

144. Tex Mex Meatloaf

"Here is a sure way to spice up a family classic. Meatloaf is a favorite in my family and now we have a new way to enjoy it."

Serving: 4 | Prep: 10 m | Cook: 1 h | Ready in: 1 h 10 m

Ingredients

- 1 1/2 pounds ground beef
- 2 eggs
- 1 (14.5 ounce) can diced tomatoes with green chile peppers
- 1 tablespoon onion powder
- 1 tablespoon ground black pepper
- 1 teaspoon salt

- 1 slice white bread, cut into cubes
- 4 slices American cheese OR your choice

Direction

- Preheat oven to 350 degrees F (175 degrees C).
- In a large bowl, combine the ground beef, eggs, diced tomatoes and green chile peppers, onion powder, ground black pepper, salt and bread. Mix together well, place in a 5x9 inch loaf pan and top with the cheese.
- Bake at 350 degrees F (175 degrees C) for 1 hour.

Nutrition Information

- Calories: 711 calories
- Total Fat: 56.9 g
- Cholesterol: 264 mg
- Sodium: 1605 mg
- Total Carbohydrate: 9.8 g
- Protein: 39.2 g

145. Tex Mex Potato Soup

"Spicy and rich potato soup."

Serving: 6 | Prep: 20 m | Cook: 35 m | Ready in: 55 m

Ingredients

- 2 potatoes, peeled and cubed
- 1 onion, chopped
- 1 green bell pepper, chopped
- 1 red bell pepper, chopped
- 2 tablespoons margarine
- 4 ounces chopped ham
- 1 tablespoon chopped green chile peppers
- 1/4 teaspoon ground white pepper
- 1/8 teaspoon cayenne pepper
- 1 (14.5 ounce) can chicken broth
- 1 egg yolk, beaten
- 1/4 cup heavy whipping cream
- 1/2 cup shredded Cheddar cheese

Direction

- Cook potatoes in boiling water until tender, about 15 minutes. Drain and reserve.
- In a skillet, sauté onion, green and red pepper in butter for 10 minutes, or until softened. Stir in the ham, green chilies, white pepper and cayenne. Cook for 1 minute longer. Reserve.
- In a blender, combine the potatoes and chicken broth and blend until smooth. Add to the sautéed vegetable mixture.
- Heat soup just to boiling. Beat the egg yolk with the heavy cream in a small bowl. Stir in 1/2 cup hot soup, stir yolk mixture back into sauce pan. Gently heat soup, but do not boil. Garnish with shredded cheddar cheese.

Nutrition Information

- Calories: 219 calories
- Total Fat: 13.2 g
- Cholesterol: 69 mg
- Sodium: 379 mg
- Total Carbohydrate: 17.7 g
- Protein: 8.2 g

146. Tex Mex Stir Fry

"My husband calls it Mexican Chinese food. Chicken is stir fried with bell peppers, black beans, and salsa. It's delicious served with rice and topped with cheese."

Serving: 4 | Prep: 20 m | Cook: 15 m | Ready in: 35 m

Ingredients

- 1 teaspoon olive oil
- 1 green bell pepper, chopped
- 1 red bell pepper, chopped
- 2 tablespoons all-purpose flour, or as needed
- 1 (1 ounce) packet taco seasoning mix
- 1 pound skinless, boneless chicken breast halves - cut into bite size pieces
- 2 teaspoons olive oil
- 1 (15 ounce) can black beans, rinsed and drained

- 1/2 cup prepared salsa
- 1 cup shredded Cheddar cheese

Direction

- Heat 1 teaspoon of olive oil in a skillet over medium-high heat until the oil is very hot, and cook and stir the green and red bell pepper until they are starting to become tender, about 5 minutes. Set the peppers aside.
- Mix flour and taco seasoning in a bowl, and stir in chicken pieces, a few at a time, to thoroughly coat with the flour mixture. Heat 2 teaspoons of olive oil in a large skillet over medium-high heat, and cook and stir the chicken until no longer pink and the coating is browned, about 5 minutes. Stir in the bell peppers, black beans, and salsa, and let the mixture simmer for about 5 minutes to blend the flavors.
- To serve, sprinkle each portion with Cheddar cheese.

Nutrition Information

- Calories: 333 calories
- Total Fat: 15.9 g
- Cholesterol: 94 mg
- Sodium: 945 mg
- Total Carbohydrate: 13.3 g
- Protein: 32.1 g

147. Texan Chicken and Rice Casserole

"Transform a chicken and rice casserole into a one-skillet meal with the addition of fire-grilled vegetables and beans seasoned to bring out the flavors of Texas and with the crunchiness of crispy tortilla strips."

Serving: 6 | Prep: 10 m | Cook: 11 m | Ready in: 21 m

Ingredients

- 1 tablespoon olive oil
- 3 skinless, boneless, chicken breast halves, cut into 1-inch cubes
- 1 tablespoon extra spicy seasoning blend, or to taste
- 2 cups frozen fire-roasted corn, peppers, and onions blend, thawed
- 1/2 cup no-salt-added black beans, rinsed and drained
- 1 cup chopped fresh tomatoes, divided
- 1 (5.6 ounce) package Knorr® Fiesta Sides™ - Spanish Rice
- Salt and black pepper to taste
- 4 tablespoons chopped fresh cilantro
- 1/2 cup tortilla strips, preferably chili-lime flavor

Direction

- Season chicken with seasoning blend. Heat skillet over medium-high heat and add oil. Carefully add chicken to oil; cook and stir until fully cooked and no longer pink inside, about 6 minutes. Transfer chicken to a bowl.
- Stir vegetable blend, beans and half of the tomatoes into the same skillet. Cook until coated with oil and vegetables begin to soften, about 3 minutes. Transfer mixture to the bowl with chicken.
- Stir together Knorr(R) Fiesta Sides(TM) - Spanish Rice and 2 cups water in the same skillet. Bring to a boil; stir. Reduce heat to low; cover and cook until rice is tender, about 7 minutes. Stir in chicken and vegetables. Cook until heated through. Season with salt and pepper.
- Stir in remaining tomatoes and chopped cilantro. Top with chili-lime flavor tortilla strips and serve immediately.

Nutrition Information

- Calories: 268 calories
- Total Fat: 5.2 g
- Cholesterol: 29 mg
- Sodium: 164 mg
- Total Carbohydrate: 24.2 g
- Protein: 18.1 g

148. Texas BBQ Chicken

"This is a SUPER easy recipe that taste GREAT and will make your home smell simply WONDERFUL while baking!! I usually serve the chicken on top a bed of rice."

Serving: 8 | Prep: 5 m | Cook: 45 m | Ready in: 50 m

Ingredients

- 8 boneless, skinless chicken breast halves
- 3 tablespoons brown sugar
- 1 tablespoon ground paprika
- 1 teaspoon salt
- 1 teaspoon dry mustard
- 1/2 teaspoon chili powder
- 1/4 cup distilled white vinegar
- 1/8 teaspoon cayenne pepper
- 2 tablespoons Worcestershire sauce
- 1 1/2 cups tomato-vegetable juice cocktail
- 1/2 cup ketchup
- 1/4 cup water
- 2 cloves garlic, minced

Direction

- Preheat the oven to 350 degrees F (175 degrees C).
- Place the chicken breasts in a single layer in a 9x13 inch baking dish. In a medium bowl, mix together the brown sugar, paprika, salt, dry mustard, chili powder, vinegar, cayenne pepper, Worcestershire sauce, vegetable juice cocktail, ketchup, water and garlic. Pour the sauce evenly over the chicken breasts.
- Bake uncovered, for 35 minutes in the preheated oven. Remove chicken breasts, shred with a fork, and return to the sauce. Bake in the oven for an additional 10 minutes so the chicken can soak up more flavor. Serve on a bed of rice with freshly ground black pepper.

Nutrition Information

- Calories: 182 calories
- Total Fat: 1.8 g
- Cholesterol: 68 mg
- Sodium: 702 mg
- Total Carbohydrate: 12.6 g
- Protein: 28.1 g

149. Texas BBQ Rub

"A staple at my house. We rub this on most anything we BBQ. It makes a glaze as it cooks. I like it best on slow smoked ribs. Rub into meat 10 to 30 minutes before cooking."

Serving: 64

Ingredients

- 3 cups sugar
- 1 cup ground black pepper
- 1 cup paprika
- 1 cup monosodium glutamate (such as Ac'cent®)
- 1/2 cup salt

Direction

- Whisk sugar, black pepper, paprika, monosodium glutamate, and salt together in a bowl. Store in an airtight container.

Nutrition Information

- Calories: 53 calories
- Total Fat: 0.3 g
- Cholesterol: 0 mg
- Sodium: 348 mg
- Total Carbohydrate: 11.4 g
- Protein: 0.4 g

150. Texas Beef Soup

"A hearty soup that even your husband will like. My husband, who thinks soups are for the faint of heart, loves this recipe! It's so quick and easy because of using the slow cooker. It's sure to be a family favorite!"

Serving: 6 | Prep: 20 m | Cook: 8 h | Ready in: 8 h 20 m

Ingredients

- 2 tablespoons olive oil
- 1 pound lean beef stew meat
- 1 tablespoon seasoning salt, or to taste
- 1/2 teaspoon ground black pepper
- 1 small onion, finely chopped
- 1/2 green bell pepper, finely chopped
- 2 1/2 cups beef broth
- 1 (15 ounce) can mixed vegetables
- 1 (11.5 fl oz) can spicy vegetable juice cocktail

Direction

- Heat the olive oil in a large heavy skillet. Season the stew meat with seasoning salt and pepper. Cook meat in the oil along with onion and bell pepper until browned. Transfer to a slow cooker, and stir in the beef broth.
- Cook on Low for 6 to 8 hours, or until meat is tender. During the last 30 minutes, stir in the mixed vegetables and vegetable juice cocktail.

Nutrition Information

- Calories: 306 calories
- Total Fat: 19 g
- Cholesterol: 66 mg
- Sodium: 1124 mg
- Total Carbohydrate: 9.4 g
- Protein: 23.4 g

151. Texas Boiled Beer Shrimp

"Family favorite. Serve with lemon wedges."

Serving: 6 | Prep: 5 m | Cook: 5 m | Ready in: 10 m

Ingredients

- 2 (12 fluid ounce) cans or bottles light beer
- 2 tablespoons dry crab boil
- 2 pounds large shrimp

Direction

- Bring beer with dry crab boil to a boil in a large pot. Add shrimp to boiling beer and place a cover on the pot. Bring the beer again to a boil, reduce heat to medium-low, and cook at a simmer for 5 minutes. Remove pot from heat and leave shrimp steeping in the beer another 2 to 3 minutes; drain. Serve immediately.

Nutrition Information

- Calories: 168 calories
- Total Fat: 1.3 g
- Cholesterol: 230 mg
- Sodium: 269 mg
- Total Carbohydrate: 4.2 g
- Protein: 25.3 g

152. Texas Brazil Nut Fruitcake

"This recipe was given to my mother in 1948 by a dear lady in Corpus Christi. There is just enough batter to hold the whole fruits and nuts together. For optimum satisfaction, leave all the fruit and nuts whole."

Serving: 36

Ingredients

- 1 cup white sugar
- 1 pinch salt
- 1/2 teaspoon vanilla extract
- 4 eggs
- 1 1/2 cups all-purpose flour
- 2 teaspoons baking powder

- 1 pound Brazil nuts
- 1 pound chopped walnuts
- 1 pound pecan halves
- 1 pound red candied cherries
- 1 pound green candied cherries
- 2 pounds pitted dates

Direction

- Preheat oven to 350 degrees F (175 degrees C). Grease three 9x5 inch loaf pans, line them with parchment paper, and grease the paper.
- Beat eggs, salt and vanilla together until very light and lemon colored. Add sugar, 1 cup of the flour and 2 teaspoons baking powder. Put brazil nuts, walnuts, pecans, red and green cherries into a large bowl. Dust with the remaining 1/2 cup flour. Then add the egg and sugar mixture. This is a very stiff mixture. Mix with hands.
- Press into 3 - 9x5 inch loaf pans which you have lined with parchment paper and have greased both pan and paper. Bake for 1 hour at 350 degrees F (175 degrees C).

Nutrition Information

- Calories: 439 calories
- Total Fat: 26.6 g
- Cholesterol: 21 mg
- Sodium: 52 mg
- Total Carbohydrate: 49.2 g
- Protein: 6.8 g

153. Texas Brisket

"This is a really easy BBQ brisket recipe that I got from Texas. There are only 3 ingredients besides the brisket, and it turns out really tender. Better with a brisket that is not too closely trimmed."

Serving: 6 | Prep: 15 m | Cook: 7 h | Ready in: 7 h 15 m

Ingredients

- 3 1/2 fluid ounces liquid smoke flavoring
- 1/4 cup ketchup
- 1 (10 fluid ounce) bottle steak sauce, (e.g. Heinz 57)
- 1 (3 pound) beef brisket

Direction

- Line a shallow roasting pan with aluminum foil. Place the brisket on the foil. Stir together the steak sauce, liquid smoke, and ketchup. Pour half of the mixture over the brisket, then turn the meat over, and pour sauce over the other side. Wrap tightly in a double layer of aluminum foil. Refrigerate for at least 24 hours.
- Preheat the oven to 250 degrees F (120 degrees C). Let the roast stand at room temperature while the oven preheats to take off some of the chill.
- Bake for 6 or 7 hours in the preheated oven. You can leave it in even longer if you turn the oven down to 200 degrees F (95 degrees C). Remove brisket from the oven, and slice across the grain. Return to the roasting pan, and serve with sauce.

Nutrition Information

- Calories: 877 calories
- Total Fat: 75.3 g
- Cholesterol: 164 mg
- Sodium: 933 mg
- Total Carbohydrate: 9.7 g
- Protein: 38.8 g

154. Texas Brownies I

"Sinfully delicious with a hint of cinnamon. Use the Texas Chocolate frosting recipe with these brownies!"

Serving: 36 | Prep: 20 m | Cook: 35 m | Ready in: 55 m

Ingredients

- 2 cups all-purpose flour
- 2 cups white sugar
- 1 cup butter
- 4 tablespoons cocoa powder
- 1 cup water
- 1/2 cup buttermilk

- 2 eggs, beaten
- 1 teaspoon baking soda
- 1 teaspoon ground cinnamon
- 1 teaspoon vanilla extract

Direction

- Preheat oven to 350 degrees F (175 degrees C). Grease a 9x13 inch baking pan.
- Combine flour and sugar in a large mixing bowl. In a medium saucepan, over medium heat, bring margarine, cocoa and water to a fast boil. Pour over flour mixture and mix well. Mix buttermilk, eggs, baking soda, cinnamon and vanilla into the flour mixture; mixing well after each addition. Spread evenly into the prepared pan.
- Bake for 35 minutes in the preheated oven, or until brownies begin to pull away from the sides of the pan.

Nutrition Information

- Calories: 121 calories
- Total Fat: 5.6 g
- Cholesterol: 24 mg
- Sodium: 79 mg
- Total Carbohydrate: 17 g
- Protein: 1.3 g

155. Texas Brownies II

"The moistest brownies ever!!!"

Serving: 12 | Prep: 15 m | Cook: 20 m | Ready in: 1 h

Ingredients

- Brownies:
- 3 cups all-purpose flour
- 3 cups white sugar
- 3/4 teaspoon salt
- 1 1/2 cups margarine
- 1 1/2 cups water
- 4 1/2 tablespoons unsweetened cocoa powder
- 1 cup buttermilk
- 3 eggs
- 1 1/2 teaspoons baking soda
- 1 teaspoon vanilla extract
- Frosting:
- 1/2 cup margarine
- 6 teaspoons milk
- 3 tablespoons unsweetened cocoa powder
- 4 cups confectioners' sugar

Direction

- Preheat oven to 350 degrees F (175 degrees C). Grease a 12x18-inch jelly roll pan.
- Sift flour, white sugar, and salt together in a large bowl.
- Combine 1 1/2 cups margarine, water, and 4 1/2 tablespoons cocoa, together in a saucepan; bring to a boil. Pour margarine mixture over flour mixture; stir to combine.
- Beat buttermilk, eggs, baking soda, and vanilla extract together in a bowl; add to margarine mixture and stir until batter is combined. Pour batter into prepared pan.
- Bake in the preheated oven until a toothpick inserted into the center of the brownies comes out clean, about 20 minutes. Cool completely.
- Heat 1/2 cup margarine, milk, and 3 tablespoons cocoa powder together in a small saucepan over low heat until margarine melts and mixture is combined; remove from heat. Beat confectioners' sugar into margarine mixture until frosting is smooth and creamy. Spread frosting over cooled brownies and cut into squares.

Nutrition Information

- Calories: 766 calories
- Total Fat: 32.2 g
- Cholesterol: 48 mg
- Sodium: 696 mg
- Total Carbohydrate: 117.1 g
- Protein: 6.6 g

156. Texas Caviar

"This is my favorite snack in the whole world; serve with tortilla chips or as a salsa. This recipe makes a ton!"

Serving: 12 | Prep: 30 m | Ready in: 1 h 30 m

Ingredients

- 4 (15 ounce) cans black-eyed peas, rinsed and drained
- 1 onion, chopped
- 1 red bell pepper, chopped
- 1 yellow bell pepper, chopped
- 1 green bell pepper, chopped
- 1/2 cup canola oil
- 1/2 cup ketchup
- 1/4 cup white wine vinegar
- 2 jalapeno peppers, minced
- 4 cloves garlic, minced
- 1 1/2 teaspoons dried oregano
- 1 teaspoon ground cumin
- 1 teaspoon salt
- 1/2 teaspoon dried basil
- 1/4 teaspoon chili powder
- 1/4 teaspoon paprika
- 1/4 teaspoon celery salt
- 1/4 teaspoon ground black pepper
- 1/4 teaspoon dried thyme

Direction

- Mix black-eyed peas, onion, red bell pepper, yellow bell pepper, green bell pepper, canola oil, ketchup, vinegar, jalapeno peppers, garlic, oregano, cumin, salt, basil, chili powder, paprika, celery salt, black pepper, and thyme together in a large bowl.
- Cover bowl with plastic wrap and refrigerate to let the flavors mingle, at least 1 hour.

Nutrition Information

- Calories: 216 calories
- Total Fat: 10.3 g
- Cholesterol: 0 mg
- Sodium: 758 mg
- Total Carbohydrate: 24.9 g
- Protein: 7.4 g

157. Texas Caviar I

"Here's a spicy Texas favorite. Black-eyed peas and black beans are marinated in a fiery, flavorful mixture. This is great with tortilla chips or bread -- and plenty of cold iced tea!"

Serving: 16 | Prep: 15 m | Ready in: 1 h 15 m

Ingredients

- 1/2 onion, chopped
- 1 green bell pepper, chopped
- 1 bunch green onions, chopped
- 2 jalapeno peppers, chopped
- 1 tablespoon minced garlic
- 1 pint cherry tomatoes, quartered
- 1 (8 ounce) bottle zesty Italian dressing
- 1 (15 ounce) can black beans, drained
- 1 (15 ounce) can black-eyed peas, drained
- 1/2 teaspoon ground coriander
- 1 bunch chopped fresh cilantro

Direction

- In a large bowl, mix together onion, green bell pepper, green onions, jalapeno peppers, garlic, cherry tomatoes, zesty Italian dressing, black beans, black-eyed peas and coriander. Cover and chill in the refrigerator approximately 2 hours. Toss with desired amount of fresh cilantro to serve.

Nutrition Information

- Calories: 107 calories
- Total Fat: 5.4 g
- Cholesterol: 0 mg
- Sodium: 415 mg
- Total Carbohydrate: 11.8 g
- Protein: 3.5 g

158. Texas Caviar II

"Here's a simple version of an old spicy Texas favorite made with black-eyed peas and salsa. Serve with tortilla chips."

Serving: 16 | Prep: 5 m | Ready in: 5 m

Ingredients

- 1 (15 ounce) can black-eyed peas, rinsed and drained
- 1/2 (16 ounce) jar picante sauce
- salt to taste

Direction

- In a medium bowl, mix together black-eyed peas, picante sauce and salt. Chill in the refrigerator before serving.

Nutrition Information

- Calories: 22 calories
- Total Fat: 0.2 g
- Cholesterol: 0 mg
- Sodium: 116 mg
- Total Carbohydrate: 3.9 g
- Protein: 1.3 g

159. Texas Caviar with Avocado

"A delicious party dip with beans, tomatoes, onions, and lots of diced avocado. A variation on 'Texas Caviar'; one bite and you won't leave the bowl. Serve with 'scoop' tortilla chips."

Serving: 32 | Prep: 15 m | Ready in: 15 m

Ingredients

- 2 (15.5 ounce) cans black-eyed peas, drained and rinsed
- 2 tomatoes, chopped
- 1 medium sweet onion, chopped
- 1/2 cup chopped jalapeno peppers
- 8 fluid ounces Italian dressing
- cayenne pepper to taste
- 2 avocados - peeled, pitted, and chopped

Direction

- In a large bowl, mix black-eyed peas, tomatoes, sweet onion, jalapeno peppers, Italian dressing, and cayenne pepper. Stir in the avocados just before serving.

Nutrition Information

- Calories: 66 calories
- Total Fat: 4.1 g
- Cholesterol: 0 mg
- Sodium: 204 mg
- Total Carbohydrate: 6.2 g
- Protein: 1.7 g

160. Texas Chicken Quesadillas

"These are quesadillas filled with chicken cooked in barbeque sauce, caramelized onions, Cheddar and Monterey Jack. Serve with plenty of guacamole, sour cream and chunky salsa!"

Serving: 8 | Prep: 20 m | Cook: 15 m | Ready in: 35 m

Ingredients

- 2 tablespoons vegetable oil, divided
- 1 onion, sliced into rings
- 1 tablespoon honey
- 2 skinless, boneless chicken breast halves - cut into strips
- 1/2 cup barbeque sauce
- 1/2 cup shredded sharp Cheddar cheese
- 1/2 cup shredded Monterey Jack cheese
- 8 (10 inch) flour tortillas

Direction

- Preheat oven to 350 degrees F (175 degrees C).
- In a large, deep skillet, heat 1 tablespoon oil over medium high heat. Slowly cook and stir onion until translucent. Mix in honey. Stir until onion is golden brown, about 5 minutes. Remove from skillet and set aside.
- Place remaining oil and chicken in the skillet over medium high heat. Cook until chicken is

no longer pink. Stir in barbeque sauce and evenly coat chicken.
- Layer 4 tortillas individually with chicken, onions, Cheddar cheese and Monterey Jack cheese. Top with remaining tortillas.
- One or two at a time, place layered tortillas on a large baking sheet. Bake uncovered in the preheated oven 20 minutes, or until cheese is melted. Do not let tortillas become too crisp. Remove from heat. Cut into quarters to serve.

Nutrition Information

- Calories: 411 calories
- Total Fat: 14.3 g
- Cholesterol: 48 mg
- Sodium: 753 mg
- Total Carbohydrate: 46.2 g
- Protein: 23.2 g

Direction

- Combine vegetable juice, chicken broth, chicken, green onions, cilantro, Worcestershire sauce, garlic powder, chili powder, and cumin in a large pot. Bring to a boil; reduce heat and simmer until flavors combine, about 25 minutes.
- Ladle into bowls and garnish with crushed tortilla chips and Monterey Jack cheese.

Nutrition Information

- Calories: 510 calories
- Total Fat: 25.9 g
- Cholesterol: 57 mg
- Sodium: 1950 mg
- Total Carbohydrate: 49.4 g
- Protein: 22.9 g

161. Texas Chicken Vegetable Soup

"Chicken vegetable soup with a Texas twist! Made from items you can keep in the panty, this soup is also a great recipe for once a month cooking. I even put a bag of cheese in the freezer alongside the soup and take it all out when I am ready to serve."

Serving: 8 | Prep: 15 m | Cook: 30 m | Ready in: 45 m

Ingredients

- 2 (46 fluid ounce) bottles vegetable juice
- 4 (14.5 ounce) cans chicken broth
- 2 cups cooked and cubed chicken
- 2 cups chopped green onions
- 1/2 bunch cilantro, chopped
- 1 tablespoon Worcestershire sauce
- 1 tablespoon garlic powder
- 1 tablespoon chili powder
- 1 tablespoon ground cumin
- 1 (14.5 ounce) package tortilla chips, crushed
- 2 cups shredded Monterey Jack cheese

162. Texas Chili Beef Slices

"This is a mildly spicy recipe that my whole family loves."

Serving: 6 | Prep: 20 m | Cook: 45 m | Ready in: 3 h 5 m

Ingredients

- 2 pounds round steak
- 1 teaspoon meat tenderizer
- 1 onion, chopped
- 2 cloves garlic, minced
- 2 tablespoons distilled white vinegar
- 2 tablespoons vegetable oil
- 2 tablespoons Worcestershire sauce
- 2 teaspoons chili powder
- 1 (8 ounce) can tomato sauce
- 1 lemon, sliced
- 2 tablespoons brown sugar
- 1/2 teaspoon mustard powder
- 1/4 teaspoon hot pepper sauce

Direction

- Sprinkle meat with meat tenderizer. Place in a shallow glass baking dish large enough to accommodate the meat. Mix together onion,

garlic, vinegar, oil, Worcestershire sauce, and chili powder, and pour over steak. Marinate for 2 or more hours in the refrigerator.
- Preheat grill for medium-low heat.
- Brush grate with oil. Transfer steak to grill, reserving marinade. Cook, covered, for 30 to 40 minutes, or to your desired degree of doneness, turning once. Allow steak to rest for a few minutes off the heat.
- While meat is cooking prepare sauce. Combine reserved marinade, tomato sauce, lemon slices, brown sugar, mustard powder, and hot sauce in a medium saucepan. Simmer for 10 minutes over medium low heat.
- Slice meat across the grain. Spoon sauce over steak, and serve.

Nutrition Information

- Calories: 283 calories
- Total Fat: 13.6 g
- Cholesterol: 76 mg
- Sodium: 404 mg
- Total Carbohydrate: 12.1 g
- Protein: 28.2 g

163. Texas Chili Dog

"Whether you're tailgating, watching the big game at home or just planning a family movie night, this Texas Chili Dog is guaranteed to please. Delicious Ball Park Brand® Franks are even better when topped with hearty Texas chili, freshly grated cheese and chopped sweet onion. You can always add a few slices of jalapeno, if you like it hot. Tater Tots or Fritos make the best sides."

Serving: 6 | Prep: 20 m | Cook: 30 m | Ready in: 50 m

Ingredients

- 8 Ball Park® Brand Franks
- 8 Ball Park® Hot Dog Buns
- Yellow mustard
- 1 cup chopped yellow onion
- 2 cups grated Cheddar cheese
- 1 jalapeno pepper, seeded and thinly sliced
- Chili:
- 1 pound ground beef
- 1 tablespoon vegetable oil
- 1/2 sweet yellow onion, chopped
- 1/2 red bell pepper, chopped
- 1 (8 ounce) can tomato sauce
- 1 tablespoon chili powder
- 2 teaspoons garlic granules
- 2 teaspoons paprika
- salt and pepper to taste

Direction

- To make chili, brown ground beef in 1 tablespoon vegetable oil in a large saucepan for about 10 minutes over medium heat.
- Add onion and red bell pepper, stirring well. Add tomato sauce and seasonings, stirring well.
- Allow mixture to bubble for about 10 minutes, then reduce heat to simmer and cook at least 30 minutes.
- To make hot dogs, cook on your grill or on a grill pan until just seared on the outside.
- Meanwhile, toast buns in a 400-degree oven for about 10 minutes, taking care not to brown.
- Swipe each bun with mustard, top with chili as desired, followed by grated cheese, onion and, if you're brave, jalapenos.
- If you'd like the cheese all melty, place chili dogs on a foil-lined cookie sheet and run under a hot broiler for 2 to 3 minutes or until cheese bubbles.

Nutrition Information

- Calories: 761 calories
- Total Fat: 48.2 g
- Cholesterol: 132 mg
- Sodium: 1638 mg
- Total Carbohydrate: 43.6 g
- Protein: 37.6 g

164. Texas Chocolate Frosting

"A delicious chocolate frosting for icing brownies and cookies! I like it especially as a topper on Texas Brownies. I like to add a dash of cinnamon to the frosting, it gives it a special flavor."

Serving: 36

Ingredients

- 1/2 cup margarine
- 4 tablespoons cocoa powder
- 4 cups confectioners' sugar
- 3 tablespoons milk
- 1 teaspoon vanilla extract

Direction

- Melt margarine over a low heat. Gradually beat in cocoa, sugar, milk and vanilla, mix well.

Nutrition Information

- Calories: 79 calories
- Total Fat: 2.6 g
- Cholesterol: < 1 mg
- Sodium: 30 mg
- Total Carbohydrate: 14.3 g
- Protein: 0.2 g

165. Texas Chocolate Mini Cake Bites

"Super chocolaty mini cupcake bites that are soft, chewy, and beautiful! Makes 4 dozen treats quickly and easily. They store and travel well. Let me know how yours turn out and how you like them!"

Serving: 48 | Prep: 25 m | Cook: 9 m | Ready in: 44 m

Ingredients

- Mini Cakes:
- cooking spray
- 1 (18.25 ounce) package devil's food cake mix
- 4 eggs
- 1 (3.9 ounce) package instant chocolate fudge pudding mix
- 1/2 cup vegetable oil
- 1/4 cup water
- Glaze:
- 2 cups confectioners' sugar
- 1/4 cup water
- 2 tablespoons unsweetened cocoa powder

Direction

- Preheat oven to 350 degrees F (175 degrees C). Grease 2 mini muffin tins generously with cooking spray.
- Combine devil's food cake mix, eggs, chocolate pudding mix, vegetable oil, and 1/4 cup water in a large bowl. Mix with a wooden spoon until batter is thick and smooth.
- Pour batter into the prepared mini muffin tins.
- Bake in the preheated oven until a toothpick inserted into the center comes out clean, 9 to 10 minutes.
- Let mini cakes cool in the tins for 1 to 2 minutes. Transfer to a wire rack.
- Stir confectioners' sugar, 1/4 cup water, and cocoa powder together in a bowl to make glaze.
- Dip tops of the mini cakes in glaze and place on a large sheet of waxed paper. Cool completely before serving, about 10 minutes.

Nutrition Information

- Calories: 102 calories
- Total Fat: 4.3 g
- Cholesterol: 18 mg
- Sodium: 118 mg
- Total Carbohydrate: 14.9 g
- Protein: 1.5 g

166. Texas Chocolate Sheet Cake

"I love this simple chocolate cake recipe!"

Serving: 20 | Prep: 15 m | Cook: 30 m | Ready in: 1 h 45 m

Ingredients

- 1 cup water
- 1 cup margarine
- 1/4 cup unsweetened cocoa powder
- 2 cups all-purpose flour
- 2 cups white sugar
- 1/2 teaspoon salt
- 2 eggs
- 1/2 cup sour cream
- 1 teaspoon baking soda
- 1/2 cup margarine
- 6 tablespoons milk
- 1/4 cup unsweetened cocoa powder
- 1 teaspoon vanilla extract
- 1 (16 ounce) box confectioners' sugar

Direction

- Preheat oven to 375 degrees F (190 degrees C). Grease a 15 1/2x10 1/2-inch jelly roll pan.
- Bring water, 1 cup margarine, and 1/4 cup cocoa powder to a boil in a large saucepan; remove from heat and stir in flour, white sugar, and salt. Beat eggs, sour cream, and baking soda in a bowl; stir into flour mixture until just blended. Pour batter into prepared jelly roll pan.
- Bake in the preheated oven until a toothpick inserted into the center comes out clean, 20 to 22 minutes.
- Meanwhile, bring 1/2 cup margarine, milk, 1/4 cup cocoa powder, and vanilla extract to a boil in another saucepan; remove from heat and stir in confectioner's sugar until icing is smooth. Spread icing over cake immediately after removing from oven. Allow cake to cool before cutting and serving.

Nutrition Information

- Calories: 358 calories
- Total Fat: 15.7 g
- Cholesterol: 21 mg
- Sodium: 292 mg
- Total Carbohydrate: 53.7 g
- Protein: 2.8 g

167. Texas Christmas Pickles

"These spicy/sweet pickles are a Texas tradition. My mother and I have made these delectable pickles for Christmas every year since I was young. We separate each batch into smaller jars and give them as gifts to friends and family. I would hate to think what would happen if we skipped a year!!"

Serving: 60 | Prep: 30 m | Ready in: 7 d s30 m

Ingredients

- 1 gallon dill pickles
- 1 (5 ounce) bottle hot pepper sauce (e.g. Tabasco™)
- 5 cloves garlic, chopped
- 1 (5 pound) bag of white sugar

Direction

- Drain the brine from the pickles and discard. Slice pickles lengthwise, and return them to the jar. Pour in the hot pepper sauce, and add the garlic. Pour in about 1/3 of the sugar. Close the lid tightly. Gently tip the jar back and forth several times to allow everything to mix well. Leave out on the counter at room temperature for about 1 week.
- During the week, add more sugar as the sugar in the jar dissolves. Gently tip the jar back and forth to mix. Continue the process throughout the week, until you have used up all of the sugar. When all of the sugar has been absorbed, pickles will be dark green and crispy. Transfer pickles to smaller sterile jars, and divide syrup between jars. Seal with lids and rings. Store in the refrigerator, and consume within one month.

Nutrition Information

- Calories: 183 calories
- Total Fat: 0.1 g
- Cholesterol: 0 mg
- Sodium: 501 mg
- Total Carbohydrate: 47 g
- Protein: 0.3 g

168. Texas Coleslaw

"One of my favorites! Goes great with barbecues and picnics. For a more mild salad, use less green onions."

Serving: 8 | Prep: 15 m | Ready in: 1 h 15 m

Ingredients

- 1 cup mayonnaise
- 1 tablespoon lime juice
- 1 tablespoon ground cumin
- 1 teaspoon cayenne pepper
- 1 teaspoon salt
- 1 teaspoon ground black pepper
- 1 medium head green cabbage, rinsed and very thinly sliced
- 1 large carrot, shredded
- 2 green onions, sliced
- 2 radishes, sliced

Direction

- In a large bowl, whisk together the mayonnaise, lime juice, cumin, salt and pepper. Add the cabbage, carrot, green onions and radishes and stir until well-combined. Chill at least an hour before serving.

Nutrition Information

- Calories: 236 calories
- Total Fat: 22.2 g
- Cholesterol: 10 mg
- Sodium: 476 mg
- Total Carbohydrate: 9.4 g
- Protein: 2.1 g

169. Texas Corn Chowder with Venison

"Hearty Texas corn chowder. Serves 6 to 8 hearty appetites. Goes great with cornbread."

Serving: 8 | Prep: 20 m | Cook: 40 m | Ready in: 1 h

Ingredients

- 1/4 cup butter
- 1 green bell pepper, chopped
- 2/3 cup chopped onion
- 3 cups whole milk
- 1 (10.75 ounce) can condensed cream of potato soup
- 1 tablespoon Worcestershire sauce
- 1 pound ground venison
- 1 (16 ounce) can cream-style corn
- ground black pepper to taste
- 4 cups shredded Cheddar cheese

Direction

- Melt butter in a large pot over medium-high heat. Sauté green bell pepper and onion until tender, 5 to 10 minutes. Stir in milk, potato soup, and Worcestershire sauce. Let soup simmer, uncovered, for 15 minutes.
- Heat a large skillet over medium-high heat. Add venison; cook and stir until browned and crumbly, 5 to 7 minutes. Drain and discard grease. Add venison to the soup; stir in corn. Season with pepper. Simmer until flavors meld, at least 15 minutes. Stir in cheese until melted.

Nutrition Information

- Calories: 472 calories
- Total Fat: 29.6 g
- Cholesterol: 128 mg
- Sodium: 867 mg
- Total Carbohydrate: 22.1 g
- Protein: 30.5 g

170. Texas Cowboy Chili Beans

"I just came up with this one day playing around in the kitchen. It's become a ranch favorite. Very unique and meaty, this is always a big hit at our potlucks. The men just love it. This will feed the cavalry. If you like Tex-Mex, you'll like this. Garnish with cheese."

Serving: 25 | Prep: 30 m | Cook: 5 h 30 m | Ready in: 6 h

Ingredients

- 8 pounds beef chuck roast
- 2 (10 ounce) cans diced tomatoes with green chile peppers
- 1 large yellow onion, diced
- 2 tablespoons garlic powder
- 2 tablespoons ground cumin
- 2 (1.25 ounce) packages chili seasoning mix
- 3 cups dried pinto beans

Direction

- In a large stock pot over high heat, brown roast on all sides. Reduce heat to medium low and add the diced tomatoes with green chile peppers, yellow onion, garlic powder, ground cumin and chili seasoning mix. Cover and simmer until meat comes apart easily, about 3 to 4 hours.
- Meanwhile, rinse the pinto beans and soak them in a bowl of warm water.
- Remove cooked roast from the pot and set aside. Rinse the pinto beans and pour them into the pot. Pour in enough water to cover the beans and bring to a boil. Cover and simmer until the beans are very tender, about 1 1/2 hours, adding extra water as needed.
- Shred roast with fork and discard the fat. Add the shredded meat to the cooked beans and pour in enough water to cover. Cover and simmer for 30 minutes

Nutrition Information

- Calories: 434 calories
- Total Fat: 26.7 g
- Cholesterol: 103 mg
- Sodium: 456 mg
- Total Carbohydrate: 17.5 g
- Protein: 30.8 g

171. Texas Crabgrass

"Serve this hot cheesy crab and spinach dip with crackers!"

Serving: 20 | Prep: 20 m | Cook: 20 m | Ready in: 40 m

Ingredients

- 1 (10 ounce) package frozen chopped spinach, thawed and drained
- 1 onion, chopped
- 1/2 cup butter
- 1/2 pound crabmeat
- 3/4 cup grated Parmesan cheese
- 1/4 cup dry sherry

Direction

- In a medium saucepan, place spinach with 1/4 cup water. Bring to a boil. Reduce heat to medium, cover and cook approximately 10 minutes, stirring occasionally.
- In a medium saucepan over medium heat, slowly cook and stir onions in butter until tender.
- Place spinach, onion, crabmeat, Parmesan cheese and dry sherry in a small baking dish. Mix thoroughly. Bake in the preheated oven 15 minutes, or until bubbly and lightly browned.

Nutrition Information

- Calories: 78 calories
- Total Fat: 5.9 g
- Cholesterol: 24 mg
- Sodium: 162 mg
- Total Carbohydrate: 1.8 g
- Protein: 4.6 g

172. Texas Curried Chicken

"Pieces of chicken are roasted with butter, then glazed with a sweet curry glaze during the last bit of cooking time for tender chicken that is full of Texas flavor."

Serving: 6 | Prep: 10 m | Cook: 1 h 5 m | Ready in: 1 h 15 m

Ingredients

- 1 (4 pound) whole chicken, cut into pieces
- 1/2 cup butter, divided
- 1/2 teaspoon salt
- 1/4 teaspoon black pepper
- 1/4 cup honey
- 1/4 cup molasses
- 1/4 cup prepared mustard
- 1 teaspoon curry powder

Direction

- Preheat the oven to 375 degrees F (190 degrees C).
- Place chicken pieces into a greased 9x13 inch baking dish. Melt 1/4 cup of the butter, and drizzle it over the chicken. Season with salt and pepper.
- Bake chicken, uncovered, for 45 minutes in the preheated oven. While the chicken is cooking, combine the honey, molasses, mustard, curry powder and remaining butter in a medium saucepan. Simmer over medium heat for about 5 minutes to blend the flavors.
- When the 45 minutes are up on the chicken, pour the curry mixture over the pieces, and bake for an additional 15 minutes, or until the chicken is no longer pink, and the juices run clear.

Nutrition Information

- Calories: 877 calories
- Total Fat: 61.4 g
- Cholesterol: 268 mg
- Sodium: 639 mg
- Total Carbohydrate: 22.7 g
- Protein: 57 g

173. Texas Egg Rolls

"These are like individual chile rellenos. Serve with salsa and or guacamole."

Serving: 6 | Prep: 15 m | Cook: 3 m | Ready in: 18 m

Ingredients

- oil for frying
- 6 canned whole green chiles
- 6 egg roll wrappers
- 6 slices Monterey Jack cheese

Direction

- Heat 1/2 inch of oil in a large skillet, or preheat a deep-fryer to 350 degrees F (175 degrees C).
- Insert a piece of cheese into each chile. Place a stuffed chile diagonally across the egg roll wrapper. Moisten all four sides of the wrapper with water. Fold the sides in and gently press to seal the ends. Starting at the bottom fold the point up and gently press around the chili. Roll up and seal the edges.
- Fry the rolls in the hot oil until golden brown on all sides, about 3 minutes. When the first side in nice and brown gently flip over and brown the other side. Work in small batches so the egg rolls don't touch while frying. Remove from the oil to drain on paper towels. Serve warm.

Nutrition Information

- Calories: 204 calories
- Total Fat: 16 g
- Cholesterol: 26 mg
- Sodium: 428 mg
- Total Carbohydrate: 6.8 g
- Protein: 7.7 g

174. Texas Eggs

"This is a great Christmas morning treat. Make it the night before and pop it in the oven in the morning."

Serving: 6

Ingredients

- 1 pound sausage
- 9 slices white bread, cut into cubes
- 9 eggs, beaten
- 1 (11 ounce) can condensed cream of Cheddar cheese soup
- 3 cups milk
- 1 1/2 teaspoons salt
- 8 ounces shredded Cheddar cheese

Direction

- Butter one 3 quart casserole dish and set aside.
- Place sausage in a large, deep skillet. Cook over medium high heat until crumbled and evenly brown. Drain and set aside.
- Place bread cubes in prepared casserole dish.
- Whisk together the eggs, soup, milk and salt; pour over bread cubes. Add sausage and sprinkle with shredded cheese. Cover with foil and refrigerate overnight.
- The next morning, preheat oven to 350 degrees F (175 degrees C) and bake for 1 hour.

Nutrition Information

- Calories: 799 calories
- Total Fat: 58.3 g
- Cholesterol: 392 mg
- Sodium: 2120 mg
- Total Carbohydrate: 30.8 g
- Protein: 36.8 g

175. Texas Enchilada Sauce

"Being from deep South Texas, I learned many ways to prepare Mexican and Tex-Mex foods. This is my all time favorite!"

Serving: 7 | Prep: 15 m | Cook: 30 m | Ready in: 45 m

Ingredients

- 2 (6.5 ounce) cans tomato sauce
- 1 (28 ounce) can crushed tomatoes
- 1/3 cup chili powder
- 1 tablespoon dried oregano
- 1 teaspoon paprika
- 2 teaspoons ground cumin
- 2 teaspoons ground black pepper
- 1/4 teaspoon salt
- 1 clove garlic, minced
- 1 tablespoon butter
- 1 onion, minced
- 1 green bell pepper, chopped

Direction

- In a medium saucepan combine tomato sauce, crushed tomatoes, chili powder, oregano, paprika, cumin, pepper, salt and garlic. Cover and cook over medium heat.
- Meanwhile, melt butter in a small skillet over medium heat. Sauté onion for about 4 minutes; stir into sauce. Cook sauce for 20 minutes, stirring occasionally. Stir in bell pepper and cook 10 more minutes.

Nutrition Information

- Calories: 100 calories
- Total Fat: 3.4 g
- Cholesterol: 4 mg
- Sodium: 582 mg
- Total Carbohydrate: 18.2 g
- Protein: 4 g

176. Texas Firehouse Dip

"This easy recipe is ridiculously addictive. One of us always makes a batch when we have a Texas get-together. Hope y'all like it. It goes great with beer and margaritas. It is especially good, served with Ritz® crackers."

Serving: 8 | Prep: 10 m | Ready in: 10 m

Ingredients

- 1 (8 ounce) package cream cheese, softened
- 1 (10 ounce) can diced tomatoes with green chile peppers (such as RO*TEL®), drain and reserve liquid
- 1/2 teaspoon Sriracha hot sauce, or more to taste
- 1 teaspoon chopped fresh cilantro, or more to taste

Direction

- Beat cream cheese and 1/2 of the drained tomato juice together in a bowl until fluffy and smooth. Beat Sriracha hot sauce into cream cheese mixture; beat in tomatoes with green chile peppers. Garnish dip with cilantro.

Nutrition Information

- Calories: 103 calories
- Total Fat: 9.8 g
- Cholesterol: 31 mg
- Sodium: 237 mg
- Total Carbohydrate: 2 g
- Protein: 2.4 g

177. Texas Ground Turkey Burrito

"Using lean ground turkey, spices, black beans, and salsa, you will create a tasty, quick burrito."

Serving: 4 | Prep: 5 m | Cook: 11 m | Ready in: 16 m

Ingredients

- 1 tablespoon olive oil
- 1 pound lean ground turkey
- 1 pinch garlic powder, or to taste
- 1 pinch onion powder, or to taste
- salt and ground black pepper to taste
- 1 cup salsa
- 1 (8 ounce) can black beans, rinsed and drained
- 4 (8 inch) flour tortillas
- 1/4 cup shredded reduced-fat Cheddar cheese

Direction

- Heat olive oil in a large skillet over medium heat. Add ground turkey and cook until no longer pink, about 5 minutes. Season with garlic powder, onion powder, salt, and black pepper. Stir in salsa and black beans; cook until heated through, about 5 minutes.
- Cover tortillas with moist paper towels; microwave on high for 30 seconds.
- Spoon turkey mixture into each tortilla. Sprinkle with Cheddar cheese.

Nutrition Information

- Calories: 441 calories
- Total Fat: 16.3 g
- Cholesterol: 86 mg
- Sodium: 995 mg
- Total Carbohydrate: 41.2 g
- Protein: 33.3 g

178. Texas Hash

"This beef, veggies and rice casserole is easy to make and a family favorite."

Serving: 6 | Prep: 15 m | Cook: 45 m | Ready in: 1 h

Ingredients

- 1 cup water
- 1 cup uncooked instant rice
- 1 pound lean ground beef
- 2 onions, chopped
- 1 large green bell pepper, chopped
- 1 (14.5 ounce) can diced tomatoes
- 1 (8 ounce) can tomato sauce
- 2 tablespoons chili powder
- 1 (8.75 ounce) can whole kernel corn, drained

- salt and pepper to taste
- 3 slices processed American cheese

Direction

- Preheat oven to 350 degrees F (175 degrees C). Lightly grease a 2 quart (8 inch round) casserole dish.
- In a medium saucepan, bring 1 cup of water to a boil. Stir in instant rice, cover and remove from heat. Let sit for 5 minutes.
- In a medium skillet over high heat, brown ground beef with onions and green pepper. Stir in diced tomatoes, tomato sauce and chili powder. Simmer for 20 minutes.
- Stir cooked rice into the beef mixture. Mix in the corn, salt and pepper.
- Pour the mixture into prepared casserole dish. Cut the American cheese slices in half and place over the top.
- Bake in preheated oven for 15 to 20 minutes or until cheese is melted and bubbly.

Nutrition Information

- Calories: 543 calories
- Total Fat: 21.1 g
- Cholesterol: 70 mg
- Sodium: 720 mg
- Total Carbohydrate: 64.5 g
- Protein: 23.8 g

179. Texas Hash in the Microwave

"One of my favorite meals growing up. I have only change up a couple of things to suit my family. The kids love it! And it's super easy and fast."

Serving: 4 | Prep: 10 m | Cook: 25 m | Ready in: 45 m

Ingredients

- 1 pound ground beef
- 1 tablespoon minced garlic
- 1 1/2 teaspoons tomato, garlic, and basil seasoning blend (such as Mrs. Dash®)
- 2 (14.5 ounce) cans no-salt-added stewed tomatoes
- 1 cup instant white rice
- 1/2 onion, chopped
- 1 teaspoon dried minced onion, or to taste
- 1/4 cup shredded mozzarella cheese, or to taste (optional)

Direction

- Crumble ground beef into a 3-quart glass, microwave-safe, casserole dish; mix in garlic and seasoning blend. Cook on high, stirring halfway through, for 5 minutes. Drain.
- Mix stewed tomatoes, rice, chopped onion, and minced onion into ground beef mixture. Cover and cook on high, stirring halfway through, until rice is cooked through, about 20 minutes. Let stand, covered, for 10 minutes. Stir and add mozzarella cheese.

Nutrition Information

- Calories: 421 calories
- Total Fat: 19.1 g
- Cholesterol: 74 mg
- Sodium: 138 mg
- Total Carbohydrate: 34.8 g
- Protein: 24.4 g

180. Texas Hickory BBQ Chicken

"Chicken leg quarters are slow cooked in barbecue sauce on the grill. Barbecued chicken with Texas size hickory smoke flavor."

Serving: 4 | Prep: 15 m | Cook: 1 h | Ready in: 1 h 15 m

Ingredients

- 2 (12 fluid ounce) cans beer
- 2 cups hickory wood chips, or as much as you like
- 4 chicken leg quarters
- 2 cups barbeque sauce
- salt and pepper to taste
- heavy duty aluminum foil

Direction

- Preheat an outdoor grill for medium heat. Coat the grill surface lightly with oil. Pour beer into a pan or bowl, and add wood chips. Let soak while the grill heats up.
- When the coals are ready, sprinkle the hickory chips over them. Place chicken pieces on the grill, cover, and cook for 15 minutes. Turn over, cover and grill for an additional 15 minutes. Remove the chicken pieces from the grill, and place each leg quarter onto a large square of aluminum foil. Cover with barbeque sauce, and fold the foil into a packet around each piece of chicken.
- Return chicken packets to the grill, and cook for an additional 15 minutes per side. Remove packets, and serve with more barbeque sauce.

Nutrition Information

- Calories: 478 calories
- Total Fat: 9.8 g
- Cholesterol: 105 mg
- Sodium: 1508 mg
- Total Carbohydrate: 51.6 g
- Protein: 31 g

181. Texas Hot Sauce

"This is a Hot Dog Sauce perfected by me in 1955. It is a must at family picnics. To Serve: Grill hot dog, toast or steam bun. With hot dog in bun, spoon chopped onion over, 1 slice dill pickle, a good horseradish mustard, and a generous amount of Texas Hot Sauce. Enjoy."

Serving: 20 | Prep: 20 m | Cook: 1 h 30 m | Ready in: 1 h 50 m

Ingredients

- 4 tablespoons vegetable oil
- 1/2 pound ground pork
- 1/2 pound lean ground beef
- 2 frankfurters, finely diced
- 1 onion, chopped
- 2 cloves garlic, minced
- 1 1/2 teaspoons browning sauce
- 1 teaspoon ground black pepper
- 1/2 teaspoon salt
- 1 (6 ounce) can tomato paste
- 8 cups water
- 1 tablespoon paprika
- 1 tablespoon chili powder
- 4 teaspoons ground cinnamon
- 1 teaspoon dried parsley
- 1 1/2 cups bread crumbs

Direction

- Heat oil in a large skillet over medium heat. Add onion and garlic and cook until soft.
- Stir in beef and pork and cook, stirring frequently until brown.
- Reduce heat to medium-low and stir in hot dogs. Sauté for 3 to 4 minutes. Drain off any excess fat.
- Stir in the browning sauce, pepper, salt, tomato paste and water. Bring mixture to a boil. Lower heat and simmer for 1 hour, uncovered. Stir occasionally.
- Stir in the paprika, chili powder, cinnamon and parsley. Taste and adjust seasoning, if necessary. Simmer for 10 minutes. Remove from heat and let cool.
- Using a hand held mixer blend the bread crumbs into the sauce and it's ready to serve!

Nutrition Information

- Calories: 143 calories
- Total Fat: 9.3 g
- Cholesterol: 19 mg
- Sodium: 254 mg
- Total Carbohydrate: 9 g
- Protein: 6.1 g

182. Texas Hot Wiener Sauce Ulster County New York Style

"The sauce was created in Ulster County, New York. The sauce turns a ordinary hot dog into a mouth-watering meal. The hot dog is served on a steamed bun with mustard, chopped onions and then the sauce. Enjoy."

Serving: 28 | Prep: 10 m | Cook: 45 m | Ready in: 55 m

Ingredients

- 1/2 (16 ounce) package hot dogs, coarsely chopped
- 1/2 cup cornstarch
- 8 cups water, divided
- 1/4 cup distilled white vinegar
- 1 tablespoon paprika
- 1 tablespoon chili powder
- 1 teaspoon sea salt
- 1 teaspoon red pepper flakes
- 1/2 teaspoon dried oregano
- 1/2 teaspoon onion powder
- 1/2 teaspoon ground cinnamon
- 1/4 teaspoon white pepper
- 1 pinch ground black pepper, or to taste

Direction

- Grind hot dogs into a chunky paste in a food processor and place into a large saucepan. Mix cornstarch with 1 cup water in a small bowl and set aside. Pour 7 more cups water over the hot dogs. Stir in vinegar, paprika, chili powder, sea salt, red pepper flakes, oregano, onion powder, cinnamon, white pepper, and black pepper and bring to a boil.
- Simmer over low heat until the sauce is slightly thickened, about 30 minutes. Gradually stir in reserved cornstarch mixture and simmer for 15 more minutes. Adjust salt and black pepper. Sauce will be thinner than chili and will thicken as it cools.

Nutrition Information

- Calories: 37 calories
- Total Fat: 2.5 g
- Cholesterol: 4 mg
- Sodium: 159 mg
- Total Carbohydrate: 2.9 g
- Protein: 1 g

183. Texas Hotdog Sauce

"When I was small we would always stop and get hot dogs smothered in a flavorful meat sauce on the way to Gram's. Dad worked and experimented, and finally came up with a sauce that tasted just as good. Be sure to spread the hot dog rolls with mustard and top them off with chopped onion."

Serving: 32 | Prep: 10 m | Cook: 30 m | Ready in: 40 m

Ingredients

- 1 tablespoon vegetable oil
- 4 ounces ground beef
- 4 ounces ground pork
- 4 beef frankfurters, diced
- 1/4 cup diced sweet onion
- 1/2 clove garlic, peeled and minced
- 1/2 teaspoon browning sauce
- 1/4 teaspoon ground black pepper
- 3/4 teaspoon salt
- 1/4 (10.75 ounce) can tomato soup
- 2 1/2 cups water
- 3/4 teaspoon paprika
- 1/2 teaspoon chili powder
- 3/4 teaspoon ground cinnamon
- 1/2 cup fine dry bread crumbs

Direction

- Heat vegetable oil in a large, deep skillet over medium high heat. Place ground beef, ground pork, frankfurters, and sweet onion in the skillet. Cook until meat is evenly brown and onion is soft. Drain and lower heat.
- Mix in garlic, browning sauce, ground black pepper, salt, tomato soup, water, paprika, chili powder, cinnamon and dry bread crumbs. Slowly simmer until thick, about 25 minutes.

Nutrition Information

- Calories: 50 calories
- Total Fat: 3.9 g

- Cholesterol: 9 mg
- Sodium: 137 mg
- Total Carbohydrate: 1.7 g
- Protein: 2.1 g

184. Texas Hurricane

"This beverage is known for its 'sneak up and blow you away' power. There are many different versions, but I believe you will find mine a very good blend of rums, other alcoholic beverages and fruit juices. If you can walk after two of these...well...you just think you can. Everything is bigger and better in Texas -- just try this and see."

Serving: 1 | Prep: 10 m | Ready in: 10 m

Ingredients

- 1 cup crushed ice
- 1 fluid ounce rum
- 1 fluid ounce coconut flavored rum
- 1 fluid ounce vodka
- 1 fluid ounce gin
- 1 fluid ounce triple sec (orange-flavored liqueur)
- 2 fluid ounces orange juice
- 1 fluid ounce pineapple juice
- 1 fluid ounce grenadine syrup
- 1 fluid ounce 151 proof rum
- 1 orange slice (optional)
- 1 lime slice (optional)
- 1 maraschino cherry (optional)

Direction

- Fill a hurricane glass with ice. Pour in the rum, coconut rum, vodka, gin, triple sec, orange juice, pineapple juice, and grenadine. Stir well with a bar spoon, then pour the 151 rum over the back of the spoon to float the liquor on top of the drink. Garnish the glass with orange, lime, and a cherry.
- Sip with a straw from the bottom for a 'sneak up on you' punch or sip from the top for a 'knock you down' twister.

185. Texas Jambalaya

"This is a hearty, filling meal with only one pot to clean up."

Serving: 6 | Prep: 10 m | Cook: 35 m | Ready in: 45 m

Ingredients

- 2 tablespoons olive oil
- 1 cup diced onion
- 1/2 cup diced green bell pepper
- 1/2 cup diced celery
- 1 1/2 teaspoons chopped garlic
- 1 cup converted long-grain white rice
- 4 ounces smoked sausage, cut into slices
- 4 ounces cooked ham, cut into bite-size pieces
- 2 (10 ounce) cans diced tomatoes with green chile peppers
- 1 cup chicken broth
- 1/4 teaspoon dried thyme
- 1 bay leaf
- 2 (15 ounce) cans ranch-style beans, undrained

Direction

- Heat oil in a large saucepan over medium heat. Sauté onion, green pepper and celery, until onions are soft and translucent. Stir in garlic, and cook another minute. Add rice, sausage and ham. Cook 2 to 3 minutes, to coat the rice with oil, stirring frequently. Pour in tomatoes with green chiles and chicken broth. Season with thyme and bay leaf. Bring to a boil, then reduce heat. Cover, and simmer 20 to 25 minutes, or until liquid is absorbed. Stir in the beans, mix well and heat through.

Nutrition Information

- Calories: 400 calories
- Total Fat: 12.4 g
- Cholesterol: 23 mg
- Sodium: 1541 mg
- Total Carbohydrate: 53.1 g
- Protein: 17.3 g

186. Texas Lime in the Coconut Muffins

"This recipe was devised when I had a lot of limes on hand. I'm sure you could use any citrus fruit you like. The key is using healthy ingredients! This muffin is a moderately sweet breakfast treat but much healthier than sweet cereal. The coconut oil is very healthy for you, and so is the flaxseed. Never use margarine! Always use non-aluminum baking powder. I use white whole wheat flour, it comes from white wheat instead of red wheat. These are always a hit at my house."

Serving: 10 | Prep: 15 m | Cook: 40 m | Ready in: 55 m

Ingredients

- 1 1/3 cups raw sugar
- 3/4 cup virgin coconut oil
- 1/4 cup grapeseed oil
- 4 eggs
- 4 limes, zested
- 1 1/2 cups whole wheat flour
- 1 1/3 cups all-purpose flour
- 3/4 cup flaked coconut
- 2 tablespoons ground flaxseed
- 1 tablespoon baking powder
- 1/2 teaspoon salt
- 1 cup milk
- 1/4 cup fresh lime juice

Direction

- Preheat oven to 350 degrees F (175 degrees C). Grease 10 Texas-size muffin cups or line with paper muffin liners.
- Whisk sugar, coconut oil, and grapeseed oil together in a bowl. Add eggs and lime zest; whisk until smooth.
- Whisk whole wheat flour, all-purpose flour, flaked coconut, flaxseed, baking powder, and salt together in a bowl. Stir milk and lime juice together in another bowl.
- Whisk milk mixture into sugar mixture. Gently fold flour mixture into sugar mixture until batter is just combined. Spoon batter into prepared muffin cups.
- Bake in the preheated oven until lightly browned and a toothpick inserted in the center comes out clean, about 40 minutes. Transfer muffins to wire racks to cool.

Nutrition Information

- Calories: 488 calories
- Total Fat: 27.4 g
- Cholesterol: 76 mg
- Sodium: 328 mg
- Total Carbohydrate: 56.9 g
- Protein: 8 g

187. Texas Lizzies

"Delicious, festive cookies almost like tiny fruitcakes."

Serving: 60 | Prep: 15 m | Cook: 10 m | Ready in: 30 m

Ingredients

- 2 1/2 cups golden raisins
- 1 1/4 cups raisins
- 1/2 cup whiskey
- 1/2 cup butter, softened
- 1 pound light brown sugar
- 3 eggs
- 3 1/2 cups all-purpose flour
- 1 tablespoon baking soda
- 1 teaspoon ground cinnamon
- 1 teaspoon ground nutmeg
- 2 cups chopped walnuts
- 1 1/2 cups chopped pecans
- 1 pound red and green candied cherries, halved

Direction

- Preheat oven to 350 degrees F (175 degrees C). Prepare cookie sheets by lining with parchment paper. In a medium bowl, toss together the golden raisins and dark raisins with the whiskey; set aside.

- In a large bowl, cream together the sugar and butter. Add the eggs one at a time, mix until light and fluffy. Sift together the flour, baking soda, cinnamon, and nutmeg; stir into the creamed mixture. Stir in the walnuts, pecans, cherries, and finally, the raisin and whiskey mixture.
- Drop cookies by rounded tablespoonfuls onto the prepared baking sheet about 2 inches apart. Bake in the preheated oven for 10 minutes. Cool on the baking sheet for 1 minute before removing to cool on wire racks.

Nutrition Information

- Calories: 165 calories
- Total Fat: 6.4 g
- Cholesterol: 13 mg
- Sodium: 81 mg
- Total Carbohydrate: 25 g
- Protein: 2.1 g

188. Texas Mess

"This is a popular make-night-before appetizer. Serve with tortilla chips."

Serving: 20 | Prep: 20 m | Ready in: 8 h 20 m

Ingredients

- 1 (16 ounce) can refried beans
- 2 tablespoons taco sauce
- salt and ground black pepper to taste
- 2 avocados - peeled, pitted, and mashed
- 1 teaspoon lemon juice
- 1/2 cup sour cream
- 1/2 cup mayonnaise
- 1/2 package taco seasoning mix
- 1 bunch green onions, chopped
- 2 tomatoes, chopped
- 2 cups shredded longhorn Colby cheese

Direction

- Mix refried beans, taco sauce, salt, and pepper together in a bowl; spread onto a large platter.
- Stir mashed avocado and lemon juice together in a bowl; spread over refried beans layer.
- Mix sour cream, mayonnaise, and taco seasoning together in a bowl; spread over avocado layer.
- Sprinkle green onions, tomatoes, and Colby cheese, respectively, over sour cream mixture layer. Cover platter with plastic wrap and refrigerate, 8 hours to overnight.

Nutrition Information

- Calories: 159 calories
- Total Fat: 12.5 g
- Cholesterol: 17 mg
- Sodium: 246 mg
- Total Carbohydrate: 7.9 g
- Protein: 4.9 g

189. Texas New Mexico Chili

"This is a hybrid of two chili recipes and it is wonderful. I serve it with tortilla chips and cheese. Makes great nachos!!"

Serving: 12 | Prep: 15 m | Cook: 1 h | Ready in: 1 h 15 m

Ingredients

- 1 onion, chopped
- 4 cloves garlic, minced
- 1 red bell pepper, chopped
- 1 pound ground beef
- 2 tablespoons ground cumin
- 1 tablespoon chili powder
- 1 teaspoon dried oregano
- 1 bay leaf
- 4 (14.5 ounce) cans chicken broth
- 1 (14.5 ounce) can peeled and diced tomatoes with juice
- 1 (15 ounce) can pinto beans
- 1 (15 ounce) can kidney beans with liquid
- 3 tablespoons cornmeal

Direction

- In a large pot over medium heat, combine the onion, garlic, red bell pepper and ground beef and sauté for 10 minutes, or until meat is browned. Add the cumin, chili powder, oregano and bay leaf and sauté for 2 to 3 more minutes.
- Then add the chicken broth and the tomatoes, mix well and cook for 30 minutes. Add the pinto beans and kidney beans and continue cooking for 10 more minutes. Finally, add the cornmeal, stirring well, until the chili thickens, about 10 to 15 minutes. Remove bay leaf.

Nutrition Information

- Calories: 219 calories
- Total Fat: 11.6 g
- Cholesterol: 32 mg
- Sodium: 667 mg
- Total Carbohydrate: 15.2 g
- Protein: 13.1 g

190. Texas Pecan Candy Cake

"This cake should be made at least two weeks ahead to allow the flavors to blend. Hint: I cheat and use the date pieces coated with sugar (instead of regular pitted dates), just taking off most of the sugar by rubbing them in my hands."

Serving: 14

Ingredients

- 1 1/2 cups red and green candied cherries, quartered
- 1 cup candied pineapple, coarsely chopped
- 1 1/2 cups dates, pitted and chopped
- 1 tablespoon all-purpose flour
- 4 1/3 cups chopped pecans
- 1 1/2 cups flaked coconut
- 1 (14 ounce) can sweetened condensed milk

Direction

- Preheat oven to 250 degrees F (120 degrees C). Grease and flour a 9 inch tube pan with a removable bottom.
- Combine cherries, pineapple, and dates; sprinkle with flour, and toss to coat. Add pecans and coconut; mix thoroughly by tossing. Stir in the sweetened condensed milk, mixing well. Spoon into prepared pan, and smooth the top.
- Bake for 1 1/2 hours. Cool the cake in pan on a wire rack. When completely cool, remove from pan. Wrap in foil tightly. Refrigerate. Cut cake when cold.

Nutrition Information

- Calories: 473 calories
- Total Fat: 29 g
- Cholesterol: 10 mg
- Sodium: 75 mg
- Total Carbohydrate: 53.3 g
- Protein: 6 g

191. Texas Pie

"Quick to make and as big as Texas."

Serving: 18 | Prep: 10 m | Cook: 40 m | Ready in: 50 m

Ingredients

- 1 (21 ounce) can cherry pie filling
- 1 (15 ounce) can crushed pineapple with juice
- 1 (18.25 ounce) package butter cake mix
- 2 1/2 cups flaked coconut
- 1 cup pecan halves
- 1 cup margarine, melted

Direction

- Preheat oven to 325 degrees F (165 degrees C).
- Pour pie filling into 9x13 inch baking dish. Top with pineapple. Do not stir. Sprinkle cake mix over pineapple. Sprinkle coconut over cake mix. Sprinkle nuts over coconut and pour melted margarine over all.
- Bake 40 minutes, until top is golden brown.

Nutrition Information

- Calories: 342 calories
- Total Fat: 19.2 g
- Cholesterol: 0 mg
- Sodium: 331 mg
- Total Carbohydrate: 42.3 g
- Protein: 1.9 g

192. Texas Pork Ribs

"This is a multiple prize-winning master recipe. It has several steps that can be used on pork spareribs, country-style ribs, or pretty much any other type of pork rib; simply adjust oven time up for meatier cuts. Use some soaked wood chips on the barbecue. The smokier the grill, the better the ribs will taste!"

Serving: 12 | Prep: 30 m | Cook: 5 h | Ready in: 13 h 30 m

Ingredients

- 6 pounds pork spareribs
- 1 1/2 cups white sugar
- 1/4 cup salt
- 2 1/2 tablespoons ground black pepper
- 3 tablespoons sweet paprika
- 1 teaspoon cayenne pepper, or to taste
- 2 tablespoons garlic powder
- 5 tablespoons pan drippings
- 1/2 cup chopped onion
- 4 cups ketchup
- 3 cups hot water
- 4 tablespoons brown sugar
- cayenne pepper to taste
- salt and pepper to taste
- 1 cup wood chips, soaked

Direction

- Clean the ribs, and trim away any excess fat. In a medium bowl, stir together the sugar, 1/4 cup salt, ground black pepper, paprika, 1 teaspoon cayenne pepper, and garlic powder. Coat ribs liberally with spice mix. Place the ribs in two 10x15 inch roasting pans, piling two racks of ribs per pan. Cover, and refrigerate for at least 8 hours.
- Preheat oven to 275 degrees F (135 degrees C). Bake uncovered for 3 to 4 hours, or until the ribs are tender and nearly fall apart.
- Remove 5 tablespoons of drippings from the bottom of the roasting pans, and place in a skillet over medium heat. Cook onion in pan drippings until lightly browned and tender. Stir in ketchup, and heat for 3 to 4 more minutes, stirring constantly. Next, mix in water and brown sugar, and season to taste with cayenne pepper, salt, and pepper. Reduce heat to low, cover, and simmer for 1 hour, adding water as necessary to achieve desired thickness.
- Preheat grill for medium-low heat.
- When ready to grill, add soaked wood chips to the coals or to the smoker box of a gas grill. Lightly oil grill grate. Place ribs on the grill two racks at a time so they are not crowded. Cook for 20 minutes, turning occasionally. Baste ribs with sauce during the last 10 minutes of grilling, so the sauce does not burn.

Nutrition Information

- Calories: 614 calories
- Total Fat: 30.9 g
- Cholesterol: 127 mg
- Sodium: 991 mg
- Total Carbohydrate: 53.1 g
- Protein: 33.4 g

193. Texas Praline Cake

"Howdy Ya'll. Ready for some darn good cake? This tasty pecan cake has the subtle flavors of chocolate and coffee, and is frosted with a rich brown sugar whipped cream. This cake prefers Texas pecans!"

Serving: 10 | Prep: 20 m | Cook: 55 m | Ready in: 1 h 30 m

Ingredients

- 1 cup butter or margarine
- 1 cup brown sugar
- 1/2 cup white sugar
- 4 eggs
- 1 1/2 teaspoons vanilla extract
- 1 1/2 cups water
- 1 tablespoon instant coffee granules
- 4 cups all-purpose flour
- 1 tablespoon unsweetened cocoa powder
- 5 teaspoons baking powder
- 1 teaspoon salt
- 1 cup coarsely chopped pecans
- 1 cup heavy cream, chilled
- 1/8 teaspoon salt
- 1/2 teaspoon vanilla extract
- 1/2 cup brown sugar, not packed
- 10 pecan halves (optional)

Direction

- Preheat the oven to 350 degrees F (175 degrees C). Grease just the bottom of a 10 inch tube pan.
- In a large bowl, cream together the butter, 1 cup brown sugar and white sugar until smooth. Beat in the eggs one at a time, mixing well after each. Stir in vanilla. Dissolve the coffee crystals in water, and stir into the creamed mixture until blended. Stir together the flour, cocoa, baking powder and salt; stir into the batter until just incorporated. Fold in pecans. Transfer the batter to the prepared pan.
- Bake for about 55 minutes in the preheated oven, or until a toothpick inserted into the center of the cake comes out clean. Cool cake in pan on a wire rack.
- In a chilled bowl, stir together the heavy cream, salt, vanilla and remaining 1/2 cup brown sugar so that the sugar is dissolved. Whip using chilled beaters until stiff. Run a knife around the outer edge of the cake in the pan, and tap it out onto a serving plate. Make sure cake is completely cool before frosting. Decorate with pecan halves if you like.

Nutrition Information

- Calories: 696 calories
- Total Fat: 38.7 g
- Cholesterol: 156 mg
- Sodium: 619 mg
- Total Carbohydrate: 80.4 g
- Protein: 9.7 g

194. Texas Praline Coffee Cake

"This is a quick and easy coffee cake with a great combination of tastes and textures. Great for breakfast, brunch, dessert or late night snack."

Serving: 12 | Prep: 15 m | Cook: 20 m | Ready in: 35 m

Ingredients

- 2 cups baking mix (such as Bisquick ®)
- 1/2 cup brown sugar
- 3/4 cup chopped pecans
- 2 tablespoons instant coffee granules
- 1 large egg
- 1 cup butter flavored shortening, melted
- 1 teaspoon vanilla extract
- 1 cup buttermilk
- 1/4 cup brown sugar
- 1/4 cup chopped pecans
- 1/4 cup graham cracker crumbs
- 1/4 cup softened butter

Direction

- Preheat an oven to 375 degrees F (190 degrees C). Grease and flour a 10 inch square cake pan.
- Mix baking mix, 1/2 cup brown sugar, 3/4 cup chopped pecans, and the instant coffee granules in a large bowl. Whisk together the

egg, shortening, buttermilk, and vanilla in a separate large bowl. Stir the dry ingredients into the wet ingredients, mixing just until completely moistened.

- Pour batter into prepared pan. Mix remaining 1/4 cup brown sugar, 1/4 cup chopped pecans, and the graham cracker crumbs in a small bowl. Sprinkle topping evenly over batter.
- Bake in preheated oven until a toothpick inserted in the center comes out clean, about 20 to 25 minutes. Immediately dot top of cake with softened butter.

Nutrition Information

- Calories: 416 calories
- Total Fat: 32.5 g
- Cholesterol: 26 mg
- Sodium: 321 mg
- Total Carbohydrate: 29.7 g
- Protein: 3.7 g

195. Texas Pralines

"Chewy Texas pralines we make every year for Christmas! Delicious!"

Serving: 56 | Prep: 10 m | Cook: 20 m | Ready in: 30 m

Ingredients

- nonstick cooking spray
- 2 cups white sugar
- 2 cups light corn syrup
- 1 pound butter
- 2 cups heavy cream
- 2 teaspoons vanilla extract
- 8 cups pecans

Direction

- Line 2 baking sheets with aluminum foil. Coat with nonstick cooking spray.
- In a large saucepan over medium heat, combine sugar and corn syrup. Heat to 250 degrees F (120 degrees C). Remove from heat, and stir in butter until melted. Gradually stir in cream. Return to heat. Cook, stirring constantly, until temperature reaches 242 degrees F (116 degrees C). Remove from heat, and stir in vanilla and pecans.
- Drop by spoonful onto prepared pans. Cool completely, then wrap with plastic.

Nutrition Information

- Calories: 255 calories
- Total Fat: 20.8 g
- Cholesterol: 29 mg
- Sodium: 57 mg
- Total Carbohydrate: 18.5 g
- Protein: 1.7 g

196. Texas Ranch Chicken

"This is a baked chicken recipe I created as a single mother one night when the cupboard seemed bare. The kids love it, and have created their own variations. Variation: In place of dressing and mozzarella cheese, use sour cream and Cheddar cheese - slices or shredded."

Serving: 6 | Prep: 10 m | Cook: 35 m | Ready in: 45 m

Ingredients

- 2 teaspoons olive oil
- 1 1/2 pounds skinless, boneless chicken parts
- 1 1/2 cups Ranch-style salad dressing
- 2 cups shredded mozzarella cheese

Direction

- Preheat oven to 350 degrees F (175 degrees C). Spread the olive oil in a 9x13 inch baking dish.
- Arrange chicken in the dish, and cover with the dressing. It's best to place chicken pieces close together so that the cheese and the dressing do not burn on the bottom of the pan.
- Bake for 20 minutes in the preheated oven. Remove from heat, top with mozzarella cheese, and return to the oven. Continue cooking for about 15 minutes, until the cheese

is melted and lightly browned and the chicken is no longer pink and juices run clear.

Nutrition Information

- Calories: 543 calories
- Total Fat: 45.8 g
- Cholesterol: 103 mg
- Sodium: 863 mg
- Total Carbohydrate: 3.5 g
- Protein: 27.6 g

197. Texas Ranch Potato Salad

"This is not your usual mustard mayo potato salad. These potatoes are slathered in a rich ranch dressing and bacon pieces. My family and friends love this potato salad! It is requested at every cook-out."

Serving: 16 | Prep: 30 m | Cook: 30 m | Ready in: 1 h

Ingredients

- 1 (1 ounce) package ranch dressing mix
- 2 cups mayonnaise
- 3/4 cup chopped green onion
- 1 pound bacon slices
- 5 pounds unpeeled red potatoes

Direction

- Bring a large pot of lightly salted water to a boil. Add whole potatoes, and cook until tender, 15 to 20 minutes. Drain, run under cold water to cool, and chop into 1 inch cubes. Transfer to a large serving bowl, and refrigerate until completely chilled, about 2 hours.
- In a small bowl, stir together the ranch dressing mix, mayonnaise and green onion. Cover, and refrigerate for about 2 hours to blend flavors.
- Wrap bacon in paper towels and place on a plate. Cook in the microwave until crisp, about 15 minutes depending on the power of your microwave. Cool.

- Stir the mayonnaise mixture into the bowl of potatoes. Crumble bacon into the bowl, and stir to distribute. Serve.

Nutrition Information

- Calories: 353 calories
- Total Fat: 25.9 g
- Cholesterol: 21 mg
- Sodium: 503 mg
- Total Carbohydrate: 24.8 g
- Protein: 6.5 g

198. Texas Rice

"It is not known where this recipe originated, but it has been used as a hot dish on outings and potlucks for at least 30 years. Rice and ground beef in tomato sauce, baked under a layer of shredded cheese. A great way to feed several with hamburger, and easy to keep on hand ingredients. Leftovers can be made into quick roll-ups by microwaving in a tortilla."

Serving: 10 | Prep: 30 m | Cook: 30 m | Ready in: 1 h

Ingredients

- 3 cups water
- 2 cups uncooked long grain white rice
- 6 slices bacon
- 1 1/2 pounds ground beef
- 1 onion, chopped
- 1/2 green bell pepper, seeded and chopped
- 1 (28 ounce) can peeled and diced tomatoes
- 1 1/2 teaspoons salt
- 1/4 teaspoon ground black pepper
- 1 1/2 cups shredded Cheddar cheese

Direction

- Combine rice and water in a saucepan, and bring to a boil. Reduce heat, cover and simmer for 20 minutes.
- Place bacon in a large, deep skillet. Cook over medium high heat until evenly brown. Drain, reserving 2 tablespoons of drippings, crumble and set aside. Add ground beef, green pepper,

- and onion to the skillet; cook over medium-high heat until the beef is evenly browned. Drain excess grease, and season with salt and pepper.
- Preheat the oven to 400 degrees F (200 degrees C).
- Place beef and cooked rice into a 9x13 inch baking dish. Stir in the tomatoes, bacon and reserved drippings, mixing until everything is well blended. Spread the shredded cheese over the top.
- Bake for 30 minutes in the preheated oven, until cheese is bubbly, and the center is heated through.

Nutrition Information

- Calories: 391 calories
- Total Fat: 17.4 g
- Cholesterol: 69 mg
- Sodium: 771 mg
- Total Carbohydrate: 33.9 g
- Protein: 22 g

199. Texas Sheet Cake I

"This is an easy and very good potluck cake. Serves several."

Serving: 20 | Prep: 30 m | Cook: 30 m | Ready in: 1 h

Ingredients

- 1 cup butter
- 1 cup water
- 4 tablespoons unsweetened cocoa powder
- 2 cups all-purpose flour
- 2 cups white sugar
- 1/2 teaspoon salt
- 2 eggs
- 1/2 cup sour cream
- 1 teaspoon baking soda
- 1/2 cup butter
- 4 tablespoons unsweetened cocoa powder
- 5 tablespoons milk
- 4 cups confectioners' sugar
- 1 teaspoon vanilla extract
- 1 cup chopped walnuts

Direction

- Preheat oven to 375 degrees F (190 degrees C). Grease a 15x10 inch jelly roll pan.
- Bring 1 cup butter, water and 4 tablespoons cocoa to a boil in a large saucepan. While still hot, remove from heat and add 2 cups flour, 2 cups white sugar, and salt. Mix well. Beat in eggs, sour cream, and baking soda. Do not beat too long.
- Pour batter into greased 15x10 inch jelly roll pan. Bake at 375 degrees F (190 degrees C) for 20 to 25 minutes, or until a toothpick inserted into center of cake comes out clean.
- To Make Icing: Bring 1/2 cup butter or margarine, 4 tablespoons cocoa and 5 tablespoons milk to a boil. Remove from heat. While still hot, add confectioners' sugar vanilla and nuts. Beat well. Ice cake while icing is still hot.

Nutrition Information

- Calories: 404 calories
- Total Fat: 19.8 g
- Cholesterol: 58 mg
- Sodium: 232 mg
- Total Carbohydrate: 55.9 g
- Protein: 3.7 g

200. Texas Sheet Cake V

"I have made this recipe for years. My children always chose it for their birthday cake over any other, and it makes enough for a crowd. Moist and delicious. Very easy to make. Enjoy!"

Serving: 32 | Prep: 10 m | Cook: 20 m | Ready in: 30 m

Ingredients

- 2 cups all-purpose flour
- 2 cups white sugar
- 1 teaspoon baking soda

- 1/2 teaspoon salt
- 1/2 cup sour cream
- 2 eggs
- 1 cup butter
- 1 cup water
- 5 tablespoons unsweetened cocoa powder
- 6 tablespoons milk
- 5 tablespoons unsweetened cocoa powder
- 1/2 cup butter
- 4 cups confectioners' sugar
- 1 teaspoon vanilla extract
- 1 cup chopped walnuts (optional)

Direction

- Preheat oven to 350 degrees F (175 degrees C). Grease and flour a 10x15 inch pan.
- Combine the flour, sugar, baking soda and salt. Beat in the sour cream and eggs. Set aside. Melt the butter on low in a saucepan, add the water and 5 tablespoons cocoa. Bring mixture to a boil then remove from heat. Allow to cool slightly, then stir cocoa mixture into the egg mixture, mixing until blended.
- Pour batter into prepared pan. Bake in the preheated oven for 20 minutes, or until a toothpick inserted into the center comes out clean.
- For the icing: In a large saucepan, combine the milk, 5 tablespoons cocoa and 1/2 cup butter. Bring to a boil, then remove from heat. Stir in the confectioners' sugar and vanilla, then fold in the nuts, mixing until blended. Spread frosting over warm cake.

Nutrition Information

- Calories: 256 calories
- Total Fat: 12.5 g
- Cholesterol: 36 mg
- Sodium: 145 mg
- Total Carbohydrate: 35.8 g
- Protein: 2.4 g

201. Texas Sheet Cake VI

"This chocolate sheet cake is made with coffee and sour cream. Included is a recipe for frosting which should be spread on the cake while it is still very warm. It is VERY rich. My daughter encouraged me to submit the recipe on-line. Hope you like it as much as we do."

Serving: 12 | Prep: 15 m | Cook: 30 m | Ready in: 1 h

Ingredients

- 1 cup hot brewed coffee
- 1 cup butter
- 5 tablespoons unsweetened cocoa powder
- 2 cups all-purpose flour
- 2 cups white sugar
- 1 teaspoon baking soda
- 1/2 teaspoon salt
- 3 eggs
- 1 (8 ounce) container sour cream
- 1 teaspoon vanilla extract
- 1/2 cup butter
- 6 tablespoons milk
- 6 tablespoons unsweetened cocoa powder
- 4 cups confectioners' sugar
- 1 teaspoon vanilla extract
- 1 cup chopped pecans

Direction

- Preheat oven to 350 degrees F (175 degrees C). Grease and flour a 12x18 inch sheet pan. In a saucepan, combine coffee, 1 cup butter and 5 tablespoons cocoa. Bring to a boil, reduce heat and stir until smooth. Remove from heat and set aside.
- In a large bowl, combine flour, white sugar, baking soda and salt. Make a well in the center and pour in eggs, sour cream and 1 teaspoon vanilla. Mix well, then beat in cocoa mixture. Spread into prepared pan.
- Bake in the preheated oven for 20 to 25 minutes, or until a toothpick inserted into the center of the cake comes out clean. Frost while still warm.
- To make the Frosting: In a saucepan, combine 1/2 cup butter, milk and 6 tablespoons cocoa. Bring to a boil, reduce temperature and stir

until smooth. Remove from heat and blend in the confectioners' sugar. Stir in 1 teaspoon vanilla and chopped pecans. Spread on cake while still warm.

Nutrition Information

- Calories: 709 calories
- Total Fat: 35.8 g
- Cholesterol: 116 mg
- Sodium: 398 mg
- Total Carbohydrate: 96.2 g
- Protein: 6.6 g

202. Texas Slaw

"This is a wonderful spicy coleslaw recipe for pot luck or bbq's. I always get asked for this recipe."

Serving: 8 | Prep: 20 m | Ready in: 20 m

Ingredients

- 1 (16 ounce) package coleslaw mix
- 1 (7 ounce) can Mexican-style corn, drained
- 1 cup shredded Cheddar cheese
- 2 fresh jalapeno peppers, seeded and chopped
- 1/2 cup chopped fresh cilantro
- 1 cup Ranch-style salad dressing
- 1/4 teaspoon ground cumin
- 1/4 teaspoon ground coriander
- 1/2 teaspoon garlic powder
- 1 lime, juiced

Direction

- In a large bowl, toss together the coleslaw mix, corn, Cheddar cheese, jalapeno and cilantro. In a separate bowl, stir together the Ranch-style dressing, cumin, coriander, garlic powder and lime juice. Pour over the coleslaw mixture, and toss to coat. Serve right away, or refrigerate until serving.

Nutrition Information

- Calories: 285 calories
- Total Fat: 23 g
- Cholesterol: 31 mg
- Sodium: 495 mg
- Total Carbohydrate: 14.4 g
- Protein: 6.2 g

203. Texas Smoked Barbecue Meatloaf

"It's dishes like this that keep up excited about food. Our love for barbecue could be a cause for worry from outsiders. And we also enjoy a great meatloaf. In fact, meatloaf is the epitome of classic home-cooking for us. Because we're no stranger to barbecuing meatloaf, we started to think about incorporating regional barbecue ingredients into different loaves."

Serving: 8 | Prep: 1 h | Cook: 6 h | Ready in: 7 h

Ingredients

- Brisket Rub:
- 3 tablespoons salt
- 2 teaspoons cayenne pepper
- 2 teaspoons garlic powder
- 1 teaspoon cumin
- 1 teaspoon dried Mexican oregano
- 1 teaspoon dried thyme
- Meatloaf:
- 2 pounds lean ground beef
- 1/2 cup almond flour
- 1 green bell pepper, shredded
- 1/2 yellow onion, shredded
- 1 fresh jalapeno pepper - stemmed, seeded, and minced
- 1 egg, beaten
- 2 cloves garlic, grated
- aluminum foil pan
- 1 tablespoon grapeseed oil, or as needed
- 2 pounds pecan wood chunks, soaked in water
- Apple Spray:
- 1/2 cup unfiltered apple juice
- 2 tablespoons apple cider vinegar
- 1 1/2 tablespoons bourbon whiskey
- 1 1/2 tablespoons water

- 1 tablespoon Worcestershire sauce
- 1 tablespoon fresh lemon juice
- Glaze:
- 1/2 cup water
- 1/3 cup ketchup
- 3 tablespoons apple cider vinegar
- 1 1/2 tablespoons Worcestershire sauce
- 2 teaspoons smoked paprika
- 1 teaspoon dry mustard
- 1 teaspoon fresh lemon juice
- 1/2 teaspoon honey, or to taste
- 1 dash liquid smoke
- 1 pinch ancho chile powder
- 1 pinch red pepper flakes
- 1 pinch ground black pepper

Direction

- Combine salt, cayenne pepper, garlic powder, cumin, Mexican oregano, and thyme in a spice grinder until powdered. Set rub aside.
- Combine beef, almond flour, bell pepper, onion, jalapeno, egg, and garlic in a bowl. Mix lightly with hands until loosely combined. Gently fold in spice rub mixture until distributed throughout.
- Punch holes in the bottom of the aluminum foil pan and coat with grapeseed oil. Form the meat mixture into a loaf and place in the prepared pan. Place in the refrigerator to chill while preparing the smoker.
- Preheat the smoker to 250 degrees F (120 degrees C). Place a water-filled pan under the grate where the meatloaf will be placed. Fill firebox with charcoal and 1 chunk pecan wood.
- Place meatloaf in the hot smoker.
- Combine apple juice, vinegar, bourbon, water, Worcestershire sauce, and lemon juice in a clean, all-purpose spray bottle. Spray the outside of the meatloaf well with apple spray every 30 minutes.
- Refill firebox with charcoal and 1 chunk pecan wood every 45 minutes to maintain temperature; ground meat absorbs smoke very easily, so use only 1 chunk of wood at a time. Smoke meatloaf until internal temperature reaches 130 degrees F (55 degrees C), about 2 hours.
- Combine water, ketchup, vinegar, Worcestershire sauce, paprika, mustard, lemon juice, honey, liquid smoke, ancho chile powder, red pepper flakes, and black pepper in a saucepan over medium-high heat. Bring glaze to a boil and reduce to a simmer. Cook until reduced, about 20 minutes.
- Discontinue apple spray; brush glaze over entire top and sides of meatloaf every 30 minutes. Continue smoking until internal temperature reaches 160 degrees F (71 degrees C), 4 to 5 hours more. Remove meatloaf from smoker and let rest 10 minutes before cutting and serving.

Nutrition Information

- Calories: 333 calories
- Total Fat: 20.6 g
- Cholesterol: 102 mg
- Sodium: 2751 mg
- Total Carbohydrate: 9.3 g
- Protein: 25.4 g

204. Texas Stuffed Grilled Burgers

"A great change to the usual grilled burgers. These burgers are stuffed with ham, cheese, mushrooms, and onions then slow grilled. Grill over hickory or mesquite wood if possible for better flavor! A sure family pleaser!"

Serving: 10 | Prep: 15 m | Cook: 15 m | Ready in: 30 m

Ingredients

- 5 pounds lean ground beef
- 6 tablespoons Worcestershire sauce
- 2 teaspoons hickory seasoning (optional)
- salt and pepper to taste
- 2 cups chopped onion
- 2 cups chopped fresh mushrooms
- 2 cups chopped cooked ham
- 3 cups shredded Cheddar cheese

Direction

- Preheat a grill for high heat. When the grill is hot, lightly oil the grate.
- In a large bowl, mix together the ground beef, Worcestershire sauce, hickory seasoning, salt and pepper until well blended. Make 20 balls, and flatten into patties. On one half of the patties, distribute the onions, mushrooms, ham and cheese. Carefully cover the piles with the remaining patties, making sure to seal all of the edges of the patties together tightly and enclose the filling.
- Grill the patties for 8 to 10 minutes per side, or until meat is well done, and cheese in the center is melted.

Nutrition Information

- Calories: 679 calories
- Total Fat: 47.5 g
- Cholesterol: 188 mg
- Sodium: 969 mg
- Total Carbohydrate: 6.4 g
- Protein: 54 g

205. Texas Stuffed Mushrooms

"These tangy and creamy stuffed mushrooms are a bit messy, but make a great appetizer."

Serving: 8 | Prep: 15 m | Cook: 15 m | Ready in: 30 m

Ingredients

- 1 (8 ounce) package cream cheese, softened
- 2/3 cup barbeque sauce
- 3 tablespoons steak sauce
- 1 (8 ounce) package fresh mushrooms, stems removed
- 1/4 cup bacon bits

Direction

- Preheat oven to 400 degrees F (200 degrees C). Lightly grease a 9x13 inch baking dish.
- In a medium bowl, mix together cream cheese, barbeque sauce and steak sauce.
- Arrange mushroom caps in the baking dish, and stuff each cap with equal portions of the cream cheese mixture. Sprinkle with bacon bits.
- Bake 10 to 15 minutes in the preheated oven, or until lightly browned.

Nutrition Information

- Calories: 151 calories
- Total Fat: 10.7 g
- Cholesterol: 33 mg
- Sodium: 509 mg
- Total Carbohydrate: 10 g
- Protein: 4.6 g

206. Texas Style Chicken Tequila

"This dish is colorful and the ingredients prepared ahead of time. Your family and friends will love this recipe! Note: the most time consuming part of this recipe is making the paste for the sauce (it gives an unique flavor and is worth the effort). The paste can be made ahead of time and stored in the fridge. Bring to room temperature before adding to the sauce. Serve with your favorite noodles (1b of dry) or with mashed potatoes (5 medium.)"

Serving: 6 | Prep: 10 m | Cook: 40 m | Ready in: 50 m

Ingredients

- 3 tablespoons unsalted butter, divided
- 2 tablespoons chopped garlic
- 2 tablespoons finely chopped jalapeno pepper
- 1/2 cup chicken stock
- 1/4 cup tequila
- 3 tablespoons lime juice
- 3 tablespoons soy sauce
- 4 skinless, boneless chicken breast halves - cut into cubes
- 1 tablespoon cooking oil
- 1/4 medium onion, thinly sliced
- 1/2 medium red bell pepper, thinly sliced
- 1 medium green bell pepper, thinly sliced

- 1 1/2 cups heavy cream
- 1/4 cup chopped fresh cilantro
- 1/3 cup freshly grated Romano cheese

Direction

- Heat 2 tablespoons of butter in a small saucepan over medium heat. Add garlic and jalapeno, and sauté until soft. Pour in chicken stock, tequila, and lime juice. Bring to a boil, then lower the heat and simmer until the mixture is reduced to a paste, about 15 minutes. Stir occasionally to make sure it is not sticking.
- While the sauce is cooking, place the chicken in a bowl, and pour soy sauce over it. Melt remaining butter in a skillet, and sauté the onion, red bell pepper and green bell pepper until soft. Remove vegetables, and set aside.
- Add oil to the skillet, and cook the chicken over medium-high heat until lightly browned. Pour in the sauce and heavy cream, and add the peppers. Bring to a boil, and simmer until chicken is cooked through, about 5 minutes. Remove from heat, and stir in Romano cheese and cilantro. Taste and adjust seasonings if desired. Serve immediately.

Nutrition Information

- Calories: 430 calories
- Total Fat: 32.9 g
- Cholesterol: 149 mg
- Sodium: 608 mg
- Total Carbohydrate: 6.2 g
- Protein: 22.6 g

207. Texas Taco Soup

"A quick and easy meal in the cold weather if you have a house full of kids. Once done, it can be left on the stove on simmer so those still hungry can graze from time to time. Serve with cornbread."

Serving: 10 | Prep: 5 m | Cook: 1 h | Ready in: 1 h 5 m

Ingredients

- 3 pounds ground beef
- 2 onions, chopped
- 2 (15 ounce) cans pinto beans
- 2 (16 ounce) packages frozen corn kernels
- 3 (10 ounce) cans diced tomatoes with green chile peppers
- 6 serrano peppers, crushed
- 1 (1.25 ounce) package taco seasoning mix
- 1 (1 ounce) package ranch dressing mix

Direction

- In a large pot over medium heat, cook beef until brown. Stir in onion and cook a few minutes more. Drain.
- Stir in pinto beans, corn, diced tomatoes with green chiles, serrano peppers, taco seasoning and ranch dressing mix. Fill the pot with water to come within two inches of the top. Bring to a boil for 30 minutes, stirring occasionally, then reduce heat and simmer 30 minutes more.

Nutrition Information

- Calories: 605 calories
- Total Fat: 20.9 g
- Cholesterol: 82 mg
- Sodium: 885 mg
- Total Carbohydrate: 67.8 g
- Protein: 40 g

208. Texas Tea III

"The Texas part of the tea comes from the tequila as opposed to a Long Island iced tea, which uses gin instead of tequila. This is the standard Bartender's recipe for a Texas Tea."

Serving: 1 | Prep: 1 m | Ready in: 1 m

Ingredients

- 1/2 fluid ounce vodka
- 1/2 fluid ounce amber rum
- 1/2 fluid ounce gold tequila
- 1/2 fluid ounce triple sec liqueur
- 1/4 cup sweet-and-sour cocktail mix
- 1/4 cup cola-flavored carbonated beverage
- 1 wedge lemon
- 1 wedge lime

Direction

- In a tall glass filled with ice, combine vodka, rum, tequila and triple sec. Top with equal parts sweet-and-sour and cola. Squeeze juice of lemon wedge and lime wedge over top; stir.

209. Texas Tomatillo Avocado Sauce

*"Uniquely delicious. A must-have for any party, luncheon, dinner, or snack!
A mean green creamy, delectable sauce! Great for dipping or on your favorite tacos or fajitas."*

Serving: 8 | Prep: 15 m | Cook: 15 m | Ready in: 4 h 30 m

Ingredients

- 1 pound tomatillos, husked
- 4 avocados, halved and pitted
- 1 (8 ounce) container sour cream
- 1 jalapeno pepper
- 2 tablespoons lime juice
- 4 cloves garlic
- 3 sprigs fresh cilantro
- 1 tablespoon red fajita seasoning
- 1 teaspoon Mediterranean sea salt

Direction

- Place tomatillos into a large pot and cover with water; bring to a boil. Reduce heat to medium-low and simmer until tender, about 10 minutes. Drain.
- Transfer tomatillos to a blender. Add avocados, sour cream, jalapeno pepper, lime juice, garlic, cilantro, fajita seasoning, and sea salt; blend until smooth.
- Refrigerate blended sauce until flavors meld, at least 4 hours.

Nutrition Information

- Calories: 246 calories
- Total Fat: 21.3 g
- Cholesterol: 12 mg
- Sodium: 296 mg
- Total Carbohydrate: 14.6 g
- Protein: 3.6 g

210. Texas Tornado Cake

"This recipe is quick and easy, and can be made with ingredients at hand. Serve it to those guests who strike unexpectedly."

Serving: 18

Ingredients

- 1 1/2 cups white sugar
- 2 eggs
- 2 cups fruit cocktail
- 2 teaspoons baking soda
- 2 cups all-purpose flour
- 1/4 cup packed brown sugar
- 1 cup chopped walnuts

Direction

- Grease and flour a 9 x 13 inch cake pan. Preheat oven to 325 degrees F (165 degrees C).

- Mix together sugar, eggs, fruit cocktail, soda, and flour. Pour batter into prepared pan.
- Mix the brown sugar and nuts together, and sprinkle mixture onto the batter.
- Bake for 40 minutes, or until done.

Nutrition Information

- Calories: 203 calories
- Total Fat: 4.9 g
- Cholesterol: 21 mg
- Sodium: 151 mg
- Total Carbohydrate: 37.8 g
- Protein: 3.2 g

211. Texas Wild Pork Roast for Two

"This recipe makes the toughest pig easy to handle with the added benefit of being healthy. Naturally low fat, this is also low sodium and easy to do in the slow cooker. Just use your favorite Texas beer to keep it authentic."

Serving: 2 | Prep: 20 m | Cook: 3 h 30 m | Ready in: 3 h 50 m

Ingredients

- 1 (1 1/2-pound) boneless pork loin roast
- 8 baby bella mushrooms
- 1/2 cup lemon juice
- 1/2 sweet onion, sliced
- 6 cloves garlic, minced, or more to taste
- salt and ground black pepper to taste
- 1 (12 fluid ounce) can or bottle dark beer

Direction

- Combine pork loin, mushrooms, lemon juice, onion, garlic, salt, and black pepper in a slow cooker. Pour beer on top.
- Cook on Low until pork is tender and an instant-read thermometer inserted into the center reads at least 145 degrees F (63 degrees C), 3 1/2 to 4 hours.

Nutrition Information

- Calories: 555 calories
- Total Fat: 18.7 g
- Cholesterol: 159 mg
- Sodium: 193 mg
- Total Carbohydrate: 22.2 g
- Protein: 62 g

212. Texas Yum Yum

"This chocolate and vanilla layered pudding pie is a perfect treat for a hot day. No baking required, and it is really easy too."

Serving: 6 | Prep: 15 m | Ready in: 45 m

Ingredients

- 1 (3.9 ounce) package instant chocolate pudding mix
- 1 1/2 cups milk
- 1 (9 inch) prepared graham cracker crust
- 1 (8 ounce) package cream cheese, softened
- 1 cup confectioners' sugar
- 1 (8 ounce) tub frozen whipped topping, thawed
- 1 (3.4 ounce) package instant vanilla pudding mix
- 1 1/2 cups milk

Direction

- In a medium bowl, mix together the chocolate pudding mix and 1 1/2 cups of milk until smooth and well blended. Pour into the graham cracker crust.
- In a clean bowl, beat cream cheese with an electric mixer until soft, then mix in confectioners' sugar. Fold in 2 cups of the whipped topping, and spread on top of the chocolate pudding layer.
- Whisk together the vanilla pudding mix and 1 1/2 cups of milk until well blended. Spread over the top of the cream cheese layer. Spread the remaining whipped topping over the top. Chill for at least 30 minutes before slicing and serving.

Nutrition Information

- Calories: 717 calories
- Total Fat: 35.4 g
- Cholesterol: 51 mg
- Sodium: 886 mg
- Total Carbohydrate: 93 g
- Protein: 9.4 g

213. TexasStyle Baked Beans

"Not your usual baked beans! Green chiles and hot pepper sauce give zest to these eat-'em up sweet-and-hot baked beans."

Serving: 12 | Prep: 15 m | Cook: 2 h | Ready in: 2 h 15 m

Ingredients

- 1 pound ground beef
- 4 (16 ounce) cans baked beans with pork
- 1 (4 ounce) can canned chopped green chile peppers
- 1 small Vidalia onion, peeled and chopped
- 1 cup barbeque sauce
- 1/2 cup brown sugar
- 1 tablespoon garlic powder
- 1 tablespoon chili powder
- 3 tablespoons hot pepper sauce (e.g. Tabasco™), or to taste

Direction

- In a skillet over medium heat, brown the ground beef until no longer pink; drain fat, and set aside.
- In a 3 1/2 quart or larger slow cooker, combine the ground beef, baked beans, green chiles, onion and barbeque sauce. Season with brown sugar, garlic powder, chili powder and hot pepper sauce. Cook on HIGH for 2 hours, or low for 4 to 5 hours.

Nutrition Information

- Calories: 360 calories
- Total Fat: 12.4 g

- Cholesterol: 43 mg
- Sodium: 899 mg
- Total Carbohydrate: 50 g
- Protein: 14.6 g

214. TexasStyle Chili Rice

"You won't be the lone star in the kitchen with this flavorful one skillet Texas-style chili."

Serving: 4 | Prep: 10 m | Cook: 20 m | Ready in: 30 m

Ingredients

- 2 teaspoons olive oil
- 1 pound flank steak, cut into 1/2-inch cubes
- 1 large onion, chopped
- 3 large cloves garlic, finely chopped
- 1 1/2 teaspoons chili powder
- 1 teaspoon ground cumin
- 1 1/2 cups water
- 1 (15 ounce) can no-salt-added tomato sauce
- 1 (5.5 ounce) package Knorr® Rice Sides™ - Beef flavor

Direction

- Season steak with salt and pepper if desired. Heat oil in large deep nonstick skillet over medium-high heat and cook steak and onions, stirring occasionally, until steak is browned and onions are tender, about 5 minutes.
- Stir in garlic, chili powder and ground cumin and cook, stirring, until fragrant, about 30 seconds. Add water and tomato sauce and bring to a boil over medium-high heat.
- Stir in Knorr(R) Rice Sides(TM) - Beef flavor; reduce heat and simmer covered, stirring occasionally, until rice is tender, about 7 minutes. Serve, if desired, with sour cream and chopped red onion.

Nutrition Information

- Calories: 411 calories
- Total Fat: 13 g
- Cholesterol: 47 mg

- Sodium: 614 mg
- Total Carbohydrate: 43.5 g
- Protein: 30.1 g

215. Texatini

"A unique way to make a margarita. Be careful! These are known to be potent!"

Serving: 1 | Prep: 15 m | Ready in: 15 m

Ingredients

- coarse salt (optional)
- 1 (1.5 fluid ounce) jigger tequila
- 1 (1.5 fluid ounce) jigger orange liqueur (Cointreau, Triple Sec or Grand Marnier)
- 1/2 cup sweet and sour mix
- 1 fluid ounce orange juice
- 1 cup crushed ice
- 1 jalapeno-stuffed green olive

Direction

- Slightly moisten rim of a large martini glass, and dip in course salt to rim the glass.
- Combine tequila, orange liqueur, sweet and sour mix, orange juice, and ice in a shaker. Shake vigorously, and strain into martini glass. Garnish with jalapeno-stuffed green olives.

216. Texified Black Beans and Brown Rice

"Made this up in my kitchen and even my meat loving husband enjoyed this and went back for more!"

Serving: 2 | Prep: 15 m | Cook: 15 m | Ready in: 30 m

Ingredients

- 1 tablespoon olive oil
- 1 onion, diced
- 1/2 cup diced red bell pepper
- 1 tomato, diced, divided
- 2 cloves garlic, minced
- 1/2 teaspoon ground cumin
- 1 (15 ounce) can black beans, rinsed and drained
- 1/2 cup water
- 1 teaspoon salt
- 1/2 teaspoon chili powder
- 1/2 teaspoon paprika
- 1/4 teaspoon ground black pepper
- 2 tablespoons minced fresh cilantro
- 1 cup cooked brown rice, or more to taste

Direction

- Heat olive oil in a 2-quart saucepan over medium heat; cook and stir onion, red bell pepper, 1/2 of the tomato, and garlic until onion is translucent, 5 to 10 minutes. Mix black beans, water, salt, chili powder, paprika, and black pepper into onion mixture; simmer until heated through, about 10 minutes.
- Remove saucepan from heat and stir cilantro and remaining tomatoes into bean mixture; serve over brown rice.

Nutrition Information

- Calories: 418 calories
- Total Fat: 8.8 g
- Cholesterol: 0 mg
- Sodium: 1998 mg
- Total Carbohydrate: 70.1 g
- Protein: 17.1 g

217. TexMex Beef and Cheese Enchiladas

"Cheese filled tortillas are covered with a spicy meat sauce and cheese before baking. Growing up all my life in South Texas, this dish was a staple!"

Serving: 6 | Prep: 30 m | Cook: 20 m | Ready in: 50 m

Ingredients

- 2 pounds ground beef
- 3 tablespoons chili powder
- 2 tablespoons paprika
- 1 tablespoon ground cumin
- 1 tablespoon garlic powder
- 1 teaspoon salt
- 1 (8 ounce) can tomato sauce
- 4 cups water
- 1/2 cup all-purpose flour, divided
- 1 1/2 teaspoons sugar
- 2 tablespoons cooking oil
- 12 (6 inch) corn tortillas
- 4 cups shredded American cheese

Direction

- Preheat the oven to 350 degrees F (175 degrees C).
- Heat the ground beef in a large skillet over medium heat. Cook, stirring to crumble, until no longer pink. Drain off grease and season with chili powder, paprika, cumin, garlic powder, and salt. Mix in the tomato sauce and 2 cups of the water. Simmer over low heat. Mix the remaining water with the flour and sugar until flour is dissolved; stir into the simmering meat sauce. Simmer until thickened, about 10 minutes.
- While the sauce is cooking, heat oil in another skillet over medium-high heat. Warm tortillas in the hot oil until pliable. Fill each tortilla with a little bit of cheese, and place in a 9x13 inch baking dish, reserving some of the cheese to sprinkle on top. Pour the meat sauce evenly over the rolled tortillas. Top with remaining cheese.
- Bake for 25 minutes in the preheated oven, until cheese is melted and lightly browned.

Nutrition Information

- Calories: 794 calories
- Total Fat: 49.1 g
- Cholesterol: 172 mg
- Sodium: 1915 mg
- Total Carbohydrate: 40.4 g
- Protein: 47.1 g

218. TexMex Beef Bowl with Avocado Cilantro Dressing

"Wow your Big Game guests with these individual-sized Tex-Mex BBQ Beef Bowls served with an avocado cilantro dressing. The below recipe is for two people but the recipe can be easily doubled or tripled."

Serving: 2 | Prep: 30 m | Cook: 8 m | Ready in: 48 m

Ingredients

- Dry Rub:
- 1/2 teaspoon garlic powder
- 1/2 teaspoon chili powder
- 1/2 teaspoon kosher salt
- 1/4 teaspoon sweet paprika
- 1/4 teaspoon ground cumin
- Bowl Ingredients:
- 1/2 pound flank steak
- 1 cup cooked white rice
- 1 cup halved cherry tomatoes
- 1 cup chopped romaine lettuce
- 1 cup tortilla chips
- 1/2 cup canned black beans
- 1 jalapeno pepper, thinly sliced
- 1 lime, cut into wedges
- 1/4 cup crumbled cotija cheese
- 1 tablespoon chopped fresh cilantro
- Avocado Cilantro Dressing:
- 2 avocados, peeled and pitted
- 1 cup water
- 1/2 cup chopped fresh cilantro
- 2 tablespoons sour cream
- 1 lime, juiced
- 1 clove garlic

- 1 pinch salt

Direction

- Preheat a grill pan or skillet over medium-high heat until just barely smoking.
- Combine garlic powder, chili powder, kosher salt, paprika, and cumin in a bowl; rub over all sides of flank steak.
- Grill flank steak in the preheated grill pan, flipping halfway through, until browned and cooked to desired doneness, about 8 minutes. Let steak rest on a work surface for 10 minutes. Thinly slice steak against the grain.
- Divide rice, tomatoes, romaine lettuce, tortilla chips, black beans, jalapeno peppers, and lime wedges between 2 serving bowls; top with steak, cotija cheese, and 1 tablespoon cilantro.
- Combine avocados, water, 1/2 cup cilantro, sour cream, lime juice, garlic, and salt in a blender; blend until dressing is smooth. Pour dressing over each bowl.

Nutrition Information

- Calories: 465 calories
- Total Fat: 16.8 g
- Cholesterol: 49 mg
- Sodium: 1091 mg
- Total Carbohydrate: 55.6 g
- Protein: 26.5 g

219. TexMex Burger with Cajun Mayo

"A jazzy way to spice up the boring basic burger that will tantalize your taste buds! Cajun spiced mayonnaise is the perfect complement to these spicy beef burgers."

Serving: 4 | Prep: 25 m | Cook: 15 m | Ready in: 40 m

Ingredients

- 1/2 cup mayonnaise
- 1 teaspoon Cajun seasoning
- 1 1/3 pounds ground beef sirloin
- 1 jalapeno pepper, seeded and chopped
- 1/2 cup diced white onion
- 1 clove garlic, minced
- 1 tablespoon Cajun seasoning
- 1 teaspoon Worcestershire sauce
- 4 slices pepperjack cheese
- 4 hamburger buns, split
- 4 leaves lettuce
- 4 slices tomato

Direction

- Preheat grill for medium-high heat. In a small bowl, mix together the mayonnaise and 1 teaspoon of Cajun seasoning. Set aside.
- In a large bowl, mix together the ground sirloin, jalapeno pepper, onion, garlic, 1 tablespoon Cajun seasoning, and Worcestershire sauce using your hands. Divide into 4 balls, and flatten into patties.
- Lightly oil the grilling surface, and place the patties on the grill. Cook for about 5 minutes per side, or until well done. During the last 2 minutes, lay a slice of cheese on top of each patty. Spread the seasoned mayonnaise onto the insides of the buns. Put burgers in the buns, and top with lettuce and tomato to serve.

Nutrition Information

- Calories: 714 calories
- Total Fat: 49.1 g
- Cholesterol: 132 mg
- Sodium: 1140 mg
- Total Carbohydrate: 28.5 g
- Protein: 38.3 g

220. TexMex Chicken Tamale Pie

"Indigenous people in Mexico make a version of this delicious pie with meat, chile peppers, and tomatoes, which is wrapped in a masa dough and foil and cooked over a campfire. This sumptuous cheese-topped pie might be considered the Tex-Mex version! It takes a lot of prep time but prep can be done a day ahead and the results are well worth the effort."

Serving: 10 | Prep: 40 m | Cook: 3 h 15 m | Ready in: 4 h

Ingredients

- 6 pounds bone-in chicken breasts
- water to cover
- 1 (15 ounce) can crushed tomatoes
- 1 onion, quartered
- 4 tomatillos - stemmed, husked, and halved (optional)
- 3 cloves garlic, peeled
- 4 New Mexico dried red chile pods, stemmed and seeded
- 1 teaspoon salt
- 1 teaspoon ground cumin
- 1/2 teaspoon dried oregano
- 1/2 cup lard
- 1 cup masa harina
- 1 (12 ounce) bag shredded Cheddar and Monterey Jack cheese blend

Direction

- Preheat oven to 350 degrees F (175 degrees C).
- Place chicken breasts in baking pans and cover with aluminum foil.
- Bake chicken in the preheated oven until tender and cooked through, 1 1/4 to 1 1/2 hour. An instant-read thermometer inserted near the bone should read 165 degrees F (74 degrees C). Cool until easily handled. Remove skin and discard. Bone chicken and chop into 1/2-inch pieces.
- Combine bones with drippings from baking pans in a large pot; add enough water to cover. Bring to a boil and simmer for 1 hour. Strain broth and discard bones.
- Place tomatoes, onion, tomatillos, garlic, and red chile pods in a blender or food processor; puree until chile pods are reduced to small flecks. Pour into a pot.
- Mix 1 cup chicken broth, salt, cumin, and oregano into pureed mixture in the pot. Bring to a boil; reduce heat and simmer, about 5 minutes. Stir in chicken. Remove from heat.
- Microwave 1 cup chicken broth and lard together in a microwave-safe bowl until lard is just melted, about 2 minutes. Mix in masa harina with your hands to make a smooth paste.
- Press paste evenly into the bottom of a 10x13-inch baking pan. Spread chicken mixture on top. Cover with aluminum foil.
- Bake in the preheated oven until chicken is heated through, about 40 minutes. Sprinkle shredded Cheddar and Monterey Jack cheese blend on top. Continue baking until cheese is melted and starting to bubble, 3 to 5 minutes. Let stand before serving, about 5 minutes.

Nutrition Information

- Calories: 593 calories
- Total Fat: 28.4 g
- Cholesterol: 198 mg
- Sodium: 691 mg
- Total Carbohydrate: 15.6 g
- Protein: 66.4 g

221. TexMex Eggs Benedict with Grilled Potato Slabs and AvocadoLime Hollandaise

"This Tex-Mex Eggs Benedict with Grilled Potato Slabs and Avocado-Lime Hollandaise recipe is courtesy of Edible Perspective, a part of the U.S. Potato Board's Potato Lovers Club Program."

Serving: 2 | Prep: 30 m | Cook: 1 h | Ready in: 1 h 30 m

Ingredients

- Avocado-Lime Hollandaise:
- 1 ripe avocado, pitted, peeled
- 1/4 cup fresh lime juice, or more to taste
- 3 tablespoons extra-virgin olive oil

- 2 tablespoons water
- Salt to taste
- Eggs Benedict:
- 2 large russet potatoes
- 2 teaspoons extra-virgin olive oil
- Salt and black pepper to taste
- 4 large eggs
- 1/2 cup thinly sliced red onion
- 1 teaspoon minced garlic
- 1/2 teaspoon ground cumin
- 1/2 teaspoon chili powder
- 1/2 large bell pepper, thinly sliced
- 1/2 cup corn kernels, fresh or frozen (thawed)
- 1/2 cup drained canned black beans
- 2 teaspoons adobo sauce from chipotle peppers

Direction

- Place hollandaise ingredients (avocado, lime juice, 3 tablespoons olive oil, water) in your blender and turn on until smooth. Scrape the sides as needed. Add salt to taste. The sauce should be thick and creamy, but if needed add a bit more lime juice, oil, and/or water to get it moving more. Refrigerate until ready to use.
- Preheat your grill to 375 degrees F. Slice the potatoes lengthwise into 1/3-inch-thick slabs. Drizzle with 2 teaspoons olive oil and rub over both sides. Generously top with salt and pepper. Place on the grill for about 12-15 minutes. Flip and continue to grill until fork tender, about 15 minutes. If your potatoes finish before you're done cooking the vegetables, turn the heat off on the grill with the lid shut and leave them there to stay warm until you're ready.
- My egg poaching method: While the potatoes grill, place about 4 inches of water in a large pot. Heat over high with the lid on until the water simmers. Uncover and reduce heat so the water is just barely simmering a few small bubbles. Maintain this heat throughout the poaching process. Place 2 paper towels on a large plate. Crack 1 egg in a small bowl. Gently swirl your water with a spatula in one direction and slowly pour the egg into the center of the pot. Gently swirl the water a few times around the egg then let it be for 4 minutes. Carefully remove with a slotted spoon and drain on the paper towels; repeat for each egg, using the same water.
- Heat a pan over medium with a drizzle of oil. Place the onion in the pan with a good pinch of salt and let it cook, stirring every minute or so, for about 8 minutes. Add the garlic, cumin, and chili powder and cook for another minute. Return the pot of water to just below a simmer. Add the bell pepper to the pan and cook for another 3-4 minutes, stirring once in a while, until just starting to soften. Add the corn and black beans and cook until hot. Stir in the adobo sauce and turn to low.
- Place all eggs gently back in the warm water and let them reheat for no longer than 1 minute. Place potato slabs on 2 plates with the veggie mixture over top. Remove eggs with a slotted spoon or place on the paper towel to drain the water and then place them on top of the veggie mixture (2 for each serving). Top with the avocado hollandaise, salt, pepper, and hot sauce if desired. Serve immediately.

Nutrition Information

- Calories: 936 calories
- Total Fat: 51 g
- Cholesterol: 372 mg
- Sodium: 595 mg
- Total Carbohydrate: 99.8 g
- Protein: 28 g

222. TexMex Enchiladas

"These are authentic Tex-Mex enchiladas as taught to me by a lady originally from Chihuahua, Mexico who then added a bit of Texas. They are super easy to put together and taste incredible! Watch out though, because there is nothing low-fat about them! I like to assemble these enchiladas in the morning or night before, come home and pop them in the oven. When cold, add 10 more minutes to the baking time. Leave out the onions for picky eaters. "

Serving: 5 | Prep: 15 m | Cook: 30 m | Ready in: 45 m

Ingredients

- 2 (11.25 ounce) cans chili without beans
- 1 cup enchilada sauce
- 1/2 cup vegetable oil
- 1 tablespoon chili powder
- 15 corn tortillas
- 1 pound shredded Cheddar cheese
- 1 onion, chopped

Direction

- Preheat an oven to 350 degrees F (175 degrees C).
- Mix the chili and enchilada sauce together in a small saucepan over medium-low heat, stirring occasionally as it simmers.
- Heat the vegetable oil and chili powder together in a small skillet over medium heat. Gently lay a tortilla in the hot oil and cook until the tortilla starts to puff. Remove with a spatula and place on a plate. Immediately sprinkle about 1/4 cup Cheddar cheese and 1 tablespoon chopped onion down the center of the tortilla; roll the tortilla tightly around the mixture and place, seam-side down, into the bottom of a 9x13-inch baking dish. Repeat this process until all the tortillas are used.
- Sprinkle about 2/3 of the remaining Cheddar cheese over the rolled enchiladas. Pour the warm chili mixture evenly over the enchiladas. Scatter the remaining Cheddar cheese over the layer of the chili mixture.
- Bake in the preheated oven until the top is bubbling, 20 to 25 minutes.

Nutrition Information

- Calories: 933 calories
- Total Fat: 59 g
- Cholesterol: 108 mg
- Sodium: 1776 mg
- Total Carbohydrate: 69.1 g
- Protein: 35.1 g

223. TexMex Macaroni and Cheese

"A quick and easy meal that tastes good and is a nice change from ordinary macaroni and cheese. Add cooked peas and grated Parmesan cheese on top if desired."

Serving: 6 | Prep: 10 m | Cook: 20 m | Ready in: 30 m

Ingredients

- 1 pound lean ground beef
- 1 (1.25 ounce) package taco seasoning mix
- 1 (7.3 ounce) package white Cheddar macaroni and cheese mix
- 2 tablespoons butter, or as needed
- 1/4 cup milk, or as needed

Direction

- In a large skillet, brown beef and drain off excess fat. Add taco seasoning and water according to seasoning package directions and simmer for 10 minutes or until liquid is absorbed. Set aside.
- Prepare macaroni and cheese according to package directions, adding butter or margarine and milk as indicated. Combine beef mixture and macaroni and cheese. Mix together and serve.

Nutrition Information

- Calories: 384 calories
- Total Fat: 21.1 g
- Cholesterol: 73 mg
- Sodium: 784 mg
- Total Carbohydrate: 27.1 g
- Protein: 19 g

224. TexMex Migas

"A favorite for breakfast or brunch in central Texas."

Serving: 6 | Prep: 10 m | Cook: 10 m | Ready in: 20 m

Ingredients

- 1 tablespoon butter
- 1 (4 ounce) can chopped green chiles
- 1/2 tomato, chopped
- 6 large eggs
- 1/4 cup crushed tortilla chips, or to taste
- 1/4 cup shredded sharp Cheddar cheese
- 6 (8 inch) flour tortillas
- 6 tablespoons taco sauce, or to taste (optional)

Direction

- Melt butter in a large skillet over medium heat; cook and stir green chiles and tomato in the melted butter until tomato is softened, about 5 minutes. Crack eggs directly into the skillet and stir until yolks break; cook until eggs are scrambled and slightly set, 2 to 3 minutes.
- Sprinkle tortilla chips over eggs; mix chips into eggs. Move egg mixture to the side of the skillet, turn off heat, and sprinkle egg mixture with Cheddar cheese. Cover skillet and set aside until cheese is melted and eggs are cooked through, about 5 minutes.
- Stack flour tortillas on a microwave-safe plate; microwave until tortillas are warmed, about 30 seconds.
- Spoon egg mixture onto each tortilla and top with about 1 tablespoon taco sauce.

Nutrition Information

- Calories: 283 calories
- Total Fat: 12.2 g
- Cholesterol: 196 mg
- Sodium: 661 mg
- Total Carbohydrate: 30.8 g
- Protein: 12.1 g

225. TexMex Pasta Salad

"I first made this for my husband to take for a guy's skiing weekend. He didn't want a 'girlie' pasta salad, so this one has taco beef and cheese. Very hearty, and a big hit with all the guys. I have since brought it to a family reunion....now they request it every year!"

Serving: 10 | Prep: 15 m | Cook: 20 m | Ready in: 1 h 35 m

Ingredients

- 2 tablespoons olive oil
- 1 teaspoon salt
- 1 (16 ounce) package fusilli pasta
- 2 pounds extra lean ground beef
- 1 (1.25 ounce) package taco seasoning mix
- 1 (24 ounce) jar mild salsa
- 1 (8 ounce) bottle ranch dressing
- 1 1/2 red bell peppers, chopped
- 6 green onions, chopped
- 3/4 cup chopped pickled jalapeno peppers
- 1 (2.25 ounce) can sliced black olives (optional)
- 1 (8 ounce) package shredded Cheddar cheese

Direction

- Fill a large pot with water; pour in the olive oil and salt. Bring to a rolling boil over high heat. Stir in the fusilli, and return to a boil. Cook the pasta uncovered, stirring occasionally, until the pasta has cooked through, but is still firm to the bite, about 9 minutes. Drain and set aside.
- Heat a large skillet over medium-high heat and stir in the ground beef. Cook and stir until the beef is crumbly, evenly browned, and no longer pink. Drain and discard any excess grease. Mix in taco seasoning mix, remove from heat, and cool completely.
- Combine salsa, ranch dressing, bell peppers, green onions, jalapenos, and black olives in a medium bowl. Toss together the cooked pasta, cooled beef mixture, Cheddar cheese, and

dressing mixture in a large bowl. Cover and refrigerate at least 1 hour before serving.

Nutrition Information

- Calories: 597 calories
- Total Fat: 34 g
- Cholesterol: 85 mg
- Sodium: 1541 mg
- Total Carbohydrate: 43.2 g
- Protein: 29.9 g

226. TexMex Patty Melts

"I saw similar burgers made on television for a sports event. I didn't have buns, so I made patty melts instead. I will never make this in plain burger form again!"

Serving: 3 | Prep: 15 m | Cook: 10 m | Ready in: 25 m

Ingredients

- 1 pound ground beef
- 3 tablespoons chili seasoning mix
- 2 chipotle peppers in adobo sauce, minced
- 1/2 fluid ounce beer
- 1/4 cup mayonnaise
- 1 chipotle pepper in adobo sauce, minced
- 6 (1 ounce) slices white bread
- 6 (1/2 ounce) slices pepperjack cheese

Direction

- Mix together the ground beef, chili seasoning mix, 2 minced chipotle peppers with adobo sauce, and the beer in a bowl. Divide the mixture evenly into three patties.
- Stir together the mayonnaise and 1 minced chipotle pepper with adobo sauce in a small bowl. Divide the mixture between the bread slices and spread evenly. Place a slice of pepperjack cheese on top of the mayonnaise mixture on each slice of bread.
- Heat a large skillet over medium-high heat. Cook the patties in the skillet until no longer pink in the center, 5 to 7 minutes each side for well done. Remove each burger to a slice of bread, sandwiching them with the remaining slices.
- Drain the skillet, reserving 2 tablespoons of the grease. Heat the reserved grease in the skillet over medium-high heat. Grill the sandwiches in the skillet until the bread is golden brown and the cheese is melted, 1 to 2 minutes per side.

Nutrition Information

- Calories: 691 calories
- Total Fat: 44.2 g
- Cholesterol: 129 mg
- Sodium: 1574 mg
- Total Carbohydrate: 35.4 g
- Protein: 37.3 g

227. TexMex Pork

"Mexican style shredded pork. Serve rolled up in tortillas, taco shells or on burger buns with shredded lettuce, diced red onion and sour cream."

Serving: 8 | Prep: 20 m | Cook: 10 h | Ready in: 10 h 20 m

Ingredients

- 1 (8 ounce) can tomato sauce
- 1 cup barbeque sauce
- 1 onion, chopped
- 2 (4 ounce) cans diced green chile peppers
- 1/4 cup chili powder
- 1 teaspoon ground cumin
- 1 teaspoon dried oregano
- 1/4 teaspoon ground cinnamon
- 2 1/2 pounds boneless pork loin roast, trimmed
- 1/2 cup chopped fresh cilantro

Direction

- In a 3 quart or larger slow cooker, mix tomato sauce, barbeque sauce, onion, green chile peppers, chili powder, cumin, oregano, and

cinnamon. Place pork in slow cooker, and spoon sauce over to coat. the meat.
- Cover, and cook on Low 8 to 10 hours, or until pork is tender.
- Remove pork to a cutting board. Using 2 forks, pull meat into shreds. Pour sauce into a serving dish; stir in cilantro and shredded pork.

Nutrition Information

- Calories: 281 calories
- Total Fat: 12.4 g
- Cholesterol: 67 mg
- Sodium: 908 mg
- Total Carbohydrate: 18.2 g
- Protein: 24.3 g

228. TexMex Sheet Cake

"Rich Mexican flavors of cocoa, cinnamon and coffee under a chocolate glaze."

Serving: 15 | Prep: 30 m | Cook: 15 m | Ready in: 45 m

Ingredients

- 2 cups all-purpose flour
- 1 1/2 cups brown sugar
- 1 teaspoon baking soda
- 1 teaspoon ground cinnamon
- 1/2 teaspoon salt
- 1 cup margarine
- 1 cup water
- 1/4 cup unsweetened cocoa powder
- 1 tablespoon instant coffee granules
- 1/3 cup sweetened condensed milk
- 2 eggs
- 1 teaspoon vanilla extract
- 1/4 cup margarine
- 1/4 cup unsweetened cocoa powder
- 1 tablespoon instant coffee granules
- 2/3 cup sweetened condensed milk
- 1 cup confectioners' sugar
- 1 cup slivered, toasted almonds

Direction

- Preheat oven to 350 degrees F (175 degrees C). Grease and flour a 10x15 inch jelly roll pan. Combine the flour, baking soda, brown sugar, cinnamon and salt. Set aside.
- In a small saucepan, melt 1 cup margarine. Stir in water, 1/4 cup cocoa and 1 tablespoon instant coffee. Bring mixture to a boil, then remove from heat.
- Make a well in the center of the dry ingredients. Pour in the cocoa mixture, then stir in 1/3 cup sweetened condensed milk, eggs and vanilla. Mix until blended.
- Pour batter into prepared pan. Bake in the preheated oven for 15 to 20 minutes, or until the cake springs back when lightly touched. Allow to cool.
- For the coffee glaze: In a small saucepan, melt 1/4 cup margarine. Mix in 1/4 cup cocoa, 1 tablespoon instant coffee and sweetened condensed milk, and confectioners' sugar. Stir until blended. Fold in the almonds. Spread glaze over warm cake.

Nutrition Information

- Calories: 449 calories
- Total Fat: 22.8 g
- Cholesterol: 32 mg
- Sodium: 379 mg
- Total Carbohydrate: 57.7 g
- Protein: 7 g

229. TexMex Squash Bake

"Great way to use up the ever-plentiful summertime squash. Very flexible recipe. Definitely a very yummy family favorite. Love to serve it over rice or millet. It can be easily adjusted to suit your tastes. I have used shredded cooked chicken in place of the beef. I have also added other garden veggies that I needed to use up."

Serving: 8 | Prep: 30 m | Cook: 40 m | Ready in: 1 h 10 m

Ingredients

- 1 pound ground beef
- 1/4 cup olive oil, divided
- 4 zucchini, cut into 1/2-inch cubes
- 1 red bell pepper, chopped
- 1 jalapeno pepper, seeded and chopped
- 4 cloves garlic, minced
- 4 green onions, chopped -- white and green parts separated
- salt and pepper to taste
- 3 tablespoons tomato paste
- 4 teaspoons chili powder, or to taste
- 2 teaspoons ground cumin, or to taste
- 1 (15 ounce) can black beans, rinsed and drained
- 1 (15 ounce) can kidney beans, rinsed and drained
- 1 cup frozen corn, thawed
- 1/2 cup grated Parmesan cheese, divided
- 1/4 cup chopped fresh cilantro

Direction

- Cook and stir the ground beef in a skillet over medium heat until brown and crumbly, breaking the meat apart as it cooks, about 10 minutes. Drain off excess grease. Set the beef aside.
- Preheat oven to 400 degrees F (200 degrees C). Spread the bottom of a 9x13-inch baking dish with about 1 teaspoon of olive oil.
- Pour the remaining olive oil into a large skillet over medium-high heat, and cook and stir the zucchini, red bell pepper, jalapeno pepper, garlic, and the white parts of the green onions until the vegetables begin to soften, 3 to 5 minutes. Sprinkle with salt and black pepper, and mix in the tomato paste, chili powder, and cumin. Allow the mixture to simmer until the spices are fragrant, about 1 minute. Remove from heat.
- Stir in the browned ground beef, black beans, kidney beans, corn, and 1/4 cup of Parmesan cheese until well combined. Adjust salt and pepper if necessary, and spread the mixture into the prepared baking dish. Top with remaining 1/4 cup of Parmesan cheese, and cover the dish with foil.
- Bake in the preheated oven until bubbling in the center, 20 to 25 minutes; remove the foil, return to oven, and bake until the cheese is browned, 5 to 10 more minutes. Sprinkle the remaining green onions (green tops) and cilantro over the top.

Nutrition Information

- Calories: 281 calories
- Total Fat: 15.8 g
- Cholesterol: 39 mg
- Sodium: 298 mg
- Total Carbohydrate: 20 g
- Protein: 17 g

230. TexMex Tuna Salad

"This is a great recipe for tuna fish tacos."

Serving: 6 | Prep: 15 m | Ready in: 15 m

Ingredients

- 2 (5 ounce) cans tuna, drained and flaked
- 1/2 cup sliced black olives
- 1/2 cup sliced green onion
- 1/2 cup sliced celery
- 2/3 cup salsa
- 1/2 cup sour cream
- 1 teaspoon ground cumin
- 1/2 head iceberg lettuce, shredded
- 12 medium taco shells

Direction

- In a large bowl, combine the tuna, olives, green onions and celery; toss together.
- In a medium bowl, whisk together the salsa, sour cream and cumin. Pour over tuna mixture; lightly toss to mix.
- Line taco shells with shredded lettuce and spoon tuna mixture into shells. Drizzle with additional salsa or top with additional sour cream if desired.

Nutrition Information

- Calories: 263 calories
- Total Fat: 12.1 g
- Cholesterol: 21 mg
- Sodium: 438 mg
- Total Carbohydrate: 24.6 g
- Protein: 14.6 g

231. TexMex Turkey Chili with Black Beans Corn and Butternut Squash

"Easy to make and ready in just 30 minutes. Butternut squash adds a twist of sweetness to this chili."

Serving: 6 | Prep: 10 m | Cook: 20 m | Ready in: 30 m

Ingredients

- 1/4 cup Mazola® Corn Oil
- 1 pound ground turkey
- 1 cup diced onion
- 1 teaspoon minced garlic
- 2 tablespoons chili powder
- 1 tablespoon ground cumin
- 1 tablespoon chicken-flavored bouillon powder or tomato-flavored bouillon
- 1 (15 ounce) can black beans, rinsed and drained
- 1 (11 ounce) can Mexi-corn, drained
- 1 (12 ounce) package frozen diced butternut squash, thawed
- 1 (28 ounce) can crushed tomatoes or tomato sauce
- 1 cup water
- 1/3 cup ketchup
- Garnishes:
- Shredded Mexican cheese, fresh cilantro, lime wedges, avocado slice

Direction

- Heat oil in large 4 to 6-quart saucepan over medium heat and add turkey. Brown turkey for 5 to 7 minutes, breaking apart.
- Add onions, garlic, chili powder, cumin and bouillon powder and cook for 3 to 5 minutes or until onions soften. Stir in vegetables, tomatoes, water and ketchup. Bring to a boil; reduce heat to low and simmer for 10 minutes. To serve, ladle into bowls and top with desired garnishes.
- Recipe note: If using fresh butternut squash, microwave for 1 to 2 minutes before adding to the chili or allow extra cooking time to ensure tenderness.

Nutrition Information

- Calories: 411 calories
- Total Fat: 17.2 g
- Cholesterol: 57 mg
- Sodium: 1039 mg
- Total Carbohydrate: 46.8 g
- Protein: 25.1 g

232. TexMex Turkey Soup

"Not only is this soup yummy, it sure beats leftover turkey sandwiches for days on end following a holiday!"

Serving: 6 | Prep: 10 m | Cook: 40 m | Ready in: 50 m

Ingredients

- 1 tablespoon olive oil
- 1/2 cup minced onion
- 3 cloves garlic, minced
- 2 teaspoons chili powder

- 1/2 teaspoon cumin
- 1/2 teaspoon oregano
- 4 cups water
- 1 (10.75 ounce) can condensed tomato soup
- 1 (28 ounce) can diced tomatoes
- 1 cup salsa
- 4 cups shredded cooked turkey
- 1 tablespoon dried parsley
- 3 chicken bouillon cubes
- 1 (14 ounce) can black beans, rinsed, drained
- 2 cups frozen corn
- 1/2 cup sour cream
- 1/4 cup chopped fresh cilantro
- Toppings:
- 6 cups corn tortilla chips
- 3/4 cup chopped green onion
- 1 cup shredded Cheddar-Monterey Jack cheese blend
- 1/2 cup chopped fresh cilantro
- 1/2 cup sour cream

Direction

- Heat olive oil in a large saucepan over medium heat. Add minced onions and cook until onions begin to soften, about 4 minutes. Add garlic, chili powder, cumin and oregano and cook, stirring, for 1 minute.
- Stir in water, tomato soup, diced tomatoes, salsa, shredded turkey, parsley and bouillon cubes. Bring to a boil, then reduce heat, and simmer 5 minutes or until bouillon cubes dissolve. Add black beans, corn, sour cream and cilantro. Simmer for 20 to 30 minutes.
- Serve soup with crushed tortilla chips, chopped green onion, shredded cheese and additional cilantro and sour cream.

Nutrition Information

- Calories: 684 calories
- Total Fat: 30.5 g
- Cholesterol: 112 mg
- Sodium: 2036 mg
- Total Carbohydrate: 59.2 g
- Protein: 45.7 g

233. The Best Natural Peach Jam or Filling

"This peach jam uses only real ingredients, no store-bought pectin. The apple provides natural pectin (especially the seeds and peel) and gives the jam a nice, firm consistency. The color is beautiful, too. Feel free to exchange the peaches with other stone fruits or berries. This makes great gifts, too. Of course, the best jam is made from Texas peaches, but I'm sure any sweet, fresh peaches will be just dandy."

Serving: 32 | Prep: 25 m | Cook: 50 m | Ready in: 13 h 15 m

Ingredients

- 4 pounds fresh peaches, peeled and chopped
- 2 pounds cane sugar
- 1 large apple with peel and core, cut into 8 wedges
- 2 lemons, juiced
- 1/4 cup water

Direction

- Heat four 8-ounce jars in simmering water until ready for use. Wash lids and rings in warm soapy water.
- Combine peaches, sugar, apple, lemon juice, and water in a large pot over high heat. Bring to a boil, stirring constantly. Cook until peaches soften and mixture thickens, about 20 minutes. Mash peaches with a potato masher. Continue cooking until a small amount of jam dropped on a plate stays in place and doesn't run, 5 to 10 minutes more.
- Remove apple wedges and seeds with a slotted spoon.
- Pack jam into hot jars, filling to within 1/4 inch of the top. Wipe rims with a clean, damp cloth. Top with lids and screw on rings.
- Place a rack in the bottom of a large stockpot and fill halfway with water. Bring to a boil and lower in jars using a holder, placing them 2 inches apart. Pour in more boiling water to cover the jars by at least 1 inch. Bring the water to a rolling boil, cover the pot, and process for 10 minutes.

- Remove the jars from the stockpot and place onto a cloth-covered or wood surface, several inches apart, until cool, about 12 hours. Press the top of each lid with a finger, ensuring that lid does not move up or down and seal is tight.

Nutrition Information

- Calories: 127 calories
- Total Fat: 0 g
- Cholesterol: 0 mg
- Sodium: 2 mg
- Total Carbohydrate: 31.5 g
- Protein: 0 g

234. Trays Spicy Texas Chili

"Being in Texas, chili is a staple on the few cold days we have each year. This is something I've come up with after years of trying to perfect an easy-to-make and delicious chili. This is a very spicy chili and the perfect meal for a chilly day. The beans are optional here as they traditionally aren't found in Texas chili."

Serving: 6 | Prep: 20 m | Cook: 3 h | Ready in: 3 h 20 m

Ingredients

- 1 1/4 pounds ground beef
- 1 yellow onion, chopped, divided
- 1 habanero pepper, chopped
- 1 jalapeno pepper, chopped
- 2 cloves garlic, chopped
- 2 (15 ounce) cans tomato sauce
- 1 (16 ounce) can kidney beans, rinsed and drained (optional)
- 1 (10 ounce) can diced tomatoes with green chile peppers (such as RO*TEL®), drained
- 2 tablespoons chili powder
- 1 tablespoon ground cumin
- 1 tablespoon cayenne pepper
- 1/2 teaspoon salt
- 1/2 teaspoon ground white pepper
- 1/2 teaspoon ground black pepper
- 1/4 (12 fluid ounce) can or bottle amber beer
- 2 tablespoons Worcestershire sauce
- 1/2 teaspoon chili powder
- 1/2 teaspoon ground cumin
- 1 cup shredded Cheddar cheese (optional)
- 1 sleeve crackers (optional)

Direction

- Heat a large skillet over medium-high heat. Cook and stir beef, half the onion, habanero pepper, jalapeno pepper, and garlic in the hot skillet until meat is browned and crumbly, 5 to 7 minutes; drain and discard grease.
- Transfer beef mixture to a large pot and add tomato sauce, kidney beans, diced tomatoes with green chiles, 2 tablespoons chili powder, 1 tablespoon cumin, cayenne pepper, salt, white pepper, and black pepper.
- Bring beef mixture to a boil; reduce heat to medium-low and simmer for 30 minutes. Stir in beer, Worcestershire sauce, 1/2 teaspoon chili powder, and 1/2 teaspoon cumin. Continue to simmer chili until flavors blend, about 2 hours.
- Spoon chili into bowls and top with Cheddar cheese, crackers, and remaining half onion.

Nutrition Information

- Calories: 463 calories
- Total Fat: 24.3 g
- Cholesterol: 79 mg
- Sodium: 1651 mg
- Total Carbohydrate: 34.7 g
- Protein: 27.6 g

235. Vietnamese Beef and Red Cabbage Bowl

"I love the bold taste of Vietnamese dishes. This is packed with flavor and spice and is just beautiful in colors. I have tried doing individual bowls but prefer a family-style serving. Serve with a quality jasmine rice and spring roll for additional savory awesomeness. Add a little sliced habanero pepper if you want to increase the heat level. (I'm from Texas and like heat.)"

Serving: 4 | Prep: 25 m | Cook: 5 m | Ready in: 30 m

Ingredients

- 1 head red cabbage
- 1 red onion, halved
- 3 tablespoons canola oil, divided
- 1 pound lean ground beef
- 1 red Fresno chile pepper, sliced very thinly
- 2 teaspoons paprika
- 1 teaspoon kosher salt
- 2 tablespoons lime juice
- 1 tablespoon fish sauce
- 1 teaspoon packed brown sugar
- 1/2 teaspoon grated lime zest
- 1/2 cup chopped fresh cilantro
- 1/4 cup chopped fresh mint
- 1 lime, cut into wedges

Direction

- Cut cabbage in half on a flat work surface. Empty one half of the core and most of the interior leaves to act as a bowl. Slice the other half thinly.
- Finely chop 1/2 the red onion and slice the other half thinly.
- Heat 1 tablespoon canola oil in a large skillet over medium heat. Add the chopped onion, ground beef, Fresno chile, paprika, and salt. Cook, breaking up and stirring occasionally, until beef is browned and crumbly, 5 to 7 minutes.
- Whisk remaining oil, lime juice, fish sauce, brown sugar, and lime zest together in a small bowl. Stir into the beef mixture and combine thoroughly. Scoop the heated mixture into the cabbage bowl. Top with the sliced cabbage, sliced onion, cilantro, and mint. Serve with lime wedges.

Nutrition Information

- Calories: 410 calories
- Total Fat: 26.6 g
- Cholesterol: 68 mg
- Sodium: 878 mg
- Total Carbohydrate: 22.5 g
- Protein: 23.8 g

236. West Texas Style Buffalo Chili

"Many of my Texan friends doubted a Canadian could make decent chili. They were wrong. Keep water and cornbread handy for the uninitiated."

Serving: 8 | Prep: 30 m | Cook: 3 h 30 m | Ready in: 4 h

Ingredients

- 1 (8 ounce) package dry black beans
- 1 (8 ounce) package dry kidney beans
- 1 tablespoon chili powder
- 1/2 teaspoon crushed red pepper flakes
- salt and pepper to taste
- 1 jalapeno pepper, seeded and minced
- 2 tablespoons vegetable oil
- 1 large sweet onion, chopped
- 2 green bell peppers, chopped
- 2 zucchini, diced
- 3 (10 ounce) cans diced tomatoes with green chile peppers
- 1 (10 ounce) can tomato sauce
- 1/2 (16 ounce) jar hot chunky salsa
- 2 tablespoons chili sauce
- 2 pounds ground buffalo

Direction

- Soak beans in water overnight. Drain and rinse.
- In a large pot, combine beans with water to cover. Bring to a boil, reduce heat, and simmer 1 to 2 hours, until tender. Once the beans have absorbed most of the water, and are starting to

soften, season with chile powder, red pepper flakes, jalapeno, salt and pepper. Reserve the seeds.
- Heat oil in a large heavy skillet over medium low heat. Sauté the onion and bell peppers for 3 minutes. Stir in diced zucchini, diced tomatoes, tomato sauce and salsa. Season with jalapeno seeds and chili sauce, stir well, and leave on medium-low heat.
- Place ground buffalo meat in a large, deep skillet. Cook over medium high heat until evenly brown. Drain excess fat. Stir buffalo and vegetable mixture into beans. Continue to simmer for 1 hour.

Nutrition Information

- Calories: 407 calories
- Total Fat: 6.7 g
- Cholesterol: 70 mg
- Sodium: 909 mg
- Total Carbohydrate: 49 g
- Protein: 39.8 g

237. White Texas Sheet Cake

"This cake is good to make a day ahead, and is very popular at pot-lucks."

Serving: 24 | Cook: 20 m | Ready in: 40 m

Ingredients

- 1 cup butter
- 1 cup water
- 2 cups all-purpose flour
- 2 cups white sugar
- 2 eggs
- 1/2 cup sour cream
- 1 teaspoon almond extract
- 1/2 teaspoon salt
- 1 teaspoon baking soda
- Frosting:
- 1/2 cup butter
- 1/4 cup milk
- 4 1/2 cups confectioners' sugar
- 1/2 teaspoon almond extract
- 1 cup chopped pecans

Direction

- Preheat oven to 375 degrees F (190 degrees C).
- In a large saucepan, bring 1 cup butter and water to a boil. Remove from heat, and stir in flour, sugar, eggs, sour cream, 1 teaspoon almond extract, salt, and baking soda until smooth. Pour batter into a greased 10x15-inch baking pan.
- Bake in the preheated oven for 20 to 22 minutes, or until cake is golden brown and tests done. Cool for 20 minutes.
- Combine 1/2 cup butter and milk in a saucepan; bring to a boil. Remove from heat. Mix in sugar, and 1/2 teaspoon almond extract. Stir in pecans. Spread frosting over warm cake.

Nutrition Information

- Calories: 344 calories
- Total Fat: 16.7 g
- Cholesterol: 48 mg
- Sodium: 193 mg
- Total Carbohydrate: 48.1 g
- Protein: 2.4 g

238. Yeah ILivedinTexas Smoked Brisket

"This is hands-down the best way I have found to cook a brisket."

Serving: 16 | Prep: 15 m | Cook: 13 h 30 m | Ready in: 1 d 13 h 45 m

Ingredients

- wood chips
- 1/4 cup paprika
- 1/4 cup white sugar
- 1/4 cup ground cumin
- 1/4 cup cayenne pepper

- 1/4 cup brown sugar
- 1/4 cup chili powder
- 1/4 cup garlic powder
- 1/4 cup onion powder
- 1/4 cup kosher salt
- 1/4 cup freshly cracked black pepper
- 10 pounds beef brisket, or more to taste

Direction

- Soak wood chips in a bowl of water, 8 hours to overnight.
- Mix paprika, white sugar, cumin, cayenne pepper, brown sugar, chili powder, garlic powder, onion powder, salt, and black pepper together in a bowl. Rub the spice mixture over the entire brisket; refrigerate for 24 hours.
- Preheat smoker to between 220 degrees F (104 degrees C) and 230 degrees F (110 degrees C). Drain wood chips and place in the smoker.
- Smoke brisket in the preheated smoker until it has an internal temperature of 165 degrees F (74 degrees C), about 12 1/2 hours. Wrap brisket tightly in butcher paper or heavy-duty aluminum foil and return to smoker.
- Continue smoking brisket until an internal temperature of 185 degrees F (85 degrees C) is reached, about 1 hour more.

Nutrition Information

- Calories: 228 calories
- Total Fat: 6.7 g
- Cholesterol: 57 mg
- Sodium: 3010 mg
- Total Carbohydrate: 16.2 g
- Protein: 26.6 g

239. Yum Yum Cake II

"A chocolaty cake similar to a Texas Sheet Cake but cooked in a 9x13 pan, rather than a cookie sheet pan. You pour the cooked icing onto the hot cake. Yum!!"

Serving: 24

Ingredients

- 2 cups all-purpose flour
- 1/2 teaspoon salt
- 1 teaspoon baking soda
- 1 tablespoon unsweetened cocoa powder
- 1 cup butter
- 1 1/2 cups white sugar
- 3 eggs
- 1 cup buttermilk
- 1 teaspoon vanilla extract
- 1 cup buttermilk
- 2 cups white sugar
- 1/2 cup butter
- 2 teaspoons vanilla extract

Direction

- Preheat oven to 325 degrees F (165 degrees C). Grease and flour a 9x13 inch pan.
- Sift together the flour, salt, baking soda and cocoa, set aside. In a large bowl, cream together the 1 1/2 cup of sugar and 1 cup butter until smooth. Add eggs one at a time, beating well after each addition. Combine the 1 cup buttermilk and 1 teaspoon vanilla, add alternately to the mixture with the dry ingredients. Pour into the prepared pan.
- Bake for about 45 minutes in the preheated oven. Prepare the topping while the cake is baking.
- In a small saucepan, combine the remaining 1 cup of buttermilk, 2 cups sugar and margarine. Bring to a boil over medium high heat, and boil for 5 minutes. Remove from the heat and cool for a few minutes before adding vanilla. As soon as the cake comes out of the oven, slowly pour the hot topping over the entire cake. It may seem like too much, but the cake will absorb it.

Nutrition Information

- Calories: 273 calories
- Total Fat: 12.6 g
- Cholesterol: 49 mg
- Sodium: 213 mg
- Total Carbohydrate: 38.4 g
- Protein: 2.6 g

240. Zekes Tortilla Soup

"An authentic, savory soup from the Mexican food capital of the world - El Paso Texas! You can cut back on some of the fat by baking the tortilla strips instead of deep-frying."

Serving: 12 | Prep: 1 h | Cook: 30 m | Ready in: 1 h 30 m

Ingredients

- 6 skinless, boneless chicken breast halves
- 3 cups vegetable oil for frying
- 36 (6 inch) corn tortillas, cut into strips
- 15 cups water
- 15 cubes chicken bouillon
- 1 (14 ounce) can peeled and diced tomatoes with juice
- 1 small onion
- 3 cloves garlic
- 1 teaspoon ground coriander
- 1 teaspoon ground cumin
- 1 teaspoon ground black pepper
- 1 teaspoon chili powder
- 1/4 cup dried oregano
- 1 cup chopped carrots
- 1 cup chopped celery
- 1 (14.5 ounce) can diced tomatoes with green chile peppers
- 3 cups shredded Monterey Jack cheese
- 3 avocado - peeled, pitted and sliced

Direction

- In a saucepan, cover chicken breasts with water and boil for 30 minutes, or until tender. Shred into small pieces; set aside. Meanwhile, heat oil in a deep-fryer or large cast-iron skillet to 375 degrees F (190 degrees C). Fry tortilla strips from about 6 tortillas at a time, stirring occasionally, until golden brown. Drain on paper towels and set aside.
- In a large stockpot, bring the water to a boil. Stir in the bouillon cubes and reduce heat to a simmer. In a blender, combine the can of tomatoes, onion and garlic. Blend on high until smooth. Pour the blended mixture into the stockpot and stir in the coriander, cumin, black pepper, chili powder and oregano. Add carrots, celery and diced tomatoes with chilies. Cover pot and simmer for about 25 minutes, until vegetables are tender. Stir in shredded chicken and cook 5 more minutes.
- Serve hot topped with fried tortilla strips, and garnish with shredded cheese and avocado slices.

Nutrition Information

- Calories: 509 calories
- Total Fat: 25 g
- Cholesterol: 60 mg
- Sodium: 1830 mg
- Total Carbohydrate: 46.3 g
- Protein: 27.9 g

Index

A

Allspice, *37–38*

Almond, *116–117, 131, 137*

Almond extract, *137*

Apple, 10, 25, 28, 32–34, 41, 51, 75, 77, 81, 116–117, 134

Apple juice, *10, 51, 116–117*

Avocado, 12, 30, 43, 93, 108, 120, 124–127, 133, 139

B

Bacon, 14–15, 35, 37, 46–47, 49, 52–53, 58–59, 68, 78, 81–82, 113–114, 118

Bagel, *34*

Baked beans, *27–28, 36–37, 122*

Baking, 10, 14, 20–24, 26–27, 29, 32, 36, 42, 44–46, 49–51, 58, 60–63, 66, 68, 71, 82, 85, 88–91, 94, 97, 99–100, 107–109, 111–112, 114–115, 118, 120–121, 124, 126, 128, 131–132, 137–139

Baking powder, *22–24, 26, 29, 36, 44–45, 89–90, 107, 111*

Balsamic vinegar, *74*

Banana, *50*

Barbecue sauce, *28, 77, 103*

Basil, *43, 53, 57, 69, 75, 92, 103*

Bay leaf, *60, 106, 108–109*

Beans, 10–12, 20, 22, 26–30, 32–33, 36–38, 41–42, 44, 46–47, 50–51, 54–56, 59–60, 65, 67–68, 70–72, 74, 76, 78–79, 83–87, 92–93, 99, 102, 106, 108–109, 119, 122–125, 127–128, 132–137

Beef, 8, 10–12, 26–28, 30, 32, 40, 42, 45–47, 50, 55–56, 59–60, 63, 65–67, 72–74, 78–80, 85–86, 89–90, 94–95, 99, 102–105, 108–109, 113–114, 116–119, 122, 124–125, 128–130, 132, 135–136, 138

Beef consommé, *80*

Beef stock, *60*

Beer, 12–14, 18–19, 25, 37–39, 44–45, 47, 52–53, 78, 89, 102–104, 121, 130, 135

Berry, *81, 134*

Black beans, 22, 32–33, 38, 51, 54–56, 83–87, 92, 102, 123–125, 127, 132–134, 136

Black pepper, 8, 10–11, 15–17, 20, 27–30, 33, 37–38, 41–45, 50, 52–53, 56–61, 63, 66–67, 74–75, 77, 79–81, 83–89, 92, 98, 100–102, 104–105, 108, 110, 113, 117, 121, 123, 127, 132, 135, 138–139

Blueberry, *36*

Brandy, *63*

Brazil nut, *89–90*

Bread, 11, 18, 21–22, 28, 39–41, 44–46, 48, 52, 55, 63, 86, 92, 101, 104–105, 130

Brisket, 40, 47–48, 56–57, 59–60, 78, 90, 116, 137–138

Broccoli, *16*

Broth, 8, 15-18, 39-40, 56, 59-61, 77, 80, 82, 84, 86, 89, 94, 106, 108-109, 126

Brown rice, *123*

Brown sugar, 21-24, 26, 28-29, 36-37, 40-41, 44-45, 53-54, 56, 77-78, 81, 88, 94-95, 107, 110-112, 120-122, 131, 136, 138

Buns, *9, 28, 77, 95, 125, 130*

Burger, *17, 33, 117, 125, 130*

Butter, 11, 15-16, 21-26, 29, 31, 35-36, 40-41, 44-46, 54, 61-62, 64-71, 73, 75, 77, 80-83, 86, 90, 98-101, 107-109, 111-112, 114-115, 118-119, 128-129, 137-138

Buttermilk, *68-69, 90-91, 111-112, 138*

Butternut squash, *61, 133*

C

Cabbage, *33-34, 52-53, 74, 98, 136*

Cake, 36, 48, 67-69, 96-97, 109, 111-112, 114-116, 120, 131, 137-138

Capers, *9-10*

Carrot, *10-11, 15, 25-26, 42, 98, 139*

Cashew, *65*

Catfish, *13*

Cauliflower, *16*

Caviar, 20, 22, 32-33, 38, 44, 49, 92-93

Cayenne pepper, 13, 15, 18, 35-36, 47, 52, 55, 63, 67, 77, 80, 86, 88, 93, 98, 110, 116-117, 135, 137

Celery, 10-12, 15-16, 18, 20, 33-34, 37, 39-40, 42, 57, 65, 73, 81-82, 92, 106, 132-133, 139

Cheddar, 21, 26, 40-41, 46, 49, 61, 66-67, 74, 76, 79, 83, 86-87, 93-95, 98, 101-102, 112-113, 116-117, 126, 128-129, 134-135

Cheese, 14-21, 26, 28, 30-31, 40-43, 46, 49, 52-53, 56, 61, 63-67, 71, 73-76, 79, 83, 85-87, 93-95, 98-103, 108, 112-114, 116-119, 121, 124-126, 128-130, 132-135, 139

Cheese sauce, *14, 19, 66*

Cherry, *90, 92, 106-109, 124*

Cherry tomatoes, *92, 124*

Chicken, 8-9, 15-20, 32, 37-40, 42-43, 50-51, 60-62, 65, 67-68, 77, 81-84, 86-88, 93-94, 100, 103-104, 106, 108-109, 112-113, 118-119, 126, 132-134, 139

Chicken breast, *20, 39, 42-43, 51, 83, 86-88, 93, 118, 126, 139*

Chicken leg, *103*

Chicken soup, *60-61*

Chicken stock, *68, 81-82, 118*

Chicken thigh, *8*

Chipotle, 13-14, 29-30, 47, 53, 55, 60-61, 68, 127, 130

Chips, 13, 17, 20-24, 26, 28-29, 38, 53, 57-58, 71-74, 76, 84-85, 92-94, 103-104, 108, 110, 124-125, 129, 134, 137-138

Chives, *27, 49, 76*

Chocolate, 22-24, 29, 68-69, 90, 96-97, 111, 115, 121, 131

Chocolate cake, *97*

Chopped tomatoes, *84*

Chorizo, *43*

Cider, 20, 28, 32-34, 54, 77, 116-117

Cinnamon, *21, 40-41, 44-45, 53, 58, 90-91, 96, 104-105, 107-108, 130-131*

Citrus fruit, *72, 107*

Cloves, *8, 10, 12, 15-16, 18, 25-26, 29, 32, 41, 43, 46-48, 51, 53, 56, 63, 67, 73, 75-77, 79,*

    81, 84, 88, 92, 94, 97, 104, 108, 116, 120-123, 126, 132-133, 135, 139

Cocktail, *25, 31, 34, 84, 88-89, 120-121*

Cocoa powder, *29, 67, 90-91, 96-97, 111, 114-115, 131, 138*

Coconut, *29, 48, 106-107, 109*

Coconut oil, *48, 107*

Cod, *82*

Coffee, *45, 78, 111, 115, 131*

Coffee granules, *111, 131*

Cola, *39, 50, 78, 120*

Coleslaw, *33-34, 98, 116*

Condensed milk, *109, 131*

Coriander, *30, 92, 116, 139*

Corn oil, *18, 43, 133*

Cornsyrup, *69, 112*

Cottage cheese, *83*

Crab, *11, 18, 89, 99*

Crackers, *35, 61, 79, 84, 99, 102, 135*

Cranberry, *81-82*

Cranberry sauce, *81*

Cream, *10, 12-14, 16-18, 24, 26-27, 29, 31, 36, 41-42, 45, 49, 52-53, 56-58, 60-61, 63-64,*

    69, 71, 73, 76, 79, 82-83, 85-86, 93, 97-98, 101-102, 108, 111-112, 114-115, 118-122,

    124-125, 130, 132-134, 137-138

  Cream cheese, *14, 17-18, 31, 49, 52, 63-64, 102, 118, 121*

Cream of tartar, *29*

Crumble, *28, 32, 43, 46, 52-53, 82, 103, 113, 124*

Cucumber, *84*

Cumin, *8, 11, 14, 17, 29-30, 32, 44-47, 49, 53-54, 59-61, 64, 70-71, 74, 79-80, 82, 84-85,*

    92, 94, 98-99, 101, 108-109, 116-117, 122-127, 130, 132-135, 137-139

Curry, *8, 79, 100*

Curry powder, *8, 79, 100*

D

Date, *90, 109*

Dijon mustard, *63*

  Dill, *17, 34, 37, 97, 104*

Dry sherry, *99*

E

Egg, *9, 16, 21-24, 26-27, 29-30, 36, 45-46, 48-49, 61, 63, 68-69, 85-86, 89-91, 96-97,*

    100-101, 107-108, 111-112, 114-117, 120-121, 126-127, 129, 131, 137-138

Egg white, *27*

  Egg yolk, *27, 86*

Evaporated milk, *67-69*

F

Fat, *9–34, 36–139*

Feta, *29–30*

Fish, *9–11, 14, 17, 51–52, 82, 132, 136*

Fish sauce, *9, 136*

Fish soup, *82*

Flank, *122, 124–125*

Flour, *9, 15–18, 21–24, 26, 28–29, 36, 39, 45–46, 48, 52, 59–60, 62, 66–69, 73, 79, 83–84, 86–87, 89–91, 93, 97, 102, 107–109, 111, 114–117, 120–121, 124, 129, 131, 137–138*

Flour tortilla, *28, 52, 73, 84, 93, 102, 129*

Frankfurter, *104–105*

French bread, *40–41*

Fruit, *70, 72, 89, 106–107, 120–121, 134*

Fruit juice, *106*

Fudge, *58, 96*

Fusilli, *129*

G

Game, *95, 124*

Garlic, *8, 10–13, 15–16, 18, 22, 24–26, 29–30, 32–41, 43–47, 49–56, 58–60, 62–64, 67–68, 73, 75–85, 88, 92, 94–95, 97, 99, 101–106, 108–110, 116–127, 132–135, 138–139*

Garlic bread, *18, 55*

Giblets, *57*

Gin, *39, 106, 120*

Grain, *60, 64, 90, 95, 106, 113, 125*

Grapes, *75*

Grapeseed oil, *33–34, 107, 116–117*

Gravy, *15, 65, 79*

Green cabbage, *33, 98*

Guacamole, *73, 76, 79, 93, 100*

H

Ham, *28–29, 34, 86, 106, 117–118*

Heart, *74, 78, 89*

Honey, *10–11, 13, 57, 67, 93, 100, 117*

Horseradish, *104*

I

Icecream, *10, 69*

Iceberg lettuce, *74, 83, 132*

Icing, *96–97, 114–115, 138*

J

Jam, *134*

Jelly, *70, 91, 97, 114, 131*

K

Kale, *25*

Ketchup, *9–10, 28, 30, 36–37, 40, 50, 54, 70–71, 78, 81, 88, 90, 92, 110, 117, 133*

Kidney, 11-12, 67, 108-109, 132, 135-136

Kidney beans, *11-12, 67, 108-109, 132, 135-136*

L

Lager, *78*

Lard, *126*

Leftover turkey, *133*

Lemon, 10, 13, 17, 37-39, 54, 62, 72, 75, 89-90, 94-95, 108, 117, 120-121, 134

Lemon juice, *13, 54, 62, 72, 75, 108, 117, 121, 134*

Lettuce, 34, 51, 73-74, 83, 124-125, 130, 132-133

Lime, 12-14, 31, 37-39, 49, 51-52, 54, 58-59, 63, 72, 75, 84-85, 87, 98, 106-107, 116, 118-120, 124-127, 133, 136

Lime juice, 12-14, 31, 49, 51-52, 54, 58-59, 84-85, 98,107,116,118-120,125-127,136

Liqueur, *25, 31, 39, 63, 106, 120, 123*

M

Macaroni, *42, 65-66, 128*

Mango, *31*

Mango juice, *31*

Maple syrup, *54-55*

Margarine, 11, 17, 23, 26, 29, 68, 86, 91, 96-97, 107, 109, 111, 114, 128, 131, 138

Marshmallow, *68-69*

Mayonnaise, 9-10, 33-34, 37, 52, 76, 79, 98, 108, 113, 125, 130

Meat,11,18,32,38,40,42,45-46,48,51,53,55-57,60, 63,65-67,73,77-80,88-90,94-95,

99, 105, 109, 117-118, 123-124, 126, 131-132, 135, 137

Milk,9,17-19,21,31,36,45-46,48,58,61-62,66-69, 73,91,96-98,101,107,109,114-115,

121, 128, 131, 137

Millet, *132*

Mint, *136*

Mixed nuts, *35*

Molasses, *54-55, 100*

Mozzarella, *16, 43, 61, 103,112*

Muffins, *36, 44, 107*

Mushroom, *25, 55, 58-61, 117-118, 121*

Mustard,9-10,28,34,40-41,54,56,59-60,63,66,77-78,81,88,94-95,100,104-105,113,

117

Mustard powder, *40, 94-95*

N

Nachos, *108*

New potatoes, *27*

Noodles, *16, 82-83, 118*

Nut, 26, 35, 40, 58, 80, 89-90, 109, 114-115, 121

Nutmeg, *21-22, 44, 107-108*

O

Oatmeal, 26

Oats, *22-24, 26, 29, 65*

Oil, 8-10, 12-14, 16-18, 20-21, 24-27, 29-30, 32-34, 37-41,43-45,48,52-57,59-61,63-65,

67-69, 71, 74-75, 77, 79, 81-87, 89, 92-96,

100, 102, 104–107, 110, 112, 116–119, 122–129, 132–134, 136–137, 139

Olive, 8–10, 12, 16–17, 20, 24–25, 29–30, 33, 37–39, 43–44, 53–56, 61, 63, 65, 74–76, 79, 83,
86–87, 89, 102, 106, 112, 122–123, 126–127, 129, 132–134

Olive oil, 8–10, 12, 16–17, 20, 24–25, 29–30, 33, 37–39, 43–44, 53–56, 61, 63, 65, 74–75,
86–87, 89, 102, 106, 112, 122–123, 126–127, 129, 132–134

Onion, 8, 10–12, 15–18, 20–22, 24–25, 27–30, 32–34, 36–47, 49–56, 58–68, 70–71, 73–87, 89,
92–95, 98–99, 101–106, 108–110, 113–114, 116–119, 121–123, 125–130, 132–139

Orange, 12, 31–32, 39, 54, 63, 72, 75, 106, 123

Orange juice, *54, 72, 75, 106, 123*

Orange liqueur, *63, 123*

Oregano, 8, 44–47, 53, 59–61, 67, 79–80, 92, 101, 105, 108–109, 116–117, 126, 130, 134, 139

Oyster, *9*

Oyster sauce, *9*

P

Pancetta, *13*

Paprika, 8–10, 34, 46–47, 51, 53–55, 79, 88, 92, 95, 101, 104–105, 110, 117, 123–125, 136–138

Parmesan, *28, 75, 99, 128, 132*

Parsley, *11, 20, 39, 46, 75, 104, 134*

Pasta, *42, 129*

Pasty, *34*

Peach, *31, 62, 134*

Peanut butter, *16, 29, 67–69*

Peanut oil, *52*

Peas, 20, 22, 32–33, 38, 44, 49–51, 92–93, 128

Pecan, 22, 26, 40–41, 58, 69, 81–82, 90, 107–109, 111–112, 115–117, 137

Pectin, *70, 134*

Peel, *18, 134*

Pepper, 8–20, 22, 25–47, 49–68, 71–89, 92–95, 97–106, 108–110, 113–114, 116–127, 129–130, 132, 135–139

Pickle, *34, 37, 79, 97, 104*

Pie, 21, 69, 109, 121, 126

Pineapple, *21, 69, 106, 109*

Pineapple juice, *69, 106*

Pinto beans, 11, 20, 28–29, 32–33, 38, 41, 47, 50, 59, 68, 70–71, 74, 78, 84, 99, 108–109, 119

Plum, *24, 39, 71*

Pork, 9, 12, 27, 30, 32, 36, 39, 41, 49, 53, 77, 81, 104–105, 110, 121–122, 130–131

Pork loin, *121, 130*

Pork shoulder, *77*

Port, *70*

Potato, 26–27, 29–30, 37, 53, 70–71, 86, 98, 113, 126–127, 134

Praline, *111–112*

Pulled pork, *77*

Pulse, *34, 65, 76, 79*

R

Radish, *98*

Raisins, *23, 40–41, 107*

Raspberry, *25*

Red cabbage, *74, 136*

Red onion, *10-12, 20, 28-29, 32, 38, 43, 51, 53, 58-59, 122, 127, 130, 136*

Red snapper, *11*

Red wine, *11, 24, 43-44, 74*

Red wine vinegar, *24, 43-44, 74*

Rice, *8, 13, 15, 18, 33, 35, 38-39, 54, 62, 64, 66, 86-88, 102-103, 106, 113-114, 122-125, 132, 136*

Rice vinegar, *13, 33, 38*

Rosemary, *27*

Rum, *31, 39, 41-42, 75, 106, 120*

Rump, *47*

S
Saffron, *64*

Sage, *57*

Salad, *20, 22, 32, 34, 37, 43, 50-51, 57, 62, 73-74, 83, 98, 112-113, 116, 129, 132*

Salsa, *12, 17, 33, 43, 49, 51-52, 58, 74, 76, 84, 86-87, 92-93, 100, 102, 129, 132-134, 136-137*

Salt, *8, 10-16, 18-28, 30, 32-38, 40-46, 48-68, 70-81, 83, 85-93, 95, 97-98, 100-105, 107-108, 110-111, 113-118, 120-127, 129, 131-132, 135-138*

Sauces, *28*

Sausage, *9-11, 14, 18, 27, 32, 36-37, 39-41, 43, 49, 53, 67, 101, 106*

Savory, *15, 80, 136, 139*

Scallop, *18*

Sea salt, *25, 28, 55, 105, 120*

Seafood, *11, 16, 33, 80*

Seasoning, *8, 18, 28, 36, 39, 42, 44, 47-48, 65, 76, 79, 82-83, 86-87, 89, 95, 99, 103-104, 108, 117-120, 125, 128-130*

Seeds, *14, 49, 134, 137*

Shallot, *9*

Sherry, *99*

Sirloin, *67, 79, 125*

Smoked fish, *17*

Snapper, *11*

Soda, *22-24, 26, 29, 58, 68, 75, 91, 97, 107-108, 114-115, 120-121, 131, 137-138*

Sorbet, *69*

Soup, *16, 19, 32, 34, 58, 60-61, 65, 72, 80-82, 86, 89, 94, 98, 101, 105, 119, 133-134, 139*

Soy sauce, *9, 118-119*

Spaghetti, *55*

Spices, *18, 38, 41-42, 44, 46-47, 53-54, 102, 132*

Spinach, *75, 82, 99*

Squash, *43, 61, 75, 132-133*

Steak, *16, 19, 21, 67, 83, 90, 94-95, 118, 122, 124-125*

Stew, *27, 30, 32-33, 42, 46, 72-73, 89*

Stock, *18, 60, 68, 73, 81-82, 99, 118-119*

Strawberry, *10, 45*

Stuffing, *11, 81-82*

Sugar, *9, 20-26, 28-29, 32-34, 36-38, 40-41, 44-45, 48, 52-54, 56, 58, 60, 62-63, 67-70, 72, 74-75, 77-78, 81, 88-91, 94-97, 107-112, 114-116, 120-122, 124, 131, 134, 136-138*

Sweet potato, *29*

Syrup, 45, 54–55, 62, 69, 97, 106, 112

T

Tabasco, 35, 97, 122

Taco, 51–52, 76, 79–80, 86–87, 108, 119–120, 128–130, 132–133

Tarragon, 37

Tea, 39, 72, 92, 120

Tequila, 12, 25, 39, 51, 54, 63, 118–120, 123

Thyme, 77, 92, 106, 116–117

Tilapia, 52

Tofu, 65

Tomatillo, 12, 57–58, 70–71, 120, 126

Tomato, 10–12, 16, 18, 22, 24, 26, 28–30, 32, 39, 41–44, 46–47, 49–51, 53–56, 58–61, 64–68, 71–74, 76, 78–79, 82–88, 92–95, 99, 101–106, 108–109, 113–114, 119, 122–126, 129–130, 132–137, 139

Tomato juice, 41, 102

Trout, 17

Turkey, 53–57, 61, 81, 102, 133–134

Turkey breast, 57

Turmeric, 8

V

Vanilla extract, 23–24, 29, 45, 58, 67–69, 89, 91, 96–97, 111–112, 114–115, 131, 138

Vegetable oil, 20, 26–27, 32, 40–41, 45, 57, 60, 64, 68–69, 77, 79, 81–84, 93–96, 104–105, 128, 136, 139

Vegetables, 18, 28–29, 32, 42, 51, 76, 80, 87, 89, 119, 127, 132–133, 139

Venison, 98

Vinegar, 10–11, 13, 20, 24, 28, 32–34, 36–38, 43–44, 54, 74, 77, 81, 84, 88, 92, 94–95, 105, 116–117

Vodka, 39, 106, 120

W

Walnut, 23, 26, 29, 63, 90, 107–108, 114–115, 120

Whipping cream, 71, 73, 86

White bread, 45, 86, 101, 130

White pepper, 34, 86, 105, 135

White sugar, 9, 20–24, 26, 29, 33–34, 36, 38, 40, 45, 48, 52, 58, 60, 62–63, 67–70, 72, 74–75, 89–91, 97, 110–112, 114–115, 120, 137–138

White wine, 10, 75, 81, 92

White wine vinegar, 10, 92

Wine, 10–11, 24, 43–44, 70, 74–75, 81–82, 92

Worcestershire sauce, 11, 19, 28, 35–38, 40, 54, 62–63, 66, 77–78, 81, 83, 88, 94–95, 98, 117–118, 125, 135

Y

Yeast, 21–22, 48

Z

Zest, 62–63, 107, 122, 136

Conclusion

Thank you again for downloading this book!

I hope you enjoyed reading about my book!

If you enjoyed this book, please take the time to share your thoughts and post a review on Amazon. It'd be greatly appreciated!

Write me an honest review about the book – I truly value your opinion and thoughts and I will incorporate them into my next book, which is already underway.

Thank you!

If you have any questions, **feel free to contact at:** *chefliamfox@gmail.com*

Lucas Neill
www.TheCookingMAP.com/Lucas-Neill